The Il
Real Estate Dictionary

Kristi Olson

Also by Michael C. Thomsett:

Investment and Securities Dictionary
How to Buy a House, Condo or Co-Op
Homeowners Money Management
Fundamentals of Bookkeeping and Accounting
Little Black Book of Business Math
Little Black Book of Budgets and Forecasts
Little Black Book of Business Reports
Little Black Book of Business Letters
Builders Guide to Accounting
Builders Office Manual
Contractors Year-Round Tax Guide
Computers: The Builder's New Tool

The Illustrated Real Estate Dictionary

Compiled by

Michael C. Thomsett

DOW JONES-IRWIN
Homewood, Illinois 60430

Published by special arrangement with McFarland & Company, Inc., Publishers, Jefferson, N.C.

©Michael C. Thomsett, 1988

Dow Jones-Irwin is a trademark of Dow Jones & Company, Inc.

All rights reserved. No part of this publication may be reproduced, stored in a retrieval system, or transmitted, in any form or by any means, electronic, mechanical, photocopying, recording, or otherwise, without the prior written premission of the copyright holder.

This publication is designed to provide accurate and authoritative information in regard to the subject matter covered. It is sold with the understanding that neither the author nor the publisher is engaged in rendering legal, accounting, or other professional service. If legal advice or other expert assistance is required, the services of a competent professional person should be sought.

From a Declaration of Principles jointly adopted by a Committee of the American Bar Association and a Committee of Publishers.

Library of Congress Cataloging-in-Publication Data

Thomsett, Michael C.
   The illustrated real estate dictionary.

   1. Real estate business—Dictionaries. I. Title.
HD1365.T46 1988   333.33'03'21   87-43196

ISBN 1-55623-165-2

Printed in the United States of America

1 2 3 4 5 6 7 8 9 0 EB 6 5 4 3 2 1 0 9

For my son, Eric J. Thomsett

Table of Contents

Introduction: What This Book Will Do for You   xi
Glossary of Terms   1
Checklists   190
Amortization Tables   196
Remaining Balance Tables   204
Abbreviations   218

Introduction: What This Book Will Do for You

The *Real Estate Dictionary* summarizes the terminology of the real estate industry. This complex field includes residential and commercial properties, investments in various forms, rules for mortgage loans, and the various rights and points of law affecting owners of real estate.

The more than 1,100 terms include words and phrases, legal concepts and rules, agencies, associations and regulatory bodies involved in real estate.

Major sections of the book include:

Glossary of Terms. This section is fully cross-referenced for complete research and includes many illustrations.

Checklists. A number of lists for owners, buyers, sellers and investors in real estate.

Amortization Tables. A handy reference section to help you figure out monthly payments on mortgages.

Remaining Balance Tables. A guide to the balance that will be outstanding on loans after a number of years.

Abbreviations. An alphabetical listing of the most common abbreviations used in the real estate industry, including agencies and phrases.

Whether you are a real estate professional or a consumer who wants to buy a home or invest in real estate, this book will serve as a convenient and complete guide for you. The *Real Estate Dictionary* will enable you to communicate with others involved in real estate, and to interpret the jargon, phrases and abbreviations used by real estate professionals. The cross-referencing feature of the glossary also allows you to gain additional information as needed.

This book will become a useful guide, for use whenever you need clarification of a term, or when you need to gain insight and understanding of a real estate subject.

Glossary of Terms

A

A-B deal description of limited partnerships offering two separate classes of securities to investors. One group assumes a debt position by lending money to the program; the other invests equity for cash flow from rental income and eventual capital gains. See also *debt instrument; equity investment; limited partnership.*

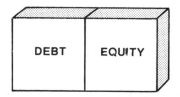

A-B deal

abandonment a voluntary action in which rights to property are surrendered or when mortgage obligations are not honored. In an abandonment, a subsequent owner, lessee or tenant is not named or assigned property rights. See also *conveyance; possession; voluntary conveyance.*

abatement a decrease in valuation or agreed rental rates. An abatement may be granted to a tenant when intended use of the property is impeded by unanticipated actions or improvements by the owner; an abatement in taxes or valuation may be won by a property owner who contests assessed valuation or the rate of an ad valorem tax. See also *ad valorem tax; assessed valuation; tenant.*

abatement of rent a contractual provision that frees a tenant from the obligation to pay full or partial rent in cases of unforeseen casualties; or an agreement between owner and tenant to reduce or suspend rent when the premises cannot be inhabited or the use of property is not possible due to improvements being performed by the owner. See also *contract; lease; tenant.*

abnormal sale the transfer of real estate under other than normal sale conditions, usually used in reference to irregularities or exceptions in the contract. See also *normal sale; sale contract.*

absentee owner an owner who does not reside in the property, or who does not regularly live or work on the site but delegates management duties to the tenant or another person or firm. See also *property manager; residential property.*

absolute sale a normal sale, one in which both buyer and seller fulfill all terms of the contract as agreed. See also *normal sale; sale contract.*

absolute title exclusive ownership of property in the absence of conditions, liens or other limitations. See also *free and clear; title.*

absorption rate the number of occupied units in a rental property, or sales of a new development. The percentage of demand is multiplied by the estimated market share to determine the number of units or homes. For example, a 200% increase in demand is expected each year. A developer expects to fill 8% of that demand, for a total of 16 home sales per year. See also *occupancy rate; supply and demand.*

absorption rate

increased demand x market share

200 x 8% = 16 units

abstract of title a summary of a property's title, including ownership, mortgage history, past and present liens and encumbrances, and present status. All recorded documents are listed in chronological order. The abstract is prepared as part of the process of granting a title insurance policy. See also *encumbrance; lien; mortgage; recording; title insurance policy.*

Accelerated Cost Recovery System (ACRS) the federal system dictating the accepted methods for recovering (depreciating) capital assets, first introduced as part of the Economic Recovery Tax Act of 1981 (ERTA). The system identifies specific recovery periods and dictates the years and depreciation methods that can be used for specific assets. See also *capital improvement; cost recovery; depreciation; Economic Recovery Tax Act of 1981 (ERTA); recovery period.*

accelerated depreciation a method for the recovery of capital asset costs, in which each year's depreciation is greater than the straight-line rate that would be allowed on the same asset. For example, an $8,000 asset with a 10-year recovery period would be eligible for $800 per year under straight-line depreciation rules. With 175% accelerated depreciation, $1,400 is allowed in the first year. In subsequent years, the basis is reduced by the amount of accumulated depreciation. Thus, during the second year, the depreciation basis is reduced to $6,600 ($8,000 less $1,400). Allowed depreciation is $1,155 (175% of $660). See also *declining balance depreciation; recovery period; straight-line depreciation.*

accelerated depreciation

YEAR	BASIS	10 YR ST-LINE	D.B. 175%
1	$8,000	$ 800	$1,400
2	6,600	660	1,155
3	5,445	545	954
4	4,491	449	786
5	3,705	371	649

acceleration clause a provision included in a deed of trust, mortgage or installment loan contract, stating that the lender has the right to demand full payment if a specific event takes place that endangers the lender's risks. Examples are failure to make an installment payment by a due date, a change in ownership without the prior consent of the lender, destruction of the property, or a lapse of a homeowner's or default insurance policy. See also *deed of trust; default; foreclosure; mortgage.*

acceptance agreement to the terms contained in an offer. Upon acceptance, a binding contract is created. Every contract, to be valid, must include both offer and acceptance. See also *contract; offer.*

access right the right of a property owner to enter and leave property by passing over public property. See also *easement; real law.*

accessory structure any building or other structure on a parcel of land, other than the primary building. See also *outbuilding.*

accretion the expansion of land as a result of the forces of nature. Accretion

accrued

may occur from the change in course of a river or stream, from flooding, or from a build-up of sand deposits. See also *littoral rights; riparian rights*.

accrued interest recognition of interest income that is earned but not yet received; or of interest expense that is due but not yet paid. When property is purchased, interest from the closing date until the date of the first payment due on a mortgage loan is accrued. For example, an $80,000, 11% loan is granted on a property that closes on June 11, with the first payment due on July 1. Interest is accrued for 19 days. See also *closing statement; interest*.

accrued interest

mortgage amount	$80,000
interest rate	11%
monthly interest	$733.33
closing date	June 11
accrued interest (19 days)	$464.44

accumulated value the appreciation in a property over time. Due to the growth in market value and gradual equity payments, real estate owners and investors gain accumulated value in their holdings. See also *appreciation; book value; market value; value*.

acknowledgement verification of a valid signature in a form acceptable under state law. Some forms of documentation, for example, require notarization or written acknowledgement from a court official, for mortgages, deeds or contracts. See also *contract; deed; recording*.

acquisition cost the total cost required to buy a property, including the purchase price and all related closing costs and expenses. See also *closing costs; title*.

action on contract a legal action to require compliance with the terms of a legal contract. See also *contract*.

Actual Cash Value (ACV) the net or fair market value of personal or real property; the replacement cost less depreciation. One form of homeowner's insurance provides for replacement of lost property on the ACV basis (so that in the event of a loss, the homeowner receives a depreciated value). A more expensive form—replacement cost coverage—covers the homeowner for actual replacement value, but is subject to certain reimbursement limitations. See also *depreciation; Fair Market Value (FMV); homeowner's insurance; market value; replacement cost*.

actual notice the direct knowledge on the part of a potential buyer of property, resulting from an examination of documents in the public record, of matters pertaining to the title, rights, liens or interests in property. See also *caveat emptor (Lt.); constructive notice; title.*

actual possession the physical occupancy of a property or direct control over it, whether title is held fully and legally or not. Actual possession is distinguished from contruction possession, which may be assumed based on registration of title. See also *constructive possession; possession; right of possession; title.*

ad valorem tax a form of tax according to the value of the property. The tax is at a fixed rate per dollar of assessed valuation. See also *tax basis; value.*

addition (1) an improvement to an existing building, as when a homeowner adds a new room or floor. (2) the construction of a subdivision of homes or other buildings. (3) the purchase of land adjoining a present parcel that increases the total holdings and value of a property. See *improvement; land; subdivision.*

add-on interest interest added to the principal amount of a loan, with a note signed for the total of payments. In comparison, the more common form of mortgage loan requires commitment to a note for the amount borrowed with a rate of interest specified, with interest computed each month on the outstanding balance of that loan. See also *amortization; full amortization; interest; mortgage.*

Adjustable Rate Mortgage (ARM) a type of mortgage loan in which the interest rate will be adjusted from time to time, based upon changes in an agreed-upon index that measures interest rates. An ARM contract should specify a rate cap per period and for the entire term of the loan. The alternative form, the Fixed Rate Mortgage (FRM), includes a rate of interest that remains unchanged as long as the loan is outstanding. See also *Fixed Rate Mortgage (FRM); interest; mortgage; rate cap.*

adjusted basis the cost of property including original cost, plus closing costs and improvements, and less depreciation. See also *closing costs; depreciation; improvement.*

adjusted sales price the sales price of property, including the actual sales value, less commissions and other closing costs paid. See also *closing costs; commission.*

adjusted tax basis the cost of a property for income tax purposes. This generally includes the purchase price plus certain closing costs (but excluding closing costs allowed as itemized deductions at the time of purchase), plus improvements made to the property, and less allowed depreciation. The basis is reduced further for any deferred profits allowed on a previous property sale. See also *capital gain/loss; deferred gain; depreciation; improvement; tax basis.*

adjustments expenses charged to sellers and buyers at the time of closing a real estate transaction, also called closing costs. See also *closing statement; settlement.* [See overleaf.]

adjustments

Adjustable Rate Mortgage (ARM)

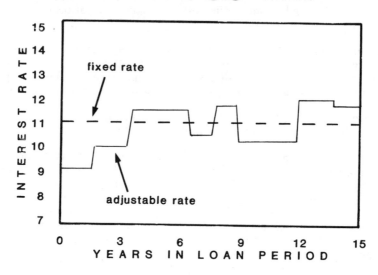

adjusted basis

original cost	$95,000
plus: closing costs	4,245
improvements	14,600
less: depreciation	(27,273)
adjusted basis	$86,572

adjusted sales price

contract price	$113,500
less: commission	(6,810)
other closing costs	(2,440)
adjusted sales price	$104,250

adverse possession a means of acquiring a property without actually holding title, described as the "open, notorious, exclusive and continuous" possession or control of that property for a specified period of time (according to the laws of the state). See also *defective title; possession; title.*

aesthetic value an intangible value assigned to a property for reasons beyond market value. For example, an apartment with an exceptional view might be rented at a rate higher than comparable units; or a home in a particularly desirable location might demand a higher market price than other homes in the same neighborhood. See also *intrinsic value; market value; value.*

affidavit a written declaration that is either notarized or affirmed by an officer of a county, often required when documents usually submitted are not available. See also *declaration.*

affidavit of title a written declaration provided by the seller, asserting that a property's title is not defective. See also *conveyance; defective title; title.*

after-tax cash flow the amount of cash an investor receives during a period of time (such as annually) after income taxes are paid. To compute this, rental receipts are reduced by deductible expenses (including mortgage interest, depreciation, insurance, and other expenses), and an applicable tax rate applied to the operating profit. The resulting after-tax profit must be further reduced by the amount of mortgage principal, and increased by the amount of allowed depreciation (a non-cash deduction). See also *cash flow; cash on cash return; depreciation; investment income.*

after-tax cash flow

rent receipts	$26,400
less: operating expenses	(6,159)
mortgage principal	(2,780)
mortgage interest	(10,859)
net taxable income	$ 6,602
less: taxes	(2,627)
after-tax income	$ 3,975
plus: depreciation	2,909
after-tax cash flow	$ 6,884

after-tax

after-tax profit   the net profit from an investment in real estate that takes into account a reduction for income tax liabilities. This should not be confused with after-tax cash flow, which allows for a reduction due to mortgage principal payments and an increase due to allowed depreciation. See also *capital gain/loss; tax basis.*

agency   descriptive of a relationship between two parties, when one (a principal) agrees to allow the other (the agent) to represent that principal's interests. The agreement may be express, or specified by contract; or it may be implied when an agent acts in accordance with generally understood terms of an agency agreement. See also *express contract; implied contract; principal.*

agency coupled with interest   a relationship between agent and principal in which the agent has or is granted an interest in a property being bought or sold. See also *equity participation; interest; principal.*

agent   an individual who acts in behalf of a principal under the terms of an agency agreement. A real estate agent represents a broker in the buying and selling of properties. See also *broker; principal.*

agreement   a meeting of the minds between two parties to a contract. Whenever a contract matter is disputed, determining the extent of agreement that was reached at the time the contract was entered is a means for arriving at an equitable resolution. See also *contract; meeting of the minds.*

air rights   the ownership or rights of access to air space above the ground. Such rights may refer to a view or direct control of air space. In the case of condominium ownership, owners of individual units are said to own the air space within the structure of their units. See also *condominium; easement.*

aleatory contract   a contract that includes conditions or contingencies. That contract is valid only upon occurrence or performance. For example, a real estate contract may be written with contingencies for obtaining financing; based on findings of a termite or home inspection; or performance of specified repairs. See also *contingency; contract.*

alienation   the conveyance of property from one owner to another, which may be voluntary or involuntary. See also *conveyance; eminent domain; involuntary alienation; title; voluntary alienation.*

allodial system   a form of ownership and property rights allowing individuals to own real estate without conditions or payments due to the government (with the exception of taxation or the government's rights in eminent domain). The allodial system is a free form of ownership, as opposed to the feudal system, under which real ownership is the right of a sovereign power. See also *eminent domain; possession; real law.*

all-risk form   a popular form of homeowner's insurance (also widely called "fire insurance") that includes protection against all perils except named exclusions. See also *fire insurance, HO-3; homeowner's insurance.*

amortization

Alternative Minimum Tax (AMT) a form of federal tax designed to ensure that individuals earning a substantial portion of certain forms of income that are tax-free or reduce taxes substantially (preference items) will pay some level of income tax. The purpose of this tax is to counteract the benefits of tax shelters. The AMT is computed as an alternative to the normal method, and the higher of AMT or normal tax liability is due. Typical preference items include accelerated depreciation and charitable contributions. See also *accelerated depreciation; income tax; tax shelter.*

American Institute of Real Estate Appraisers (AIREA) an organization that applies standards for appraiser members. It tests and grants licenses for the MAI (Member Appraisal Institute) designation, a recognized qualification for appraisers; and for the RM (Residential Member) designation. The AIREA is associated with the National Association of Realtors and publisher the Appraisal Journal and information for its members. Address: 430 North Michigan Avenue, Chicago IL 60611. See also *appraiser; Member Appraisal Institute (MAI); Residential Member (RM).*

American Land Title Association (ALTA) an association of title companies and related service providers (attorneys and abstract specialists). The organization has designed and recommended standardized forms and coverage standards. See also *abstract of title; title company.*

American Society of Appraisers (ASA) a trade association of appraisers, ASA publishes a biannual journal and other material for members. Address: P.O. Box 17265, Washington, DC 20041. See also *appraiser.*

American Society of Home Inspectors (ASHI) a trade association for home inspectors. ASHI standards include extensive experience in home inspections, and adherence to a code of standards. For example, an ASHI inspector may not perform any needed repairs or refer customers to contractors. Address: 655 15th Street N.W., Washington, DC 20005. See also *home inspection; inspection clause.*

American Society of Real Estate Counselors (ASREC) association founded in 1953 and affiliated with the National Association of Realtors since 1954. ASREC awards qualified members the designation Counselor of Real Estate (CRE), and publishes a journal twice per year. The organization's objectives include identification of qualified counselors and consultants in the real estate field, and to apply a Code of Professional Ethics and Standards of Professional Practice. Address: 430 North Michigan Avenue, Chicago IL 60611. See also *Counselor of Real Estate (CRE).*

amortization the process of paying down a loan through periodic installments, until the balance has been completely eliminated. Residential mortgage loans are examples of loans amortized with equal monthly payments. See also *full amortization; level debt service; mortgage.*

amortization table a table that summarizes the monthly payment required to repay loans, arranged in one of two ways. The first type lists the amount of a loan and shows the actual monthly payment required for different terms (such

anchor

as 10, 15, or 30 years). The second type lists a factor for a number of payment periods, which is multiplied by the actual amount of the loan to arrive at a monthly payment. In a book of amortization tables, there is one table for each rate of interest. See also *interest; level debt service; mortgage.*

amortization

(15-year term, 11% interest)

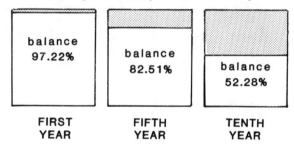

	FIRST YEAR	FIFTH YEAR	TENTH YEAR
balance	97.22%	82.51%	52.28%

amortization table

11% INTEREST

Loan Amount	MONTHLY PAYMENT		
	10 years	15 years	30 years
$50,000	$ 689	$ 568	$ 476
60,000	827	682	571
70,000	964	796	667
80,000	1,102	909	762
90,000	1,240	1,023	857
100,000	1,378	1,137	952

anchor tenant a key tenant in a commercial or retail park or shopping center, also known as the triple-A or magnet tenant. This tenant may be granted a lower lease rent because it will attract other renters to the center. See also *lease; tenant.*

annual compounding a method of computing interest on a balance once every 12 months. This seldom-used method calls for application of the nominal, or stated interest rate to the balance. In the following period, interest is computed on the new balance, including previous interest earned. See also *compound interest; interest; time value of money.*

annual compounding

YEAR	8% INTEREST	BALANCE
		$1,000.00
1	$ 80.00	1,080.00
2	86.40	1,166.40
3	93.31	1,259.71
4	100.78	1,360.49
5	108.84	1,469.33

Annual Percentage Rate (APR)   the actual rate of interest earned or charged, when a compound method more frequent than annual compounding is applied to the balance. For example, monthly compounding at 8% will produce an APR of 8.3%. APR is computed in the following manner:

a) divide the stated rate of interest by the number of periods (12 for monthly compounding, 4 for quarterly, and 2 for semiannual).
b) add 1
c) multiply the sum times itself for the first period
d) multiply by the sum for the number of applicable compound periods in the year

example: monthly compounding at 8%:

a) $\frac{.08\%}{12} = .0067$
b) $1 + .0067 = 1.0067$ (1st month)
c) $1.0067 \times 1.0067 = 1.0134$ (2nd month)
d) $1.0067 \ldots 1.0067$ (12 times) $= 1.0830$ or 8.30% APR

The multiplier of 12 is used because this is an example of monthly compounding, and there are 12 months in a year. In a computation of APR for quarterly compounding, the multiplier 4 is used; and for semiannual compounding, the multiplier is 2. See also *compound interest; interest.* [See overleaf.]

Annual Percentage Rate (APR)

$$\left(1 + \frac{\text{rate}}{\text{periods}}\right)^{\text{periods}} = \text{APR}$$

$$\left(1 + \frac{.08}{12}\right)^{12} = 8.30\%$$

annuity an arrangement under which periodic payments are made for a specified period of time, or for the remainder of the annuitant's life. A sum of money is deposited, usually with an insurance company, over a period of years or in a lump sum. Then, upon annuitization, monthly or quarterly payments are made to the individual at a fixed amount or in variable amounts but with a minimum guaranteed amount. As applied to real estate, homeowners may receive payments for their accumulated home equity through a Reverse Annuity Mortgage (RAM). See also *Reverse Annuity Mortgage (RAM)*.

annuity method an appraisal method, more commonly known as the cost approach. See also *appraisal by summation; appraisal method; cost approach; depreciation; present value; replacement cost*.

anticipated value the expectation of future profits from a real estate investment, based on assumed outside influences. For example, an investor may purchase raw land on the expectation that development will move in that direction; or one may add an improvement to a home expecting value to meet or exceed cost. See also *market value; present value*.

anticipation a theory in the valuation of properties that increases or decreases in market value may occur in anticipation of a future change. For example, if owners or prospective buyers believe a future zoning change will occur, property values could rise or fall in anticipation of that rumor. See also *change; competition; conformity; contribution; diminishing returns; highest and best use; increasing returns; plottage; regression; substitution; supply and demand*.

anticipatory breach notice in advance of a contract deadline by a party to the contract that he or she will not see the transaction through. This may occur, for example, during an escrow period. Either a buyer or seller informs the other that they do not intend to complete and close the purchase or sale. See also *breach of contract; contract*.

appraisal

apartment   a collective group of residential units, numbering from a few to hundreds. None of the units are individually owned, but are rented to tenants and managed collectively by the owner or a resident manager. During a conversion, some or all of the apartment units are sold to occupants and become condominiums or cooperative units. Generally, a residential rental development is classified under the following terms:

one unit	house
two units	duplex
three units	triplex
four units or more	apartments

See also *multiple dwelling; resident manager; residential property.*

apparent authority   a form of authorization that is believed to be held by an agent in an agency relationship. For example, a home buyer or seller believes that a real estate agent has the right to represent the broker's interests. See also *agency; implied contract.*

appliance   a removable item that is operated by gas or electric power. An appliance may be taken from a property upon change in owners or tenants, depending upon the terms of the contract. For example, a buyer agrees to include the refrigerator, electric range, washer and dryer in the sales price. An appliance is distinguished from a fixture in its portability. For example, a plug-in air conditioner is an appliance, and a central air conditioning system is a fixture. See also *fixture; personal property.*

application fee   a closing cost charged by a lender to investigate the credit and financial strength of a potential borrower, also called a loan origination fee. See also *closing costs; loan origination fee.*

appointments   the appliances, fixtures and design features within a property that add to value or set a tone or mood. See also *fixture; personal property.*

appraisal   an estimate of the fair market value of property, for the purpose of establishing a reasonable sales or purchase price range. An appraisal should be conducted by a neutral individual who does not hold an interest in the property. Professional appraisers use one of three methods—the cost, income or market comparison approach—or a combination of the three. See also *cost approach; income approach; market comparison approach; valuation.*

appraisal by summation   an alternative term meaning the same as the cost approach of appraisal. See also *annuity method; cost approach; depreciation; present value; replacement cost.*

appraisal method   one of the three common methods used by professional appraisers for placing a value on real estate. See also *cost approach; income approach; market comparison approach.*

appraisal report   a formal or informal summary of an appraiser's opinion as to the value of a piece of real estate. The report may be in the form of a written letter, or an affidavit. When an appraisal is requested as part of a sale and

appraised

purchase, the cost is included as a closing cost. The report contains the legal description and street address of the property; the date of the appraisal; descriptions of all structures and improvements; the purpose of the appraisal and individual or firm requesting it; a discussion of comparable values, highest and best use of the property, and a history of the property and the area; the appraiser's licenses and qualifications; appraisal method(s) used; and the appraised value. See also *closing costs; highest and best use; legal description; valuation.*

appraised value the current market value of a property in the opinion of an appraiser. See also *Fair Market Value (FMV); market value; valuation.*

appraiser any individual who gives an opinion as to the current market value of property. A recognized license qualifying a person to perform appraisals is the MAI (Member Appraisal Institute), although there is no national requirement stating who may or may not act in the capacity of an appraiser. See also *Member Appraisal Institute (MAI); market value; valuation.*

appreciation growth in market value of real estate, due to improvements, increased demand or a positive transition in a neighborhood. See also *capital gain/loss; market value.*

area the size of a parcel of land, a building or a room, usually expressed in square feet. A square or rectangular shape's area is computed by multiplying the length (in feet) by the width (in feet). A triangle's area is one-half the sum of the base multiplied by the height. For irregular shapes, break down into squares, rectangles or triangles, and then compute partial areas and add the sum. See also *legal description; parcel.*

---

area

> length x width

> 175' x 75' = 13,125 square feet

---

artificial tax loss a loss that is not economic, but claimed as a means for reducing a tax liability. Such losses were seen in many real estate limited partnerships in the past, and were known as abusive tax shelters. See also *Alternative Minimum Tax (AMT); investment income; tax shelter.*

as is   a condition included in some contracts specifying that no warranties or guarantees are made, and that the property is being sold exactly in the existing condition. A purchaser who signs an as is contract has no recourse upon later discovery of defects in the property. See also *contingency; contract; home inspection; settlement.*

asking price   the listed price of real estate, also considered a starting point for a negotiated offer. See also *listing; negotiation; offer to sell.*

assessed valuation   the basis for assessment of real estate taxes. The asset valuation of a property is usually substantially lower than actual market value. See also *ad valorem tax; market value; tax basis; value.*

assessment   the amount due for ad valorem tax as calculated by the taxing agency, or a special one-time additional tax, as for sidewalks or sewer installation. See also *ad valorem tax; property taxes.*

assessment ratio   a comparison between the assessed value and the market value of a property, expressed as a percentage. Divide assessed value by market value to arrive at the ratio. See also *market value; tax basis.*

---

assessment ratio

$$\frac{\text{assessed value}}{\text{market value}}$$

$$\frac{54{,}000}{120{,}000} = 45\%$$

---

assignment   the transfer of property rights or obligations from one person or company to another. Assignment refers to transfers of title through a deed of trust, lease and sublease arrangements, and liability related to a mortgage. See also *deed of trust; lease; mortgage; sublease.*

assumable mortgage   a mortgage liability that, by terms of the contract, may be transferred from the original borrower to a subsequent buyer of the property. The effective rate of interest and other terms of the mortgage may also be transferred, or may be renegotiated at the time of transfer. See also *Fixed Rate Mortgage (FRM); interest; mortgage.*

assumed

assumed mortgage   a mortgage loan that is taken over by a buyer when property is transferred, often with the same terms and conditions that the original owner had by contract. See also *contract; debt service; interest; loan.*

assumption fee   a form of closing cost assessed by a lender for the cost of transferring an existing loan from the original borrower (seller) to the new borrower (buyer). See also *closing costs; loan origination fee.*

at risk   a concept in tax law limiting the deductibility of certain expenses. Deductions may be claimed to no more than the amount an individual has at risk in a program. As a general rule, at risk includes cash paid to the program, plus the total of recourse loans. Nonrecourse loans are not included in the at risk limitation, subject to exceptions. See also *investment program; limited partnership; nonrecourse loan; recourse loan; tax basis.*

attorney in fact   any individual who has been granted written permission to represent another, said to have been given the power of attorney. See also *agent; power of attorney.*

attorney's fee   the fee paid to an attorney for reviewing contracts, performing title search, or otherwise advising a buyer or seller in a real estate transaction. This fee is usually included as a closing cost. See also *closing costs.*

attractive nuisance   descriptive of hazards on or near a property that may endanger children. A purchaser may include as a contingency in a purchase offer the requirement that attractive nuisances be eliminated or mitigated. See also *contingency; real estate; vacant land.*

attribution   the method by which commonly held property in a pooled real estate program is assigned to individual owners. For example, investors in a Real Estate Investment Trust (REIT) do not own individual pieces of property, only shares in the entire trust. Owners of cooperatives and condominiums own air space in individual units as well as attributable shares of common elements. Allocation of ownership is made by way of an attribution formula. See also *condominium; common elements; cooperative housing; beneficial interest; Real Estate Investment Trust (REIT).*

B

bad faith   the intentional failure to live up to the terms of a contract, or to deal honestly with another. See also *breach of contract; contract.*

bad title   a title that fails to deliver what is promised, such as a real estate title that does not convey ownership. See also *clear title; cloud on the title; defective title; good title.*

balance sheet   a financial statement that shows the summarized assets (properties owned), liabilities (debts), and net worth. The sum of liabilities and net worth is equal to total assets. For example, the basis in real estate is listed as an asset, while the outstanding balance of the mortgage is a liability. The difference is an individual's equity (or, net worth) in the property. See also *equity; net worth.*

balance sheet

balloon mortgage   a form of mortgage calling for a series of payments over a period of time, to be followed by a single, lump-sum payment to retire the entire debt. The initial series of payments may consist of interest only, or a small portion of principal. Also called a Renegotiated Rate Mortgage (RRM), the balloon arrangement may take the following form: a loan is granted with payments set on a 30-year amortization schedule. However, the entire balance of the loan is repayable after five years—requiring a balloon payment at that time. See also *creative financing; interest only; mortgage; Renegotiated Rate Mortgage (RRM).*

balloon payment

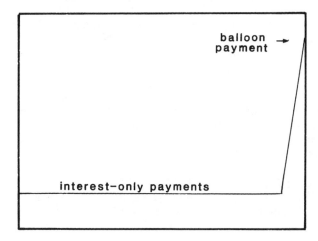

Bank

Bank for Cooperatives (Co-Op) an agency affiliated with the Farm Credit Administration (FCA) that finances real estate purchases for farmers and farm cooperatives. See also *Farm Credit Administration (FCA); financing.*

base rent the amount charged in a lease or rental agreement that is paid at a set level each month. The agreement may also call for additional payments above base rent, according to the level of gross receipts, or for property taxes, utilities, maintenance or other charges paid by the owner. See also *percentage lease; tenant.*

basic policy a form of homeowner's insurance providing coverage only for limited, named perils, also called HO-1. See also *fire insurance; HO-1; homeowner's insurance.*

basis the original cost of property, plus closing costs paid by the buyer, plus any capital improvements, and less depreciation claimed. See also *capital gain/loss; depreciation; tax basis.*

---

basis

purchase price	$105,000
closing costs	6,150
improvements	22,000
depreciation	(19,400)
basis	$113,750

---

basis adjusted cost for tax purposes, the basis in property. The basis adjusted cost is subtracted from the sales price to compute a gain (or the sales price is deducted from basis adjusted cost to arrive at a net loss) to compute a capital gain or loss. See also *capital gain/loss; capital improvement; depreciation; improvement; tax basis.*

basis point one one-hundredth of one percent. Movement in interest rates are described in terms of the number of basis points, with 100 points between whole numbers. For example, there are 25 basis points between 11.00% and 11.25%. See also *interest rate; mortgage.*

before-tax cash flow the amount of money available when total operating expenses and mortgage payments are deducted from rents received, but before income tax liabilities are computed. See also *cash flow; cash on cash return; investment income.*

before-tax cash flow

gross rents	$19,000
operating expenses	(5,800)
mortgage payments	(11,428)
cash flow	$ 1,772

---

beneficial interest   interests in real estate or a real estate program, when a trustee holds title to properties in behalf of others. Although title is held by the trust, profits and operating policies accrue to those with beneficial interests. See also *legal title; power of attorney; Real Estate Investment Trust (REIT); shares of beneficial interest.*

beneficial owner   individuals who own shares in a trust-held real estate investment, such as a Real Estate Investment Trust (REIT) or other pooled investment. Legal title is in the name of the trustee, while beneficial owners hold shares in the trust itself. See also *legal title; Real Estate Investment Trust (REIT); shares of beneficial interest.*

betterment   an improvement considered part of the capital value of property and not maintenance; the addition of structures of internal appointments that add to the property's market value. See also *appointments; capital improvement; improvement; market value.*

bid   the amount suggested as payment for real estate. A bid may be made in response to an offer or counter-offer. Once both sides agree on the price through negotiation, a contract is created. See also *contract; counter-offer; offer to purchase.*

bilateral contract   a form of contract in which both sides agree to perform in some way. A real estate contract is bilateral, as the seller transfers title in exchange for a sum of money the buyer agrees to pay. This exchange represents equal consideration. The bilateral contract differs from a unilateral contract, in which one party promises to perform to induce the other to act. This is not legally binding until the second party does act. For example, a homeowner offers to pay $30 to a neighbor for cutting lawns and trimming hedges. If the neighbor responds by doing that work, a contract is created. See also *consideration; contract; meeting of the minds; unilateral contract.*

bill of sale   a written document used for the transfer from one person to another of personal property. When appliances, fixtures and other non-real estate are included in the sales price of a home, a separate bill of sale is prepared. See also *instrument; personal property; sale.*

binder 20

binder **(1)** a provisional agreement between two people to the general terms of a contract. For example, a purchaser submits a written binder with an earnest money, or good faith deposit, and the seller accepts it, so that the property cannot be sold to another buyer. **(2)** a title insurance report on title to a property as of a specified date, that also lists conditions under which a title insurance policy will be issued by a deadline date. This report is also called a commitment. See also *agreement; commitment; contract; deposit; down payment; earnest money; good faith deposit; title insurance binder.*

blanket mortgage a mortgage secured by more than one parcel of real estate, often granted to developers of subdivisions. In some circumstances, a blanket mortgage covers future real estate holdings in addition to present ones, and is called a general mortgage. See also *general mortgage; mortgage; parcel; subdivision.*

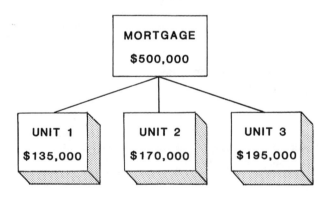

blanket mortgage

blended rate a rate of interest between the current rate being charged by a lender, and an old rate on an outstanding loan. A blended rate may be offered to borrowers as incentive to replace a below-market rate loan. See also *interest; mortgage; weighted average.*

blind pool descriptive of a limited partnership program in which individual properties are not identified specifically. Management of the program indicates it will invest in properties with certain attributes (for example, multi-unit residential properties in urban areas, or commercial and retail parks and centers in suburban areas). The blind pool contrasts with a specified program, which is formed to buy an identified property or properties. See also *limited partnership; risk factor; specified program.*

blended rate

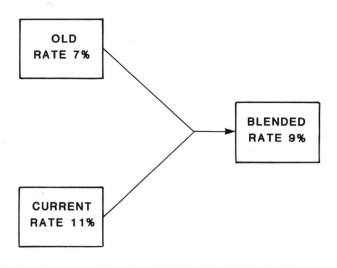

blockbusting illegally encouraging homeowners to sell their homes in response to fears that minorities are moving in. Homeowners are told that minority families are moving to the area, and are offered a deflated price for their homes. The buyer then resells the property at market value and gains a profit. See also *market value; steering.*

blue sky laws state laws restricting representations of value that can be made to the general investing public. The term is a reference to valueless or intangible assets which, like the blue sky, have no value. Salespeople are required under blue sky laws to make full disclosure of risks and valuation of assets in investment programs. See also *full disclosure; investment program; limited partnership.*

bona fide (Lt.) good faith, such as an offer made sincerely and with honest intentions. See also *contract; good faith; offer.*

book value the value of an asset as it is carried on the books. Real estate held by companies is always listed at purchase price, and is reduced by depreciation. Improvements are also carried at a book value equal to cost, regardless of the amount of increase in market value. In situations where market value is greater than net book value, the difference is not reflected on a company's balance sheet. See also *balance sheet; depreciation; improvement; market value.*

boot the difference when real estate is exchanged and agreed upon market values are unequal. One side in the transaction must include an amount of cash or other consideration to boot the value. See also *exchange; market value.*

boundary

boundary rights   the various rights to possession and access a property owner holds. See also *interest; right of possession; right of way.*

bounds   property lines, specified in a legal description of property by points and angles. See also *legal description; metes and bounds description.*

breach of contract   a failure to comply with the provisions in a legal contract, by not performing as promised; not making an agreed upon payment; not delivering title; or otherwise acting contrary to the agreement. See also *anticipatory breach; bad faith; contract.*

breakeven   the level of occupancy in a rental property at which the investor earns enough money to pay operating expenses and mortgages. The total of payments is divided by maximum rental income (assuming 100% occupancy), and the breakeven is expressed as a percentage. For example, annual operating expenses and mortgage payments total $47,835; and fully occupied, rents total $68,000. Breakeven is 70.3%. See also *investment income; occupancy rate; risk factor.*

breakeven

$$\frac{\text{total payments}}{\text{maximum rent}}$$

$$\frac{\$47,835}{\$68,000} = 70.3\%$$

bridge loan   interim financing, applicable when one loan ends but another has not yet started. As a general rule, bridge loans are granted for periods of four months or less. See also *down payment; financing; mortgage.*

brief of title   a document explaining the history of a property and its mortgages, liens and other encumbrances. See also *abstract of title; encumbrance; lien; mortgage; title company.*

broad form   a form of homeowner's insurance, also referred to as HO-2, that protects against 18 named perils. See also *fire insurance; HO-2; homeowner's insurance.*

broker one who facilitates the buying and selling of properties for another. See also *agent; principal.*

brokerage the practice of representing and matching buyers and sellers, and charging a commission for the service. See also *agent; commission; principal.*

broker's statement to seller a billing given to the seller for expenses paid by the broker. The seller is liable for these expenses, often as a form of closing cost. See also *closing costs.*

budget loan a mortgage that includes monthly estimates for property taxes and homeowner's insurance, as well as principal and interest. For example, the mortgage payment is $761.86 per month. Property taxes are estimated at $814.23 per year, and homeowner's insurance at $350. One-twelfth of these estimates is added to the payment each month, and the lender then makes payment directly for insurance and taxes. See also *homeowner's insurance; mortgage; Principal, Interest, Taxes and Insurance (PITI); property taxes.*

budget loan

principal and interest	$761.86
property taxes	67.85
homeowner's insurance	29.17
total monthly payment	**$858.88**

builder warranty a warranty against defects that is offered by a builder to purchasers of new homes. The warranty lasts only a limited period of time, usually one year. See also *condominium; development; subdivision.*

building code detailed rules and regulations governing standards of construction in a city or county. A local code applies to new construction as well as to improvements in existing properties. See also *improvement.*

building lien also called a Mechanic's Lien, an encumbrance on a property to ensure a contractor will be paid as specified in a contract. See also *encumbrance; lien; Mechanic's Lien.*

building permit a form of written permission required for the construction, renovation or improvement of property. See also *improvement.*

build-up

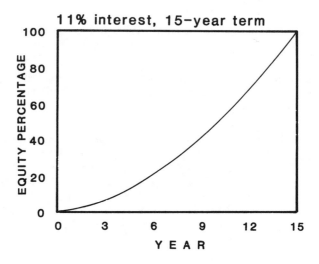

build-up the increase over time in equity in a real estate investment, resulting from accumulated principal payments. See also *equity build-up; mortgage acceleration; principal.*

built-in permanent fixtures or appliances added to a home or other property. A built-in is distinguished from personal property or appliances in its permanent attachment. For example, an oven is an appliance, whether included in the sale or removed, because it is removable; but a permanently installed dishwasher is permanent, and is a built-in. See also *appliance; fixture.*

bundle of rights the collective rights that property owners have, including the rights of possession and occupancy and the right to give away, sell, lease, or mortgage real estate. See also *allodial system; real law; right of occupancy; right of possession.*

business day a day during which business is conducted. A deadline for making a deposit, or the terms of escrow may specify the number of business days allowed. In that case, weekends and holidays are excluded. See also *contract; deposit; escrow.*

business trust a form of organization that operates in behalf of individuals holding shares of beneficial interest, such as a Real Estate Investment Trust (REIT). This is an unincorporated entity that generally passes profits to shareholders with equitable title, and is not directly liable for income taxes. The trust is responsible for the selection and management of holdings in behalf of the

buy back an agreement included in a contract that the seller will buy back a property at a specified price if an event takes place within a specified period of time. The contingency may relate to the buyer's status. For example, a contract may state that the seller will repurchase a property if the buyer's employer terminates or relocates him within one year. See also *agreement; contingency; contract.*

buy-down mortgage an arrangement to facilitate the purchase of property when the buyer cannot otherwise qualify for financing, or provided as an incentive to purchase. The buyer is offered below-market interest for a stated period of time, such as three years. The seller (a developer or builder) agrees to pay the lender the difference. At the end of the term, the loan reverts to either an agreed fixed rate or to a prevailing adjustable rate. In a buy-down agreement, the price of the property is probably raised to offset the advantages of lower interest. See also *Adjustable Rate Mortgage (ARM); creative financing; Fixed Rate Mortgage (FRM); mortgage.*

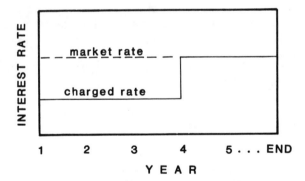

buy-sell agreement an agreement between two or more people or groups of people to repurchase properties if a specified event occurs. See also *agreement; contingency; contract.*

buyer's broker one who represents the buyer in a real estate transaction. In a normal brokerage arrangement, the real estate broker represents the seller. See also *broker; commission; selling agent.*

buyer's

buyer's instructions   a document listing all of the closing costs the buyer must pay, the deadline for submitting payment, and all other actions the buyer must take to successfully complete escrow on a purchase. See also *closing costs; escrow; purchase price.*

buyer's market   descriptive of a condition in which the supply of properties exceeds demand. In that situation, the buyer may choose from a variety of available properties, usually at attractive prices. See also *seller's market.*

C

call provision   a provision in a mortgage contract that gives the lender the right to declare that the entire balance is due and payable. It may be exercised if a specified event takes place, such as sale or destruction of the property. See also *acceleration clause; contract.*

cancellation   a provision in some sale or lease contracts enabling one party or the other to cancel the agreement if a specified event occurs. In a lease, a cancellation clause may state that the owner can cancel the lease if the property is sold. A seller in a real estate transaction may cancel the contract if the buyer is unable to obtain financing by a specified date. See also *contingency; contract; lease; release clause; transfer clause.*

cap   a maximum amount or rate included in some Adjustable Rate Mortgage (ARM) contracts. A rate cap limits the rate of interest the lender can raise during a certain period of time, or during the entire term of the loan. A payment cap limits the total amount of payment a borrower can be required to make each month. See also *Adjustable Rate Mortgage (ARM); mortgage; negative amortization; payment cap; rate cap.*

capacity   the legal ability or potential to enter into a legal contract. See also *contract; ready, willing and able; voidable contract.*

capital gain/loss   the difference between the basis in property and the net sales price. If the sales price is greater, a capital gain results. If less, it is a capital loss. "Capital" is distinguished from "ordinary" gains and losses as a distinction in tax basis. Capital gains before the Tax Reform Act of 1986 were taxed at lower rates than ordinary gains. See also *gain; loss; ordinary gain/loss; tax basis; Tax Reform Act of 1986.*

capital improvement   an improvement to property that adds permanently to structures and, according to tax rules, adds value to the adjusted basis of the owner. See also *adjusted basis; improvement.*

capitalization   the total funding of a company. It may consist of debt (through loans) or equity (represented by shareholder or investor payments). The sum of all capitalization is available to the company's management to operate the concern. In an investment program, capitalization may consist of general and limited partner investments and borrowed money. See also *debt; equity; investment program; limited partnership.*

capitalization rate a percentage estimating a profit considered likely or reasonable in a real estate program, used to base future market value, notably for commercial properties. The annual net income (consisting of annual gross rents less estimated vacancies and operating expenses) is divided by the property's purchase price. See also *commercial property; market value; occupancy rate; purchase price; rate of return.*

capitalization rate

$$\frac{\text{annual net income}}{\text{purchase price}}$$

$$\frac{\$52,000}{\$580,000} = 8.97\%$$

carryover basis the tax basis in a property when gain on a sale or exchange is deferred for tax purposes. The new property's basis is reduced in the amount of gain that is deferred, to be taxed upon sale of the new property. See also *adjusted basis; deferred gain; exchange; tax basis.*

carryover clause a provision often included in an exclusive listing contract. The listing broker would be entitled to a commission if the seller comes to an agreement with a buyer initially shown the property by that agent, following expiration of the exclusive listing term. The clause is effective for a specified and limited time following the exclusive agreement. See also *commission; exclusive listing; listing broker.*

cash flow the amount of cash actually available to an investor in real estate, considering gross income less cash-basis operating expenses and mortgage payments (and excluding depreciation, which is a non-cash expense). The term may be used to indicate either after-tax or before-tax cash. See also *after-tax cash flow; before-tax cash flow; debt service; investment program; negative cash flow; risk factor.* [See overleaf.]

cash flow

gross income	$184,000
less: operating expenses	(21,196)
loan payments	(68,196)
cash flow	$ 94,608

---

cash flow per share the amount of cash produced from an income program, divided by the number of shares outstanding. See also *after-tax cash flow; before-tax cash flow; investment program; Real Estate Investment Trust (REIT)*.

---

cash flow per share

$$\frac{\text{cash flow}}{\text{outstanding shares}}$$

$$\frac{\$94{,}608}{250{,}000} = 37.8 \text{ cents}$$

---

cash on cash return a term describing return on invested capital or return on equity in a real estate investment program. The cash flow during a period of time is divided by cash invested, and the result is expressed as a percentage. See also *investment income; rate of return; return on equity*.

cash value an estimate of market value on a property that will result from an immediate sale, barring a delay that could be expected by setting a higher or firm price. See also *asking price; firm price; market value*.

casualty insurance any form of insurance against unexpected losses from weather and other natural causes, vandalism or theft, fire and other events. In a homeowner's insurance policy, casualty insurance is one of two types, the other being liability protection. See also *fire insurance; homeowner's insurance; liability insurance*.

cash on cash return

$$\frac{\text{cash flow}}{\text{cash invested}}$$

$$\frac{\$94{,}608}{\$512{,}830} = 18.4\%$$

---

caveat actor (Lt.)   a legal term meaning "let the one who takes action beware," a reference to the concept that taking action in a contract carries with it certain contingencies. See also *contract*.

caveat emptor (Lt.)   a term meaning "let the buyer beware," a reference that buyers assume certain risks. In entering a real estate contract, the buyer is advised to exercise caution by evaluating and inspecting properties before signing. See also *contract*.

caveat vendor (Lt.)   a term meaning "let the seller beware," a reference to contingent liabilities assumed by sellers of property. For example, a seller has the duty to disclose defects to buyers before a contract is signed. Failure to do so could result in a future liability to correct the problem not disclosed. See also *contract*.

ceiling price   the highest possible price that a property will bring on the market, given the best possible presentation under current conditions of supply and demand; or the maximum amount of rent that can be charged for a rental property under present market conditions. See also *asking price; market value; supply and demand*.

certificate of limited partnership   a public notice announcing the formation and disclosing the structure of a new limited partnership offering, which is a requirement under terms of the Uniform Limited Partnership Act (ULPA). See also *full disclosure; investment program; limited partnership; public offering; Uniform Limited Partnership Act (ULPA)*.

certificate of occupancy   a notice from a local building inspection department verifying that the property is in compliance with all code and zoning specifications. See also *building code; zoning*.

certificate

certificate of sale a document given to the buyer in a tax foreclosure sale. It states that the buyer paid property taxes that were due and that the title was passed following the redemption period. The instrument itself does not convey actual title to the property. See also *conveyance; foreclosure; property taxes; redemption period.*

certificate of title a document sometimes used in place of an abstract of title, expressing an opinion on the insurability of a property, following an examination of title recordings. See also *abstract of title; title insurance policy.*

Certified Commercial Investment Member (CCIM) a professional designation given to members of the Realtors National Marketing Institute (RNMI). See also *Realtors National Marketing Institute (RNMI).*

Certified Mortgage Banker (CMB) a designation given to members of the Mortgage Bankers Association (MBA). See also *Mortgage Bankers Association (MBA).*

Certified Property Manager (CPM) a designation awarded to qualified members of the Institute of Real Estate Management (IREM). See also *Institute of Real Estate Management (IREM).*

Certified Residential Broker (CRB) a designation awarded to members of the Realtors National Marketing Institute (RNMI). See also *Realtors National Marketing Institute (RNMI).*

chain of title the unbroken and fully accounted record of ownership, transfers, liens and mortgages for a particular property. See also *abstract of title; conveyance; encumbrance.*

change one of the basic principles in the valuation of real estate, stating that conditions do not remain unchanged. A change in the economic climate (factors of supply and demand), physical condition (deterioration or improvement), or natural occurrence (disasters and casualties) will affect a property's market value. See also *anticipation; competition; conformity; contribution; diminishing returns; highest and best use; increasing returns; plottage; regression; substitution; supply and demand.*

chattel tangible personal property, as compared with fixtures (permanently attached to property) or real estate. See also *personal property; tangible property.*

chattel mortgage a loan in which personal property serves as collateral. See also *collateral; encumbrance; mortgage; personal property; secured debt.*

Civil Rights Act of 1866 a law intended to enforce provisions of the 14th Amendment to the U.S. Constitution. The Act states, "All citizens of the United States shall have the same right in every state and territory as is enjoyed by white citizens thereof to inherit, purchase, lease, sell, hold, and convey real and personal property." See also *allodial system; personal property; real property.*

Civil Rights Act of 1964 a law banning discriminatory practices in the purchase or sale of housing that is part of a federally funded program. See also *Department of Housing and Urban Development (HUD); steering.*

clear title descriptive of title held without clouds or disputes. See also *cloud on the title; encumbrance; quiet enjoyment; title.*

close (1) the date on which escrow is completed and title is passed. (2) the process of signing documents and transferring title from the buyer to the seller. See also *contract; conveyance; escrow; execution.*

closed-end mortgage a form of mortgage in which the borrower has no rights to borrow additional money as part of the same contract. See also *conventional loan; mortgage; open-end mortgage.*

closing costs all costs associated with the close in a real estate transaction. Buyers must pay loan and title search fees, title and homeowner's insurance premiums, appraisal fees, and recording and transfer expenses. Sellers must pay broker costs and commissions, inspection fees, and transfer costs. In some cases, certain costs may be negotiated and split between buyers and sellers, or paid by one or the other. See also *adjusted basis; escrow; settlement.*

closing date the actual date on which title to a property is transferred from the buyer to the seller. See also *conveyance; sale; settlement; title.*

closing statement a document given to each side in a real estate transaction summarizing the total amount due or payable and accounting for the payment of all funds in escrow, including all closing costs. See also *adjusted basis; escrow; settlement.*

cloud on the title descriptive of a title that includes a defect of some kind, such as an unsettled claim. A cloud inhibits the current owner's ability to sell the property. See also *clear title; conveyance; defective title; encumbrance.*

cluster an arrangement of homes in a development in which a series of parcels are grouped, or clustered. The plan allows for open space and parking room. See also *curvilinear system; development; gridiron pattern; loop streets; Radburn Plan; subdivision.*

Code of Ethics the principles by which members of an association agree to abide. The purpose of a Code is to set minimum standards for professional and ethical performance; professionalism; education; and dealings with customers and the public. See also *National Association of Realtors (NAR).*

co-insurance a principle under which an insurer will carry a limited portion of total coverage on a policy. For example, homeowner's insurance carriers generally will directly insure 80% of a home's replacement value. See also *homeowner's insurance; replacement value.*

collateral assets pledged as security in a loan. For example, real estate serves as collateral in a mortgage. See also *mortgage; secured debt.*

Collateralized

Collateralized Mortgage Obligation (CMO) a form of debt instrument. Income from a mortgage pool of unlike mortgages is invested in the CMO so that payments to investors are leveled out over time. See also *debt instrument; investment program; mortgage security.*

color of title a title that appears to be good but is actually defective. See also *cloud on the title; defective title; good title.*

commercial property investment real estate that usually includes office space, often combined with retail or industrial outlets. See also *investment property; residential property.*

commission an amount of money paid by the seller to a real estate broker, for the successful sale of property. The commission is usually a set percentage of the final sales price, but may be negotiated to either a lower than standard rate, or to a flat amount. See also *agent; broker; salesperson.*

commitment (1) a promise to perform in the future. For example, a developer may promise a lender that a specific portion of occupancy will be achieved in a new development by a specific date. (2) a firm commitment by a lender regarding terms and rate on a mortgage loan. In some instances, a commitment might be conditional upon verification of a borrower's credit rating. (3) indicated future capital requirements in a Real Estate Investment Trust (REIT). For example, an REIT committed to the funding or purchase of property (less operating expenses and other obligations) requires a calculable amount of cash in coming months and years. See also *contingency; mortgage commitment; occupancy rate; Real Estate Investment Trust (REIT); stand-by commitment; take-out commitment.*

common area maintenance the amount charged to owners of condominium or cooperative units for maintenance, insurance and other expenses of areas held not individually, but by the condominium development as a whole. See also *condominium; cooperative housing.*

common elements the areas of condominium or cooperative housing developments that are owned as undivided interests by all owners, including the outside of buildings, parking lots, swimming pools, elevators and stairways, and grounds. See also *condominium; cooperative housing; undivided interest.*

community property a concept of law in some states that all assets accumulated during a marriage are owned jointly by both husband and wife, regardless of whose efforts produced those assets. See also *joint tenancy; separate property; tenancy in common; unity of ownership.*

comparative method an appraisal method in which market value is estimated based on the replacement value of a similar property. See also *appraisal method; market value; replacement value.*

compensating balance a form of collateral required by lenders, to be held in an account until the loan is paid. See also *collateral; loan; secured debt.*

competition a principle in computing value of properties, that opportunities for profit invite competition. If demand is stable, the additional competition will dilute earnings for all competitors. Thus, the potential for growth in value is limited. See also *anticipation; change; conformity; contribution; diminishing returns; highest and best use; increasing returns; plottage; regression; substitution; supply and demand.*

competitive market analysis a method of estimating current market value of a property based upon a study of final sales prices on recently sold, similar properties, or current listings. This is often used to set an initial listing price on a home, in recognition of the limits in market value that are set by recent sales. See also *Fair Market Value (FMV); listing; market value.*

completion bond a bond protecting the homeowner when a contractor is completing a home improvement. The bond ensures completion of the job as agreed. See also *improvement; performance.*

component building a building that is made of prefabricated sections. See also *manufactured home; modular home; prefabricated housing.*

compound interest a method of computing interest on a total balance. Interest may be computed under one of several methods:

method	periods per year
daily	360 or 365
monthly	12
quarterly	4
semiannual	2
annual	1

See also *annual compounding; daily compounding; monthly compounding; quarterly compounding; semiannual compounding; simple interest.*

compound interest

YEAR	8% COMPOUND INTEREST ON A $100 DEPOSIT			
	MONTHLY	QUARTERLY	SEMI-ANNUAL	ANNUAL
1	$108.30	$108.24	$108.16	$108.00
2	117.29	117.17	116.99	116.64
3	127.02	126.82	126.53	125.97

comprehensive

comprehensive   a policy form of homeowner's insurance including protection against all perils except specifically named exceptions, also known as HO-5. See also *fire insurance; HO-5; homeowner's insurance.*

concurrent authority   a situation in which an open listing is available to many brokers at the same time. Any of the brokers has concurrent authority to present offers from prospective buyers. See also *broker; commission; open listing.*

conditional sale   a form of sale in which title remains with the seller until certain conditions have been met, usually payment of a loan carried by the seller. However, the buyer may take possession during the conditional period. See also *contingency; contract; installment contract; land contract; possession; title.*

condominium   a form of housing in which multiple units are contructed on commonly owned land, but units are owned individually. That portion of property not directly a part of each unit is owned in common by all unit owners. See also *cooperative housing; multiple dwelling.*

condominium policy   a policy form of homeowner's insurance designed specifically for owners of condominiums. Also known as HO-6, it provides coverage for personal property but not for the building itself, which is included on a policy held by the condominium association. See also *fire insurance; HO-6; homeowner's insurance.*

condominium regime   the self-ruling principles under which a condominium development operates. The undivided interests of individual owners are subject to rules set by the association in the interest of all residents of the development. See also *multiple dwelling; undivided interest.*

conduit tax treatment   a method of assigning tax liabilities for pooled investments, such as Real Estate Investment Trust (REIT) or limited partnership forms. The conduit organization passes all profits through to investors and, as an entity, pays no direct income tax. See also *limited partnership; Real Estate Investment Trust (REIT); tax basis.*

conformity   one of the basic principles of valuation; a property's market value is most enhanced when it conforms with other properties in the same area in terms of construction and style. For example, a house should be of the same age, style, layout, and construction quality as other houses on the same street. See also *anticipation; change; competition; contribution; diminishing returns; highest and best use; increasing returns; plottage; regression; substitution; supply and demand.*

consideration   value, as a basic test of a contract's validity. Without equal consideration, a contract cannot stand. For example, a seller offers to convey title to real estate in consideration of an agreed amount of money. See also *contract.*

construction and development REIT   a type of Real Estate Investment Trust (REIT) formed for the purpose of lending money to developers and contractors

conduit tax treatment

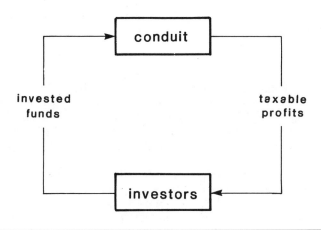

involved in the construction of new real estate projects. See also *equity REIT; hybrid REIT; Real Estate Investment Trust (REIT); risk factor.*

constructive eviction   an act by a landlord in a rental situation, or by a seller in a transaction of real estate, that prevents a tenant or buyer from holding or taking possession. For example, a landlord may remove a staircase leading to the entrance to an apartment during a renovation, making it impossible for the tenant to occupy the unit. See also *clear title; eviction.*

constructive notice   the assumption that a person in a transaction should know something, and that actual notice is not required. For example, in a real estate transaction, a title search will reveal the existence of recorded documents. If an outstanding lien exists on a property, and the title search would reveal it, there is an assumption that constructive notice has been given to a prospective buyer. See also *actual notice; legal notice.*

constructive possession   a situation in which someone holds title to a property, but does not necessarily occupy the property physically. See also *actual possession; possession; title.*

contingency   a provision that makes a contract subject to a specified condition. For example, a buyer offers to purchase a property, contingent upon approval of financing; or an offer is made contingent upon the satisfactory completion of an independent home inspection. See also *contract; financing; home inspection.*

contingent 36

contingent interest   a reference to a liability for interest on a loan that will be payable only if a specified condition is met. See also *contract; interest.*

contingent sale   a conditional sale, one that is final if a specified event occurs or action is taken. If the contingency is satisfied, the sale is final. See also *conditional sale; sale.*

contract   a legal agreement resulting from the acceptance of an offer. To be valid, a real estate contract must be in writing, and must exist between two parties of legal age; it must be dated and must include a full description of the property being conveyed; it must be signed; it must specify the date, time and place for final closing of the sale; all other terms and contingencies must be spelled out in full; and there must be equal consideration. See also *acceptance; agreement; closing date; consideration; conveyance; legal description; offer.*

contribution   a theory that the relative value of improvements and additions to a property is limited. The real value is not equal to cost, but to the amount an improvement adds to market value. See also *anticipation; change; competition; conformity; diminishing returns; highest and best use; increasing returns; plottage; regression; substitution; supply and demand.*

conventional loan   a mortgage loan from a bank, savings and loan association or other non-government lender or individual, that contains no unusual or exceptional provisions. See also *creative financing; lending institution; mortgage.*

conversion   **(1)** a change in ownership of property, either voluntarily (through a sale, for example) or involuntarily (by way of foreclosure). **(2)** a change in the purpose and use of property, as when apartment units are converted and sold as condominiums. See also *alienation; condominium; foreclosure; highest and best use; involuntary alienation; voluntary alienation.*

conveyance   **(1)** a written document that transfers title to property from one party to another. **(2)** the act of changing the title to real estate, from the seller to the buyer. See also *instrument; title.*

cooperative housing   a form of indirect ownership of real estate. Buyers of co-op's have the right of occupancy to a unit but, unlike a condominium, do not own property directly. The ownership is limited to shares in the co-op. The development is governed by an association. See also *condominium; multiple dwelling; right of occupancy.*

co-ownership   a form of owning in unity with other investors or owners. In a partnership, each partner owns units of the whole. In a joint tenancy in real estate, each owner has a share of ownership in the entire property. See also *joint tenancy; partnership; tenancy in common; unity of ownership.*

corner lot   a parcel with frontage on two streets. See also *lot and block description; parcel.*

corporate equivalent yield   the yield that is equal to the level of payments from a pass-through investment. See also *Ginnie Mae pass-through; pass-through investment.*

cost approach   an appraisal method in which an estimate is made of the cost to acquire a property of equal value to the property in question. The method involves four steps:
   1. The value of land is estimated on the basis of its being put to its highest and best use.
   2. The cost to construct the building is estimated by today's construction costs.
   3. A factor is subtracted for physical, functional and locational obsolescence.
   4. The estimates of land and building value are added, and depreciation is subtracted.
See also *appraisal by summation; curable depreciation; functional obsolescence; highest and best use; locational obsolescence; physical depreciation; replacement cost; substitution.*

cost recovery   the system under which capital assets may be depreciated for tax purposes, introduced as part of the ACRS depreciation program within the Economic Recovery Tax Act of 1981 (ERTA). See also *Accelerated Cost Recovery System (ACRS); depreciation; Economic Recovery Tax Act of 1981 (ERTA); recovery period.*

cost-to-carry   a computation of the debt service on a non-earning asset held by a Real Estate Investment Trust (REIT) until that asset can either be sold or brought to earning status. For example, an REIT is holding an office building that is being renovated. It is estimated that no tenants will move in for another eight months. The total of payments due on the mortgage for the next eight months, plus any deficiency for partial occupancy beyond that date, is the cost-to-carry. See also *debt service; interest; Real Estate Investment Trust (REIT).*

Counselor of Real Estate (CRE)   a designation held by members of the American Society of Real Estate Counselors (ASREC). Membership requires experience in counseling and proof of professional conduct. See also *American Society of Real Estate Counselors (ASREC).*

counter-offer   a response to an offer in which different terms are proposed. See also *acceptance; contract; negotiation; offer.*

creative financing   descriptive of the terms of a loan that are other than accepted and traditional terms. Many forms of creative financing are devised to enable borrowers to qualify for loans when they would otherwise not qualify. For example, a loan calls for low monthly payments for the first three years, with gradually increasing payments later. Or the terms of a loan require interest payments only, with a balloon payment due in five years. Most forms of creative financing result in higher interest costs or a higher home price than traditional loans. See also *conventional loan; financing; interest only; mortgage.*

credit

credit report fee the fee charged by a lender to a borrower for the investigation of credit, usually included as a closing cost. See also *closing costs; financing.*

cubic foot method an estimate of the construction cost per cubic foot, used to calculate replacement cost during an appraisal. The total construction cost is divided by the number of cubic feet in a building. See also *appraisal method; replacement cost; reproduction cost.*

cubic foot method

$$\frac{\text{total construction cost}}{\text{cubic feet}}$$

$$\frac{\$128{,}000}{48{,}450} = \$2.64$$

curable depreciation a form of depreciation when upgrades would restore the property's value. See also *depreciation; incurable depreciation.*

current yield the current cash received from an investment, divided by the amount invested. See also *investment income; yield.*

current yield

$$\frac{\text{annual income}}{\text{investment basis}}$$

$$\frac{\$7{,}150}{\$85{,}000} = 8.4\%$$

curvilinear system a pattern of layout in a housing development, in which quiet, less traveled streets are planned and arranged around roads and streets that are more heavily traveled. See also *cluster; development; gridiron pattern; loop streets; Radburn Plan; subdivision.*

D

daily compounding a method of compounding interest that involves either 360 or 365 periods per year. The computation involves dividing the annual rate by the number of days in the year (360 or 365). For example, if 12% is compounded daily with the 360-day method, the rate for one day is .0333% per day. To compute the second day, add one to the rate and multiply by itself:

$$1.0333 \times 1.0333 = 1.06667$$

Interest on $100 at 12%, compounded daily for two days will be 6.7 cents:

$$\$100.00 \times .00067 = 6.7 \text{ cents}$$

When the computation is carried out for 360 days, the annual percentage rate is calculated. Because this is a time-consuming procedure, daily interest tables provide annual factors for computation. For example, $100 at 12% compounded daily under the 360-day method yields $12.94, or a compounded rate of 12.94%. See also *compound interest; interest; simple interest.*

daily compounding

YEARS	COMPOUND FACTOR (360 DAYS)			
	6%	8%	10%	12%
1	1.0627	1.0845	1.1067	1.1294
2	1.1294	1.1761	1.2248	1.2754
3	1.2002	1.2755	1.3554	1.4404

dealer an individual who speculates in property, buying it for the purpose of reselling it at a profit. See also *investment property; tax basis.*

debt the amount owed to another, through a commitment on account, a note, a mortgage, or other liability. See also *loan; mortgage.*

Debt Coverage Ratio (DCR) a ratio showing the relationship between Net Operating Income (NOI) and the commitment to debt service on a related loan.

debt

Net Operating Income (NOI) consists of income from rentals during the year, minus cash-basis expenses exclusive of interest and principal. As is true with all ratios, the significance of this computation becomes clear only when reviewed as part of a trend, or in comparison with an assumed norm. An example: Annual rents are $16,830 and operating expenses are $3,420, leaving NOI of $13,410. Debt service (payments of principal and interest) totals $12,680. Dividing NOI by debt service produces a DCR of 1.06 (to 1). See also *debt service; investment property; Net Operating Income (NOI)*.

Debt Coverage Ratio (DCR)

$$\frac{\text{Net Operating Income (NOI)}}{\text{debt service}}$$

$$\frac{\$13{,}410}{\$12{,}680} = 1.06$$

debt instrument   a mortgage, promissory note or other document that is signed by the person borrowing money, and is presented for payment on the due date. For investors, the debt instrument is a debt investment certificate, just as a stock certificate is evidence of ownership of an equity position in a company. See also *mortgage; promissory note*.

debt service   the amount of money required each year to amortize a loan. The amount, usually broken down into monthly payments for a mortgage, is the total of principal and interest, and is based upon three factors: The amount of the loan, the rate of interest, and the number of months or years allowed until pay-off. See also *amortization; interest; principal*.

debt service coverage ratio   an alternate title of the Debt Coverage Ratio (DCR). See also *investment property; Net Operating Income (NOI)*.

declaration   a document used in certain real estate transactions that specifies the terms of use or occupancy of a building or unit. For example, a condominium declaration stipulates all conditions and restrictions governing the use, sale, lease and occupancy of a unit in the development. See also *condominium; contract*.

declaration of homestead a declaration filed by a homeowner claiming a homestead exemption, which protects home equity in the event of a foreclosure. In some states, limits are placed on the amount of equity that can be protected under the declaration; in others, there is no set limit. See also *forced sale; homestead.*

declaration of trust a series of regulations for the management and operation of a business trust. See also *business trust; investment program; Real Estate Investment Trust (REIT).*

declining balance depreciation an accelerated form of depreciation. Under the straight-line method, the same amount is recovered each year. Declining balance allows a greater amount each year. Common declining balance computations allow 175% or 200% of straight-line rates. For example, on a $10,000 asset with a five-year recovery period, straight-line will allow $2,000 each year. A 175% declining balance will allow $3,500 in the first year and the following year will be computed on a reduced basis. ($10,000 original basis less $3,500 claimed = $6,500. So the 175% rate is $2,275, or 175% of $1,300.) The same technique is used for 200-DB, with the factor of 200% used. Declining balance depreciation cannot be applied against real estate, which must be recovered over 27.5 years (residential property) or 31.5 years (commercial property). See also *accelerated depreciation; depreciation; personal property; straight-line depreciation; Tax Reform Act of 1986.*

declining balance depreciation

YEAR	BASIS	ST-LINE	200-DB
1	$10,000	$ 2,000	$ 4,000
2	6,000	1,200	2,400
3	3,600	720	1,440
4	2,160	432	864
5	1,296	259	518

dedication the appropriation of private property for public use, or the gifting of property to a public agency. See also *eminent domain; private property.*

deed an instrument that conveys title. It must be a legal transfer in order for the deed to be valid, and the conveyance must occur between parties competent to enter an agreement. See also *consideration; conveyance; quitclaim deed; special warranty deed; warranty deed.*

deed

deed in lieu of foreclosure a conveyance of fee simple ownership, such as when a property owner surrenders property to a lender without going through a foreclosure procedure. See also *conveyance; fee simple; foreclosure.*

deed of conformation an instrument that corrects errors in another instrument. For example, a deed is issued with an incorrect legal description. To rectify this and create good title, a deed of conformation is issued. See also *good title; legal description.*

deed of release a deed that releases a borrower from an encumbrance. This is often used when more than one property is included in a single mortgage. For example, a developer sells one unit covered under a blanket mortgage. The lender issues a deed of release for that property. See also *blanket mortgage; lien; mortgage.*

deed of trust a document that conveys and reconveys property, used in place of a mortgage in some states. The deed places ownership with a trustee while the loan is outstanding. Upon full payment, ownership is conveyed to the borrower. See also *conveyance; legal title; mortgage; reconveyance; title.*

default a breach of contract resulting from the failure to perform. Not keeping up payments on a mortgage is default on the contract, and may result in an action of foreclosure. See also *breach of contract; foreclosure.*

default insurance a form of insurance the borrower may be required to carry, that protects the lender. In the event of default on the loan, the policy ensures that the borrower will receive back the amount it loaned. Lenders granting loans above 80% will sometimes require the borrower to continue payments on a policy until equity is equal to or greater than 20% of the property's market value. This insurance is often referred to in error as mortgage insurance, which is a form of life or disability coverage based on the balance outstanding on a mortgage loan. See also *default; lending institution; mortgage insurance.*

defeasance the cancellation of the terms in an agreement upon fulfillment of a specified event. A defeasance clause is included in certain mortgage or lease contracts. For example, the obligation of indebtedness is cancelled by the defeasance clause upon full payment of the loan. And the obligation under a lease is cancelled upon expiration of the lease period and payment of the agreed amount. See also *lease; mortgage.*

defective title a title containing a flaw or a cloud, making that title invalid and unmarketable. See also *cloud on the title; good title; title.*

deferred gain a gain that would be taxable but, when certain conditions are met, is not taxed until future years. For example, a home is sold for $126,000, producing a taxable profit of $79,000 over and above the purchase price. If, within two years of the date of sale, another house is constructed or bought that costs $126,000 or more, the entire gain is deferred and the basis in the new home reduced by the profit of $79,000. If a new house costs less than $126,000, only the difference is taxed; the rest of the profit is a deferred gain. See also *adjusted basis; tax deferred.*

deferred gain

FIRST HOUSE

sales price	$126,000
purchase price	47,000
profit	$ 79,000

SECOND HOUSE

purchase price	$135,000
deferred gain	79,000
adjusted basis	$ 56,000

deferred maintenance condition requiring repair that has not been performed, causing physical depreciation to the property. This is taken into account by an appraiser when establishing market value. See also *maintenance; market value; physical depreciation.*

deferred payment an allowance provided to a borrower, that certain payments will be delayed until a specified later date. Commercial and investment grade property mortgages may include a deferral provision. Homeowners are allowed a form of deferred payment through a grace period. An installment payment plan is a form of deferred payments. See also *commercial property; debt service; grace period; installment payment.*

deficiency dividend a dividend paid by a Real Estate Investment Trust (REIT) to shareholders after the close of the year. In some cases, the books are not closed in time to accurately calculate income; yet, an REIT is required to pay out 95 cents of every dollar of income. See also *investment income; Real Estate Investment Trust (REIT).*

deficiency judgement a personal judgement against a borrower when the equity in a foreclosed property is less than the amount of outstanding debt. The judgement is for the difference. See also *foreclosure; secured debt.*

deflation a condition in which supply outpaces demand to the extent that prices fall. See also *inflation.*

demand mortgage a form of mortgage in which the lender can call for full payment at any time, without advance notice to the borrower. See also *mortgage.*

density 44

density a measurement of the number of units in a given area. As an ordinance, a density rule sets either the minimum size of parcels in a subdivision, or the maximum number of homes that can be built per acre. See also *parcel; subdivision; zoning.*

Department of Housing and Urban Development (HUD) a federal agency created in 1965 to oversee federal home development and financing. See also *non-investment property; residential property.*

depletion the exhaustion of a natural resource. Timber, oil and minerals are depleted when removed from land. Tax treatment allows a depletion allowance that is claimed in a manner similar to depreciation. See also *depreciation; tax basis.*

deposit money pledged as evidence of good faith or sincere intention (earnest money), such as a deposit left by a buyer when making an offer. The deposit represents performance under the offer of a contract. If the offer is accepted, it serves as initial consideration on that contract. See also *consideration; down payment; earnest money; good faith deposit; performance.*

deposit receipt a document that is signed by buyer and seller at the time a deposit is made and the offer accepted. It serves as an initial agreement until the time that a formal and more complete contract can be drawn. The deposit receipt should include the agreed upon price, any and all contingencies, and other terms of the agreement. See also *acceptance; agreement; binder; contingency; contract; offer; purchase offer.*

depreciation (1) a deduction the owner of an asset is allowed to claim each year. The depreciable basis of property is depreciated over a recovery period specified by tax law, with some elections available to claim depreciation over longer periods of time. Land is not eligible for depreciation, and real estate must be taken on a 27.5-year period (residential) or a 31.5-year period (commercial). Real estate must be depreciated on a straight-line basis, meaning the same amount is claimed every year. Personal property can be claimed under shorter recovery periods and at accelerated rates. Under accelerated depreciation, a larger amount is allowed during the early years of ownership, and the deduction is reduced each year. The present system for recovery of asset investments was first introduced as part of the Economic Recovery Tax Act of 1981 (ERTA). Rules were modified by subsequent tax legislation, with the most notable adjustments occurring as part of the Tax Reform Act of 1986. Depreciation is always based on the adjusted cost of property, regardless of actual current value. For example, investment real estate may be increasing in value, while book value (cost less accumulated depreciation) shows a decreasing value. (2) physical depreciation, a reduction in value due to wear and tear, obsolescence, or neglect. This condition describes actual decrease in value, as opposed to a tax-based deduction. Some forms of physical depreciation are curable, such as that caused by failure to maintain property; other forms are incurable. See also *accelerated depreciation; curable depreciation; declining balance depreciation; Economic Recovery Tax Act of 1981 (ERTA); incurable depreciation; physical depreciation; recovery period; straight-line depreciation; Tax Reform Act of 1986.*

depreciation

YEAR	$10,000 ASSET, 5 YEARS		
	ST-LINE	175% DB	200% DB
1	$2,000	$3,500	$4,000
2	2,000	2,275	2,400
3	2,000	1,479	1,440
4	2,000	961	864
5	2,000	625	518

determinable fee estate a form of estate specifying an inheritance that is subject to a specific condition. Upon a change in status, the property is conveyed to an alternate owner. For example, a deed gives a school district the right to operate a building as a school under a determinable fee estate. Several years later, the school district has a decline in enrollment, and it converts the building to a meeting hall. When this occurs, the estate is said to be determined, or ended. The school district loses its rights to the property. See also *conversion; conveyance; estate in land; fee simple; freehold estate; leasehold estate; life estate.*

developed land any land on which an improvement has been made, such as a building, streets, grading, a sewer system, utility hook-ups, or artificial lake. See also *improved land; raw land.*

development a subdivision or area under any type of construction. In general, a development is done under a common theme, such as residences, apartments, a shopping center, or industrial park. See also *improvement; subdivision.*

diminishing returns a basic principle in valuation, that over-improvement of real estate will not produce a corresponding increase in market value under all conditions. For example, three-bedroom homes in one neighborhood sell in the range of $95,000 to $103,000. The addition of a $20,000 room will not increase market value by a full $20,000, based on the average market value of similar homes in the same area. See also *anticipation; change; competition; conformity; contribution; highest and best use; increasing returns; plottage; regression; substitution; supply and demand.*

direct participation program a limited partnership or syndicate. Investors purchase units directly from the program management, and are liable only to the *directional* 46

extent of the amount at risk as limited partners. While investments are made directly, the term may be deceiving, as individuals have no direct voice in the selection or management of properties purchased by the program. See also *investment program; limited partnership; syndicate; tax shelter.*

directional growth   descriptive of a growth pattern in a community. An investor in raw land tries to anticipate the direction so that an investment will grow in value as demand rises. The risk of speculating in land is that growth could shift or cease. In that case, raw, unimproved land will not increase in value. See also *land; raw land; risk factor; speculation.*

disability insurance   protection against the economic consequences of total and permanent disability. One form, mortgage disability insurance, provides a benefit equal to the amount of a homeowner's monthly mortgage payment. If that homeowner is disabled, the insurance company will make payments directly to the lender. See also *mortgage insurance.*

discount   **(1)** a reduction in a liability to induce prompt payment. **(2)** reduced interest on a mortgage, offered to consumers to induce them to contract for an Adjustable Rate Mortgage (ARM). The discount, often called a "teaser," is removed a few months after signing, and a higher rate takes effect. **(3)** a technique used by some lenders as a sales ploy. Consumers are offered loans at rates lower than market rates, but with extra discount points. This makes the yield to the lender equal to or higher than other loans sold at market rates. See also *Adjustable Rate Mortgage (ARM); cash value; face value; lending institution; point; teaser.*

discount broker   a broker who represents sellers or buyers in real estate transactions for a commission rate far below the 6% average. A discount broker may represent an individual for as little as 2% of the final sales price. Discount brokers offer no personalized advice or assistance in locating financing, executing documents during escrow, or other matters usually associated with full service brokerage agreements. See also *broker; commission; selling agent.*

discount rate   a rate of return on investment property that makes an adjustment for the time value of money. Yields have relative value. For example, an investor holds a rental property for five years, producing $10,000 in cash after expenses each year. If that $10,000 is invested elsewhere each year, the first year's discount rate is higher than other years', because it has more time to earn. The discount rate declines with each subsequent year. See also *cash flow; investment income; rate of return; time value of money.*

discount yield   the yield on an investment purchased at a discount, computed from purchase date until maturity. For example, an investor receives the proceeds on the sale of a rental property, and wants to invest the money for three months or less, while he looks for another rental property. He buys a Treasury Bill at a 2% discount ($9,800). There are 85 days remaining until maturity. The yield is 8.5%. See also *investment income; rate of return.*

discount rate

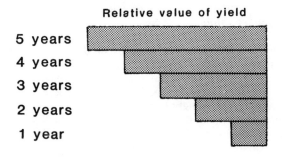

discount yield

$$\frac{\text{discount}}{\text{face value}} \times \frac{360}{\text{days to maturity}}$$

$$\frac{\$200}{\$10{,}000} \times \frac{360}{85} = 8.5\%$$

discounted cash flow a method for computing the return on invested capital that includes adjustments for the present value of available cash, tax benefits of the investment, and the expected holding period. See also *cash flow; future value; investor basis; present value; rate of return; tax basis; time value of money.*

disinterested appraisal an appraisal performed by someone with no interests in the property or ties to the person or firm requesting an estimate of market value. When an appraisal of property is given to prospective investors, the status of the appraiser should be determined. For example, an appraiser who is employed solely by the general partners of a program cannot give a disinterested appraisal. See also *appraisal; interest; market value.*

dissolution (1) the complete cancellation of a contract, as when both parties agree to void it; or when one party breaches agreed upon conditions. (2) the termination of an investment program by the sale of all assets and distribution of profits to all investors. A finite-life REIT dissolves when the dissolution date has been reached. See also *anticipatory breach; breach of contract; contract; Real Estate Investment Trust (REIT); voidable contract.*

distressed

distressed property a property whose market value is falling rather than rising, due to neglect, poor location, or the inability of an owner to find a tenant; or a property for which the owner is unable to keep up with mortgage payments, one that is in imminent danger of being foreclosed. See also *foreclosure; investment income; market value.*

double declining balance a form of accelerated depreciation in which the annual recovery allowance is equal to 200% of the straight-line rate that would be allowed against the same basis. The basis is reduced each year by the amount of depreciation claimed. For example, the basis in property is $8,000. In a five-year recovery period, the straight-line period is $1,600 each year. Under the double declining balance method, the first year is 200% of that amount, or $3,200. In the second year, the basis is reduced by depreciation claimed ($8,000 less $3,200 = $4,800). Straight-line depreciation on that basis would be $960; double-declining balance doubles that to $1,920. See also *accelerated depreciation; depreciation; straight-line depreciation.*

double declining balance

YEAR	BASIS	ST-LINE	200-DB
1	$8,000	$1,600	$3,200
2	4,800	960	1,920
3	2,880	576	1,152
4	1,728	346	692
5	1,036	207	414

down payment an amount of money paid by the buyer of real estate. Lenders will carry a specified percentage of the property's value, and expect the buyer to also have a vested interest. For example, a home's agreed price is $87,500. The lender agrees to finance 80%, or $70,000. The borrower is required to pay a down payment of 20%, or $17,500. The amount may be reduced if the borrower is able to obtain a second mortgage to offset part of the 20%. Payment of a good faith deposit is evidence of willingness to perform under an offer, and serves as consideration with the assumption that it will be possible to obtain financing for the balance. See also *consideration; deposit; good faith deposit; performance; second mortgage.*

drainage natural or artificial system by which water or waste matter is moved from raw land or improved real estate. See also *improved land; parcel; raw land.*

dual agency a situation in which a broker represents and is compensated by both the buyer and the seller in a real estate transaction. This may occur without the knowledge of the individuals who retain the broker. Dual agency creates a conflict of interest for the broker, and is considered an unethical practice. See also *agency; buyer's broker; selling agent.*

duplex a two-unit residence or apartment sharing a common wall or ceiling/floor. In some regions of the country, a duplex is considered a form of individual housing, distinct from apartments. In other regions, the term is used to describe any structure containing two units, either owned or rented. See also *apartment; multiple dwelling; residential property.*

E

earned increment growth in market value as a result of the owner's care, maintenance and management. For example, a homeowner who improves a property's appearance with attractive landscaping, paint, and fixtures will bring about increases in value directly. Other factors, such as the supply and demand for property, are unearned increments in market value. See also *market value; supply and demand; unearned increment.*

earnest money a deposit placed by a potential buyer at the time a serious offer is made and accepted. It is a sign of good faith within an offer to purchase, and may be applied against a down payment on the transaction. The earnest money deposit is usually accompanied by a signed deposit receipt that serves as an agreement, pending signing of a more complete contract at a later date. See also *deposit receipt; down payment; good faith deposit; offer to purchase.*

easement a privilege, interest or other right that one person has in the land of another. An easement is a right but not an estate in land. There are two broad types: easement appurtenant and easement in gross. See also *interest; right of way.*

easement appurtenant an easement granted by one property owner to another who owns an adjacent tract. The easement benefits the owner of the adjacent land and may increase property value. For example, one parcel fronts on a beach. Another, set behind the first, has an easement appurtenant that provides a right of way across the first tract, to the beach. See also *market value; parcel; right of way; tract.*

easement by necessity an easement created when a parcel has no access of its own to a street or other public way without crossing the land of another. A form of easement appurtenant, a typical example is the use of a common driveway by tenants of a property behind the owner's. See also *egress; ingress; right of way.*

easement

easement by prescription an easement acquired by visible, open and notorious use over a period of years. The required term varies by state and may be as long as 20 years. One who claims an easement by prescription must establish that use was continuous and exclusive, and that it occurred without the permission of the land's owner. See also *implied easement; right of way.*

easement in gross a personal interest in real estate. A personal easement in gross cannot be assigned or inherited in most cases. However, a commercial easement in gross can be conveyed to others or assigned. See also *commercial property; residential property; right of way.*

economic life the estimated years that a property will continue to be profitable. As a concept in investment property, it is the real, physical depreciation and not the deduction allowed by prescribed recovery of capital costs. See also *depreciation; physical life; useful life.*

economic obsolescence a loss of value in a property resulting from conditions apart from the quality of management of the property itself. This may come about due to zoning changes, changes in supply and demand, or movements in population and traffic. For example, an investor buys a service station on a major roadway. A few years later, a new interstate freeway is built and traffic is diverted several miles away. See also *depreciation; highest and best use; locational obsolescence; market value; obsolescence; supply and demand.*

Economic Recovery Tax Act of 1981 (ERTA) a major tax law that changed many rules for individual and business deductions; curtailed abusive tax shelter investments; reduced minimum individual tax rates to 50% of taxable income; established a maximum tax rate on long-term capital gains of 20%; and replaced the previous system for depreciation with ACRS. See also *Accelerated Cost Recovery System (ACRS); capital gain/loss; depreciation.*

economic rent an estimate of the amount of rent a property should bring, based on average rental values for similar properties in the same area. See also *market rent; rental value.*

effective age the assigned estimate of a building's age, based not on the year it was built but upon the present condition. A well-maintained older building may have a lower effective age than newer, poorly maintained buildings, thus a higher current market value. See also *appraisal; depreciation; physical depreciation.*

effective borrowing cost the true cost of borrowing money, with all factors considered. For example, a loan is granted with the condition that a compensating balance must be left on deposit in the lending institution. The borrower estimates that money could have produced a higher yield if put to work in another investment. The effective borrowing cost is the amount of interest paid on the loan, plus the difference between earning potential and the rate paid on the compensating balance. See also *compensating balance; debt; financing; lending institution.*

effective date   the date of origination or termination of an agreement. See also *closing date; escrow; origination.*

egress   the means of exit from a parcel of land to a public way. See also *easement; ingress; parcel.*

11 common perils   the casualties that are covered in all types of homeowner's insurance policies. They are:

1. fire or lightning
2. loss of property removed from the premises due to fire and other perils
3. windstorm and hail
4. explosion
5. riots and civil commotions
6. aircraft
7. vehicles
8. smoke
9. vandalism and malicious mischief
10. theft
11. breakage of glass constituting a part of the building.

See also *casualty insurance; homeowner's insurance.*

eminent domain   the right reserved by governments and their agencies to acquire private property for public use. Expropriation requires fair compensation to the owner. See also *allodial system; right of way.*

encroachment   a violation of boundaries by structures of improvements. The encroachment may affect marketability of title, or, if known for a necessary period of time, may represent implied easements. For example, a homeowner builds a brick wall that is several feet beyond the rightful boundary of a neighbor's parcel. The improvement encroaches upon the neighbor's land. See also *boundary rights; implied easement; property line; right of way.*

encumbrance   an interest, lien, mortgage, or other claim against a property. The existence of an encumbrance reduces the owner's equity. See also *interest; lien; mortgage.*

endorsement   a signature, as on a mortgage loan or contract. See also *contract; debt; lending institution; mortgage.*

Equal Credit Opportunity Act (ECOA)   a federal law that prohibits discrimination in lending on the basis of race, color, religion, national origin, sex, marital status, age, or dependence upon public assistance. The ECOA became law in 1974. See also *lending institution; mortgage.*

equal 52

equal dignity the status of mortgages and other liens that share priority in the event of a default, as opposed to one lien being senior to the others. See also *junior lien; mortgage; priority; senior lien.*

equitable lien a lien that is derived from the signing of a contract or entering into a commitment. See also *involuntary lien; statutory lien; voluntary lien.*

equitable title an interest in land. Such title cannot be acquired merely by the signing of a contract, as title can be conveyed only by deed. See also *conveyance; deed; fee simple; right of possession; title.*

equity **(1)** the interest an owner holds in the property; the unencumbered portion. For example, a homeowner put a down payment of $35,000 on a home several years ago, and has made combined principal payments of $10,100. On that basis, equity is $45,100. However, if the market value of the property has increased, so has the degree of equity. Current equity value is computed by subtracting the balance of loans from market value. **(2)** the legal theory of fairness, as opposed to strict laws as written. See also *market value; mortgage; net worth; value.*

equity build-up the amount of principal paid on a loan over time. For example, a homeowner is paying on a 30-year mortgage. Equity build-up is slow during the early years. At 10% interest, only 3.4% of that loan is repaid after five years. And 58.7% is repaid after 25 years. If the homeowner repaid a 10% loan over 15 years, equity build-up is more rapid. After 5 years, 18.7% of the loan is repaid. See also *build-up; down payment; mortgage acceleration.*

equity capital money available to an investment program derived from shareholders, as opposed to borrowed money. Total capital may consist of both equity and debt. For example, a limited partnership is formed to purchase a $12 million building. Investors pay in $8 million, and the balance comes from borrowed funds. In that event, the $8 million represent equity capital. The leveraged portion, $4 million, is debt capital. See also *debt; investor basis; leverage; limited partnership; net worth.*

equity conversion descriptive of a Reverse Annuity Mortgage (RAM). A homeowner owns a home free and clear, but needs funds for living expenses. By arrangement with an insurer, an annuity will be paid to that homeowner each month, as a form of reverse mortgage loan. Upon the death of the homeowner or expiration of an agreed period, the home is sold and the insurer reimbursed. See also *annuity; free and clear; mortgage; Reverse Annuity Mortgage (RAM).*

equity dividend rate the rate of earnings computed by dividing cash flow (pre-tax profit) by the amount of money invested. For example, an investment yields $4,350 in one year. The investor had put $50,000 into the property. The equity dividend rate is 8.7%. See also *cash flow; investment program; pre-tax profit.*

equity investment a direct ownership of real estate, or investment in a program that in turn takes an equity position in property. For example, a Real Estate Investment Trust (REIT) or limited partnership is formed to purchase property.

equity build-up

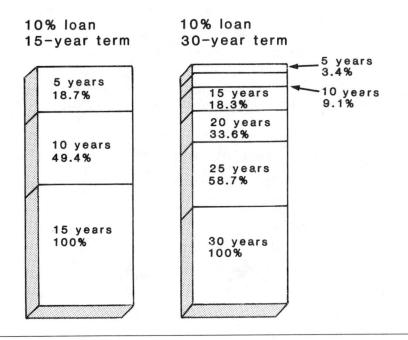

equity dividend rate

$$\frac{\text{cash flow}}{\text{investment}}$$

$$\frac{\$4{,}350}{\$50{,}000} = 8.7\%$$

See also *debt; investment program; limited partnership; Real Estate Investment Trust (REIT).*

equity line of credit an arrangement with a lending institution in which a homeowner is allowed to borrow money up to specified limits. Those limits are based on home equity, and all borrowed funds are secured by real estate. See also *debt service; lending institution; mortgage.*

equity

equity method a method used by some investment programs to report to shareholders. Instead of showing the amount of profit, shares are reported on the basis of current market value. This is a practice for publicly listed REIT's as well as limited partnerships in many cases, and reflects a trend toward liquidity and public listing in the real estate investment industry. See also *investor basis; limited partnership; Master Limited Partnership (MLP); Real Estate Investment Trust (REIT); Real Estate Mortgage Investment Company (REMIC); real estate stock corporation.*

equity participation a provision included by some limited partnerships, enabling investors to gain a portion of profits upon sale of property held for the long term, or when rental values rise. See also *investment income; limited partnership.*

equity REIT a type of Real Estate Investment Trust (REIT) that limits its activities only to taking of equity positions in real estate. In comparison, a mortgage REIT is formed to loan money, either to existing properties or for the construction and development of new properties. And a hybrid REIT may include equity and mortgage activities. See also *hybrid REIT; mortgage REIT; Real Estate Investment Trust (REIT).*

equity return the calculated rate of return on a real estate investment, based on actual cash flow plus reduction of a loan's principal. For example, gross income for one year is $18,800. Expenses are $11,430, leaving cash income of $7,370. In addition, principal is reduced by $2,050 in the same year. The original investment was $95,000. The combined cash income and principal reduction ($7,370 plus $2,050), divided by the investment of $95,000, produces an equity return of 9.9%. See also *cash flow; principal; rate of return.*

equity return

$$\frac{\text{cash income} + \text{principal reduction}}{\text{investment}}$$

$$\frac{\$7,370 + \$2,050}{\$95,000} = 9.9\%$$

escalator clause a provision in a lease contract specifying an increase in payment in the event that increases occur in specific expenses. Such clauses may be included for property taxes, utilities, and operating or maintenance expenses. See also *graduated lease; lease.*

escape clause a clause included in some contracts allowing withdrawal or modification of terms. See also *agreement; conditional sale; contract.*

escrow a period between an agreement of terms and final settlement of conditions. During escrow, a title search is conducted; financing is arranged for the buyer; all required forms and documents are completed and delivered; and any contingencies are settled. The escrow agent holds paperwork and deposit funds pending the completion of all terms, conditions and investigations. See also *closing costs; contingency; contract; title search.*

escrow account an account established to hold funds pending a final transaction of property. At the close of escrow, all funds are disbursed. See also *closing costs; sale.*

escrow agent an individual or company appointed to hold deposits and other funds while a final sale is pending. The agent has the responsibility of safekeeping funds and documents and disbursing to the buyer, seller, borrower and others involved in the transaction. See also *closing costs; down payment; lending institution.*

escrow agreement (1) the agreement appointing a third party to hold funds and documents while the investigations, payments and contingencies of a sale are pending. (2) a contingency specified by buyer or seller that is to be satisfied during the escrow period and before the final sale is completed. See also *contingency; contract.*

escrow fee the charge assessed by an escrow company or an individual for safekeeping cash and documents during the escrow period. See also *closing costs.*

estate at sufferance an estate that comes into being when an individual with title and in possession of property retains those rights beyond a specified period of time. See also *possession; tenancy at sufferance.*

estate at will an indefinite estate created by mutual agreement between two parties. It may terminate at any time that one or both parties to the agreement modify the terms, as in a month to month rental agreement. See also *lease; month to month; possession.*

estate by the entirety a joint tenancy, as between a husband and wife. Upon the death of either tenant, the entire estate becomes solely owned by the survivor. It is not inherited; ownership is automatically transferred to the one person. While living, the joint tenants are jointly in possession of the entire property. See also *joint tenancy; unity of possession.*

estate for years an estate that sets a specific limit in duration. Such an estate must have both a starting and ending date, and will not renew automatically upon expiration of its term, but must be reestablished by the holder. The term may be tied to the lifetime of another person, or may depend upon a future contingency. See also *life estate; personal property; real property.*

estate 56

estate in land interests and extent of rights in land. There are two types, the freehold estate (including fee simple, defeasible fee, life estate, and legal life estate) and leasehold estate (estate for years, from period to period, at will and at sufferance). See also *freehold estate; interest; land; leasehold estate.*

eviction actual removal of a person from physical possession of property. Actual eviction is total, whereas constructive eviction results from an act that makes the use of property impractical or impossible; and partial eviction restricts or limits a tenant's ability to fully utilize the premises. See also *constructive eviction; partial eviction.*

evidence of title proof of actual ownership. A deed conveys title, but does not prove it is held legally, nor that the seller had the right to convey. There are four forms of evidence: abstract of title; a certificate of title; title insurance policy; and a Torrens certificate. See also *absolute title; abstract of title; certificate of title; conveyance; title insurance policy; Torrens certificate.*

exchange the simultaneous purchase and sale of one property for another. If properties are of equal value, no money exchanges hands. But if one is of higher value, the holder of lower valued property must include a sum of money (known as boot) to equalize the transaction. See also *basis; boot; conveyance.*

exchange program limited partnerships allowing investors to exchange currently held units in a program for interests in another program, or for shares in a corporation. See also *investment program; limited partnership; Master Limited Partnership (MLP); Real Estate Mortgage Investment Corporation (REMIC).*

exclusion rule an allowance included in federal tax law under which anyone aged 55 or older may exclude up to $125,000 in capital gains from tax, upon the sale of their principal residence. This is allowed only once in a lifetime. A "principal" residence is defined as one in which the family lived most of the year for no less than three of the past five years. For example, a home is sold for $184,000 and the adjusted purchase price was $45,000. Of the $139,000 profit, only $14,000 is taxed after claiming the exclusion. See also *capital gain/loss; principal residence; tax basis.*

exclusive agency a form of agreement between a seller and a real estate broker, in which the broker is granted exclusive rights to sell the property. This provision normally lasts for a specified period of time, after which other brokers may show the property as well. See also *commission; listing broker.*

exclusive listing the contractual agreement between an exclusive agent and the seller. Under its terms, the broker is entitled to a specified commission during the exclusive period, regardless of who actually sells the property. See also *concurrent authority; Multiple Listing Service (MLS); open listing.*

exculpatory clause a provision included in some lease contracts that releases the owner/landlord from all liability in the event that tenants or their guests are injured, or property is damaged or lost. Such clauses do not eliminate liability

exclusion rule

	EXAMPLE 1	EXAMPLE 2
sale price	$184,000	$120,000
purchase price	45,000	50,000
gain	$139,000	$ 70,000
exclusion	125,000	125,000
taxable gain	$ 14,000	$ 0

under the law. If a loss results from conditions under the owner's control and responsibility, or are due to the owner's negligence, he or she is liable in spite of this disclaimer. Tenants generally are responsible for insuring their own personal property and personal liabilities, while landlords generally insure against casualties to the structure itself. See also *contract; homeowner's insurance; lease.*

execution completion of the terms of a contract; performance. For example, conveyance of legal title is execution by the seller, and payment of the purchase price is execution by the buyer of their respective contractual requirements. See also *conveyance; legal title; performance.*

executory contract descriptive of the status of a contract with outstanding provisions yet to be satisfied. In a real estate contract, title cannot be conveyed until all conditions have been met. See also *contract; conveyance; title.*

expected return (1) a rate an investor can theoretically earn if money is left invested over a long enough period of time, but that might not be realized in the event that money is withdrawn early. (2) a forecast an investor makes concerning income, based upon assumptions about a property or a similar property. See also *investment income; rate of return.* [See overleaf.]

express contract a contract in which all terms are spelled out exactly and agreed upon by both sides. In comparison, an implied contract is one in which some terms are assumed to be understood. See also *contract; implied contract; meeting of the minds.*

extended coverage insurance included in a policy beyond basic coverage. In homeowner's insurance policies, extended coverage specifies perils covered beyond the 11 common perils. And the homeowner may purchase replacement cost coverage rather than less expensive Actual Cash Value (ACV) protection. See also *Actual Cash Value (ACV); casualty insurance; 11 common perils; fire insurance; homeowner's insurance; replacement cost.*

extension

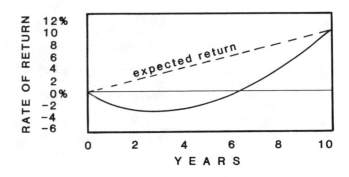

expected return

extension (**1**) in a lease agreement, additional time added onto the original lease term. For example, a tenant requests a six-month extension to the terms of a lease. (**2**) in a contract, allowance of additional time to satisfy agreed upon terms. For example, a home purchase contract includes a contingency that the seller will repair damages. Before escrow closes, the seller asks for a two-week extension to satisfy the contingency. (**3**) in a building, an addition to the existing structure. For example, a homeowner adds an extension off the existing building to make room for an additional bedroom. See also *addition; closing date; effective date; improvement; lease; performance.*

F

face value the value reflected on the books of a company, or carried by an investor or homeowner. The face value may differ considerably from market value. For example, a company invests in real estate at a cost of $250,000. Several years later, the book value is $172,000 (after deducting depreciation). However, market value of the property has risen to $325,000. See also *book value; depreciation; market value.*

failure of consideration a failure to perform under the terms of a contract, or the loss of value in a property or asset transferred. For example, a potential buyer makes an offer and accompanies it with a good faith deposit. However, the buyer later stops payment on the check. See also *breach of contract; consideration; contract; good faith deposit.*

failure to perform not living up to the agreed terms of a contract. For example, a buyer agrees to make monthly payments on a mortgage loan. However, payments are not made for three months. The lender will begin foreclosure proceedings in response to the failure to perform. See also *breach of contract; default*.

Fair Credit Reporting Act (FCRA) a law giving borrowers the legal right to review the contents of credit bureau and agency files regarding their credit history, and to correct erroneous information. See also *credit report fee; financing; lending institution*.

Fair Housing Act of 1968 a section of Title VII of the Civil Rights Act of 1968, establishing guidelines for non-discriminatory practices in housing. The Act prohibits discrimination on the basis of race, color, religion, sex, or national origin. It covers practices in the negotiation, leasing, selling, advertising, conditions, and representations made by sellers or agents. See also *blockbusting; Federal Fair Housing Act (FFHA); steering*.

Fair Market Value (FMV) the estimated best possible market price, assuming a seller is willing to make a sale in a reasonable period of time. FMV is calculated based on recent sales in the same area of similar properties, and will vary at different points in the real estate cycle, depending upon factors of ever-changing supply and demand trends. See also *market value; real estate cycle; supply and demand; value*.

Fannie Mae acronym for the Federal National Mortgage Association (FNMA), an agency that forms mortgage pools in the secondary mortgage market. See also *Federal National Mortgage Association (FNMA); mortgage pool; secondary market*.

Fannie Mae debenture a debt instrument that is not secured directly, but is guaranteed by the FNMA. The debentures are sold to investors, and funds used to purchase home mortgages from lending institutions. See also *debt instrument; Federal National Mortgage Association (FNMA); mortgage pool; secondary market*.

farm a parcel of land used for raising crops, specific animals, or for the production of dairy products. See also *land; parcel*.

farm cooperative an organization formed to invest in farm property, or to farm directly. The cooperative may be formed as a partnership or a corporation. See also *investment program; partnership*.

Farm Credit Act of 1933 a law that established the Farm Credit Administration (FCA) and its 12 administrative districts. See also *Bank for Cooperatives (Co-Op)*.

Farm Credit Administration an agency that oversees activities of the Bank for Cooperatives (Co-Op) and the Federal Intermediate Credit Bank (FICB). See also *Bank for Cooperatives (Co-Op); Federal Intermediate Credit Bank (FICB)*.

Farm Loan Act of 1916 a law that established the Federal Land Bank (FLB) system, to administer financing of agricultural land and projects. See also *Federal Land Bank (FLB); financing*.

Farmer's Home Administration (FmHA) an agency of the U.S. Department of Agriculture that grants real estate mortgage loans to individual owners in rural areas. One qualification is that the applicant has not qualified for conventional financing elsewhere. See also *conventional loan; financing; mortgage.*

farmstead collectively, the primary structural improvements of a farm. See also *improvement; land.*

Federal Fair Housing Act (FFHA) a federal law defining and banning discrimination in housing. See also *Fair Housing Act of 1968; steering.*

Federal Farm Credit Banks (FFCB) an agency of the Farm Credit Administration (FCA), founded to consolidate three other agencies: the Bank for Cooperatives (Co-Op); the Federal Intermediate Credit Bank (FICB); and the Federal Land Bank (FLB). See also *Bank for Cooperatives (Co-Op); Farm Credit Administration (FCA); Federal Intermediate Credit Bank (FICB); Federal Land Bank (FLB).*

Federal Farm Mortgage Corporation (FFMC) an agency established in 1932, with the purpose of granting loans to owners of defaulted farm mortgages. See also *default; lending institution; mortgage.*

Federal Home Loan Bank (FHLB) an agency that grants mortgage loans through savings and loan associations, to companies in the home building industry. See also *development; lending institution.*

Federal Home Loan Mortgage Corporation (FHLMC) an agency, also known by the acronym "Freddie Mac," that purchases existing mortgages, creates mortgage pools, and resells shares to investors. See also *Freddie Mac; investment program; mortgage pool; secondary market.*

Federal Housing Administration (FHA) an agency founded as part of the National Housing Act of 1934, to insure the mortgage risks undertaken by lending institutions. See also *lending institution; risk factor.*

Federal Intermediate Credit Bank (FICB) an agency of the Farm Credit Administration (FCA) that lends money to finance agricultural activities. See also *Farm Credit Administration (FCA).*

Federal Land Bank (FLB) a branch of the Farm Credit Banks Consolidated System-Wide Banks, created as part of the Farm Loan Act of 1916. The agency finances farm, ranch and agricultural activities through first mortgage loans. See also *Farm Loan Act of 1916; financing; mortgage.*

Federal National Mortgage Association (FNMA) an independent corporation supervised by the federal government, also known by the acronym "Fannie Mae," that purchases existing mortgage loans from lending institutions, forms mortgage pools, and sells shares to investors. This activity enables individuals to spread risks by diversifying their money, and still participate in the mortgage lending market. The FNMA also facilitates home financing by purchasing mortgages from lenders. See also *Fannie Mae; investment program; mortgage pool; risk factor; secondary market.*

fee simple the greatest possible legal interest in real estate; ownership without conditions. This unencumbered, absolute title entitles the owner to sell, lease, bequeath or encumber the property. See also *absolute title; allodial system; encumbrance; title.*

fee simple defeasible a form of ownership that is dependent upon a condition. There are two major types: the conditional fee estate, one that can be inherited and will be determined (ended) upon the occurrence of a specified event; and the fee simple subject to a condition subsequent, in which title will revert to the original owner or the owner's heirs if a specified event occurs, or if a condition is violated. See also *estate for years; title.*

fence a barrier, constructed on or near a property line. See also *boundary rights; improvement; parcel.*

FHA mortgage a loan granted by a conventional lender and insured by the Federal Housing Administration (FHA). See also *conventional loan; Federal Housing Administration (FHA); financing; lending institution.*

fiduciary an individual placed in a position of trust, primarily in the management of safekeeping of someone else's money or property. For example, a real estate broker is authorized to represent a seller in the arranging of financing for a qualified buyer. In this case, the seller depends upon the broker's good faith, and creates a fiduciary relationship. See also *agency; broker; escrow agent; good faith; power of attorney.*

finance charge **(1)** generally descriptive of interest and other costs of borrowing money. **(2)** a fee charged for late payment in a mortgage loan, also called a late charge. See also *interest; lending institution.*

financial statement a document showing either the current status of assets, liabilities and net worth, either of an organization or an individual (balance sheet) or the income, expenses and net profit or loss for a specified period of time (income statement). See also *balance sheet; income statement; net worth.* [See overleaf.]

financing broadly descriptive of the means of funding real estate purchases beyond the down payment the buyer pays. Financing from conventional lending institutions may include a fixed rate of interest or a flexible, or variable rate. Financing provided by the Veteran's Administration (VA) or the Federal Housing Administration (FHA) is for a period of 30 years (sometimes more), is offered at a fixed rate, and is assumable. Creative variations of traditional financing may be possible, and are more popular when buyers cannot qualify for a lender's terms under more accepted forms of lending. See also *creative financing; debt service; Federal Housing Administration (FHA); interest; lending institution; mortgage; Veteran's Administration (VA).*

finder's fee a fee paid by one person or company to another for a referral or other service. Finder's fees may be paid for listings, locating and arranging a mortgage loan, or referring buyers. The fee is normally paid upon successful

financial statement

BALANCE SHEET	INCOME STATEMENT
assets	revenues
=	− costs
liabilities	− expenses
+ net worth	= net profit

---

completion of a transaction. See also *brokerage; commission; listing; prospect.*

fire insurance   a term applied to the broader homeowner's insurance, which includes protection against a number of casualties besides fire losses, as well as liability coverage. The majority of claims are due to fire losses, however. See also *casualty insurance; homeowner's insurance; liability insurance; risk factor.*

firm contract   a legal, binding, complete contract that contains the necessary elements required by law, and absent any conditions. See also *conditional sale; contract; escape clause; voidable contract.*

firm price   a price the seller demands for a property, allowing no room for a lower offer or a negotiated price. See also *acceptance; asking price; market price; negotiation; offer.*

first deed of trust   the senior lien on a property, having priority over all subsequent liens. See also *deed of trust; lien; senior lien.*

first lien   a lien having priority over all other liens and encumbrances. A lien may include a variety of claims, including mortgages and other encumbrances secured by the property. See also *collateral; encumbrance; junior lien; lien; priority; senior lien.*

first mortgage   the original mortgage, having priority of claim over other mortgages and liens in the event of default. In cases where a second mortgage remains outstanding after full payment of the first mortgage, the remaining debt becomes a first, or senior claim. See also *junior mortgage; mortgage; priority; second mortgage; senior mortgage; voluntary lien.*

first refusal   **(1)** the right held by the lender of a senior lien, mortgage or other encumbrance on property. The lender with this right has priority of claim against property when it goes into default. **(2)** the right held by a cooperative, and sometimes by a condominium. In the event that one of the owners wants to sell his or her interests, the association has first refusal rights to purchase the property from the owner. See also *condominium; cooperative housing; default; mortgage; priority.*

FISBO abbreviation used in the real estate industry for an individual who sells property without the assistance of a commissioned broker—"For Sale by Owner." See also *broker; buyer's broker; commission; selling agent.*

Fixed Rate Mortgage (FRM) the traditional form of financing real estate purchases. A homeowner will be required to pay an interest rate higher than rates on a Flexible Rate Mortgage (FRM). In exchange, the homeowner has the security of knowing his or her rate cannot rise during the term of the loan. This fixed interest rate represents a reduced real cost of financing over time, due to the effects of inflation. For example, a mortgage payment of $700 per month is equal to 23% of a $3,000 monthly salary. If the homeowner's salary increases over several years to $5,000 per month, the fixed rate payment then is equal to only 14% of monthly income. An FRM protects the home buyer when interest rates rise. See also *financing; Flexible Rate Mortgage (FRM); inflation; interest rate; mortgage.*

fixing-up expenses certain qualified expenses undertaken in anticipation of a sale. If incurred within 90 days before the sale date and paid for within 30 days after the sale date, fixing-up expenses reduce the adjusted sales price of the residence and, thus, may reduce the taxable gain. However, these expenses are not deductible from gross income. Typically, fixing-up expenses include painting, plastering, and other repairs, maintenance and replacements intended to make the home ready for market. Capital improvements (such as the addition of a new room) are not considered as fixing-up expenses. See also *adjusted sales price; capital gain/loss; deferred gain; improvement; tax basis.*

fixture a permanently attached, integral part of real estate, added to enhance appearance, aesthetic value, utility, or marketability of a property. A fixture is distinguished from an appliance by its permanent nature. Although it becomes fixed as part of the real property, a fixture is considered a form of personal property. See also *aesthetic value; appliance; improvement; personal property; real property.*

flat lease a lease that includes a provision for regular, unchanging payments. See also *graduated lease; lease; straight lease; variable lease.*

Flexible Rate Mortgage (FRM) also called an Adjustable Rate Mortgage (ARM) or Variable Rate Mortgage (VRM), a form of real estate financing that first came into popular use during the late 1970's. A traditional Fixed Rate Mortgage (FRM) includes protection for the buyer in the fact that interest rates do not vary; this also adds to the lender's risk in the event that market interest rates rise. Under a Flexible Rate Mortgage agreement, the rate may be changed periodically, based upon movement of rates in a pre-agreed independent index of interest rates. Most contracts include either a payment cap (placing a maximum on the amount of monthly payment the homeowner will be required to make) or a rate cap. A rate cap may include a maximum increase that can be charged per period (six months, one year, two years, etc.) as well as a maximum increase the lending institution may assess during the life of the contract.

Lenders may offer FRM's at rates much lower than current market rates for Fixed Rate Mortgages, but may increase the rate within six months to two years after the start of the contract. The initial, lower rate, referred to as the "teaser," is intended to attract borrowers, but ultimately, the loan is more expensive than a Fixed Rate Mortgage.

A danger of FRM's that include a payment cap is that interest rates will rise beyond the limit set by contract. In that event, the amount required to pay interest each month exceeds the payment cap, so that the outstanding balance of the loan rises instead of falling each month. This condition is called negative amortization.

Use of an independent index (such as the National Cost of Funds Index, Six-month Weekly Treasury Bill Rate Index, or a bank's prime rate) adds a degree of risk to long-term financing, mitigated only by a rate cap. For example, a contract specifies that the interest rate can be raised by no more than 2% per year, with a maximum for the entire contract of 2.5%. During the fifth year of the contract, the index rises to the point that an increase in the rate would exceed the 2% annual limit; so interest is frozen at 2% above the previous rate. The following year, another increase in the index would raise the rate beyond the 2.5% maximum; the loan rate is frozen at that point.

Some contracts include a provision that excess interest above cap rates are to be recaptured in the event index rates fall, until the lending institution recovers the excess. In that case, borrowers will continue paying a higher rate on an FRM contract, even when index rates fall. See also *Adjustable Rate Mortgage (ARM); cap; financing; Fixed Rate Mortgage (FRM); interest rate; lending institution; mortgage; negative amortization; payment cap; rate cap; risk factor; teaser; Variable Rate Mortgage (VRM)*.

float the use of cash flow pending clearance by another bank. A bank's float consists of funds for uncleared checks or funds collected in advance of payment deadlines, and may be invested to earn interest. For example, a lender collects impound funds for payment of homeowner's insurance and property taxes over several months. The collective value of this fund earns interest until payments are due. See also *cash flow; impound; lending institution*.

floater policy a form of homeowner's insurance, also called the all-risk form, that gives maximum coverage against loss. See also *all-risk form; HO-3; homeowner's insurance*.

floating rate descriptive of the interest rate in an Adjustable Rate Mortgage (ARM), so called because it is subject to change based on movement of rates in an independent index. See also *Adjustable Rate Mortgage (ARM); financing; interest rate; mortgage*.

flood plain an area of land that is subject to flooding periodically or each year (annual flood plain). A form of casualty, flooding can be insured against; however, this form of coverage is too expensive for many homeowners. See also *casualty insurance*.

Flexible Rate Mortgage (FRM)

YEAR	INDEX BASE	% INCREASE	MORTGAGE RATE
1	100.0	– %	8.00%
2	104.6	4.6	8.37
3	108.2	3.4	8.65
4	109.7	1.4	8.77
5	135.3	23.3	10.27 (a)
6	142.6	5.4	10.50 (b)

(a) 2% maximum per period
(b) 2.5% maximum increase

Floor-Area Ratio (FAR) a calculation of the relationship between a building's total area and the area of the land. For example, a building's area is 22,500 square feet, and the total parcel measures 30,000 square feet. The Floor-Area Ratio (FAR) is 75%. See also *area; land; parcel.*

Floor–Area Ratio (FAR)

$$\frac{\text{building area}}{\text{land area}}$$

$$\frac{22{,}500}{30{,}000} = 75\%$$

floor

floor loan that portion of a loan that may be granted with lower qualifications than the full amount. For example, a lender agrees to fund 65% of a construction loan upon substantial or near completion of the project. However, the balance will not be granted until some other condition (such as a specified level of lease commitment or occupancy) is achieved by the developer. See also *gap financing; loan; mortgage.*

forced sale an event that results when a homeowner or other property owner is unable to keep up mortgage payments, or whose property is sold as part of a bankruptcy proceeding. A forced sale can be brought about due to lapsed payments on a mortgage, or in satisfaction of other outstanding liens and encumbrances. See also *alienation; default; involuntary alienation; voluntary alienation.*

foreclosure a legal proceeding undertaken by the holder of a mortgage or lien on property, to sell that property in satisfaction of the unpaid amount. The foreclosure ends the rights of the borrower. A statutory foreclosure proceeding may or may not involve the courts, but must proceed in conformity with state law. See also *alienation; breach of contract; consideration; deed of trust; default; failure of consideration; mortgage.*

fraudulent concealment the intentional nondisclosure of important information regarding a matter at issue under a contract. A contract may be canceled upon proof of fraudulent concealment. For example, a seller fails to advise the buyer that a home's foundation must be raised to counteract chronic annual flooding, and that the cost of the change will be $35,000. Upon discovery, even after consummation of the sale, the buyer may rescind the contract and recover the amount invested and other costs. See also *bad faith; contract; home inspection.*

fraudulent conveyance the sale, lease or other granting of rights in property with the intentional purpose of defrauding the buyer or a legal creditor. For example, a property owner has pledged real estate as collateral on a major loan, which is not disclosed during a title search. The purpose in conveying this property is to avoid responsibility for the debt, and to transfer it to the owner or a title insurance company. See also *bad faith; conveyance.*

Freddie Mac acronym for the Federal Home Loan Mortgage Corporation (FHLMC), an agency that purchases existing mortgages and creates mortgage pools in the secondary market. See also *Federal Home Loan Mortgage Corporation (FHLMC); investment program; mortgage pool; secondary market.*

free and clear descriptive of title to property that is completely unencumbered. See also *clear title; encumbrance; lien; marketable title; mortgage; unencumbered property.*

freehold estate an estate of unspecified length, including fee simple, defeasible, and life estates. Examples include estates created for a lifetime or forever. See also *estate in land; fee simple; life estate.*

full amortization the process of paying down a loan until the debt is completely eliminated. In a long-term mortgage loan, the rate of amortization begins slowly, and accelerates as time progresses. Each month's payment is divided between interest and principal, with interest computed on an ever declining loan balance. The rate of amortization is more rapid for shorter-term loans. For example, a $5,000 loan at 10% interest, requires a monthly payment of $106.24 for full amortization in five years. Books of amortization tables list monthly payments for various interest rates and loan amounts. See also *amortization; financing; interest; mortgage; principal.*

full amortization

YEAR	$5,000 LOAN 10%, 5 YEARS	
	INTEREST	PRINCIPAL
1	$ 464	$ 811
2	378	897
3	285	990
4	182	1,093
5	66	1,209
		$5,000

full disclosure the revealing of all pertinent and material facts, especially during the negotiation of a contract. One form of full disclosure is calling for a complete and independent home inspection, with a written report made available to the seller. The document will disclose all discovered flaws and maintenance deficiencies of a property. See also *contract; fraudulent concealment; good faith; home inspection.*

full faith and credit a form of guarantee as to an investment's degree of safety. For example, the U.S. government pledges its full faith and credit that investors will receive full principal and interest on Treasury bills, bonds and notes. And securities issued by the Government National Mortgage Corporation (GNMA) also are made on the same terms. See also *Government National Mortgage Association (GNMA); investment program; mortgage security; risk factor; secondary market.*

fully diluted earnings a calculated rate of return that would be earned by an investor, assuming that all outstanding convertible debts and rights were converted to common stock at the beginning of the reporting period. This event *functional*

rarely occurs, so the calculation is theoretical only. See also *investment income; rate of return.*

functional obsolescence a decline or loss of value caused by deterioration, lack of maintenance, lack of validity, or any other cause other than physical depreciation in a property. For example, an apartment house is designed with high ceilings and excessive window space. The cost of heating and cooling rises and makes the design inappropriate for the climate, and impossible to operate profitably. The building has become functionally obsolescent. See also *economic obsolescence; locational obsolescence; obsolescence; physical depreciation; useful life; value.*

functional utility the highest and best use of a property, assuming that the building is safe, in compliance with current zoning and safety rules, and continues to meet standards for other, similar properties. See also *highest and best use; obsolescence.*

future interest a right held by a person or organization in a property, to take effect at some point in the future. For example, a property is willed to a minor with the stipulation that it may not be taken possession of until a specified age. See also *estate for years; interest; leasehold estate; life estate; right of possession.*

future value the actual dollar value of either a sum of money or the sum of periodic deposits, at a specified rate of interest and for a specified period of time. For example, $1,000 is to be left on deposit at 5% interest (compounded quarterly) for five years. At the end of the five-year period, it will have grown to $1,282.05, the future value of $1,000. It may also be said that the $1,000 is the present value of $1,282.05 under the same conditions. See also *compound interest; interest; present value; value.*

future value

YEAR	5% (A)	BALANCE
		$1,000.00
1	$50.95	1,050.95
2	53.54	1,104.49
3	56.27	1,160.76
4	59.14	1,219.90
5	62.15	1,282.05

(A) compounded quarterly

G

gain an increase in value, such as the profit a homeowner earns when selling a home for a higher amount than the purchase price. See also *capital gain/loss; investment income; return on equity; yield.*

gap financing temporary financing for a period of time after a previous mortgage ends and before a new mortgage is granted; or from the beginning of a construction project until full lending terms (such as occupancy or lease commitments) have been met. Gap financing is often arranged for developers of commercial properties or major residential subdivisions, and may be used in a construction and development REIT to pay lenders, with repayments to be made upon finalization of a more permanent mortgage. See also *bridge loan; construction and development REIT; financing; mortgage; Real Estate Investment Trust (REIT).*

gap insurance (1) a form of insurance granted to lenders for a period between the closing of title and actual recording of a deed. A title insurance policy protects the subject property for any undisclosed liens prior to the closing date. (2) a form of default insurance a lender may require of a borrower during the period of gap financing on a yet uncompleted construction project. See also *default insurance; financing; mortgage; title insurance policy.*

general agent an agent with the right to represent a principal in a range of matters. For example, a real estate agent is presumed to have the right to represent a broker in matters pertaining to the successful close of a real estate transaction, including negotiation, terms of sale, and financing. A universal agent, in comparison, has the right to represent a principal on all matters. And a special agent is empowered to represent another for one specific matter only. See also *agent; broker; power of attorney; special agent; universal agent.*

general lien a form of lien that encompasses all personal and real property rather than one specific property. It may be said that a general lien is secured by the total net worth of the individual, rather than by the market value of that individual's property. See also *collateral; lien; personal property; real property; secured debt; specific lien.*

general mortgage (1) a blanket mortgage, one granted on a range of properties. For example, a developer is granted a single mortgage on a number of units under development. (2) a mortgage secured by all properties of the borrower, both personal and real, and not just by a single property. See also *blanket mortgage; collateral; mortgage; personal property; real property; secured debt.*

general partnership a form of organization in which two or more individuals or companies act together in the direct management of a business or venture. Partners share in profits and losses according to an agreed upon ratio, often tied to the amount of initial capital invested. See also *limited partnership; partnership; Uniform Partnership Act (UPA).*

Ginnie Mae acronym for the Government National Mortgage Association (GNMA), a federal agency whose purpose is to organize mortgage pools and insure investors' income and safety of principal. See also *Government National Mortgage Association (GNMA); investment program; mortgage pool; secondary market.*

Ginnie Mae pass-through a debt instrument in a pool sponsored by the Government National Mortgage Association (GNMA). Investors share in a pool of residential mortgages purchased from conventional lenders, the earnings on which are passed from the homeowner to the original lender; from the lender to the GNMA; and then distributed to the investor. See also *debt instrument; Government National Mortgage Association (GNMA); investment program; lending institution; mortgage pool; residential mortgage; secondary market.*

Ginnie Mae pass-through

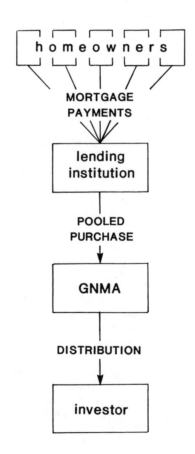

good faith acting with honesty and integrity, abiding by the agreed upon terms of a contract. See also *bad faith; contract; full disclosure.*

good faith deposit an amount of money given at the time an agreement is reached, pending the signing of a more complete contract. At the time the good faith deposit is paid, the basic terms are put into writing, and both sides sign. The deposit is intended as a binder, showing the buyer's intention and good faith in entering the contract. See also *agreement; binder; contract; earnest money; offer to purchase.*

good record title descriptive of title found to be clear of encumbrances other than those already known. For example, a seller offers a home for sale with an existing first mortgage. A title search shows that no other mortgages, liens or other encumbrances on that property are outstanding. See also *clear title; encumbrance; fee simple; title search.*

good title a marketable title, one that is free of disputes and undisclosed encumbrances. See also *clear title; encumbrance; marketable title; title.*

Government National Mortgage Association (GNMA) a federal agency that facilitates the financing of residential properties. The GNMA purchases existing mortgage loans from lending institutions, specifically low-interest loans granted as part of federally subsidized programs. It organizes these mortgages into pools and sells shares to investors, including full faith and credit guarantees. The GNMA was originally part of the Federal National Mortgage Association (FNMA), and is directed by the Department of Housing and Urban Development (HUD). See also *Department of Housing and Urban Development (HUD); Federal National Mortgage Association (FNMA); full faith and credit; Ginnie Mae; lending institution; mortgage pool; residential mortgage; secondary market.*

grace period a period of time after a payment due date, and before default. For example, the terms of a mortgage specify that payments are due on the first of each month. A late charge will be assessed if payment is not received by the 16th. The period between these two dates is the grace period. See also *default; late charge; mortgage; performance.*

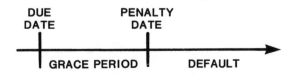

Graduate

Graduate Realtors Institute (GRI) a designation granted by the National Association of Realtors, to qualified members. See also *National Association of Realtors (NAR).*

graduated lease a lease that includes a provision for scheduled increases over time. The levels of increases are established at the time the lease is signed, with the timing of increases spelled out. For example, a lease calls for $50 increases from a base of $500 per month, to occur every three years for a total lease period of 12 years. See also *lease; variable lease.*

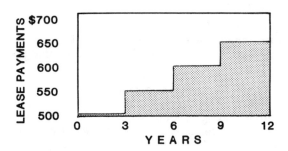

graduated lease

Graduated Payment Mortgage (GPM) a form of creative financing involving a scheduled increase in monthly payments over an initial period between five and 10 years. The payments then level out, often at a variable rate of interest. The purpose of this loan is often to enable a buyer to qualify when income is below the required level for a more traditional form of mortgage loan. See also *Adjustable Rate Mortgage (ARM); amortization; creative financing; financing; mortgage acceleration.*

gridiron pattern a pattern of housing layout in a subdivision, involving rectangular blocks, wide streets, and smaller access or service alleys. See also *cluster; curvilinear system; development; loop streets; Radburn Plan; subdivision.*

gross area the total area of a building, including exterior walls and unrentable space (halls, elevators, stairwells). This is computed to develop a relationship of total area to net rentable space. See also *area; Floor-Area Ratio (FAR); rentable area.*

gross income the total amount received before deduction of operating expenses, mortgage interest, depreciation or taxes. See also *investment income; net income.*

Graduated Payment Mortgage (GPM)

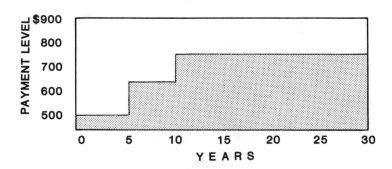

gross lease a residential lease requiring the tenant to make level payments for the agreed term. The landlord is responsible for all taxes, maintenance, insurance and other operating expenses. See also *apartment; lease; multiple dwelling; net lease.*

gross profit the portion of installment payments that are attributed to capital gain rather than a return of invested capital. For example, a homeowner paid $45,000 for a home several years ago, and sold it for $68,000 on an installment sale. The basis is divided by the sales price to develop the gross profit of 66%. Periodic payments of $7,000 in this example would be broken down as follows: $4,620 (66%) would be taxable as a capital gain, and the balance of $2,380 represents a non-taxable return of the basis. See also *basis; capital gain/loss; installment sale; investment income; tax basis.*

gross profit

$$\frac{\text{basis}}{\text{sales price}}$$

$$\frac{\$45,000}{\$68,000} = 66\%$$

Gross

Gross Rent Multiplier (GRM) a factor used to estimate the market value of rental properties. The sales price is divided by monthly rent to determine the GRM. An appraiser may estimate the market value of a home by comparing GRM factors on four or more similar properties that were sold in the same area during recent months. For example, a rental property is going on the market, and an appraiser compares the GRM on four similar homes. On one property, the sales price was $90,000 and monthly rent was $700. On this property, the GRM was 128.6. When added to GRM's for other homes, an area average is established as the basis for determining market value. For example:

Sales price	rent	GRM
$90,000	$700	128.6
89,600	650	137.8
92,400	600	154.0
95,000	725	131.0

The average GRM among these recently sold properties is 137.9. Monthly rent of the subject house is $650, so an estimated market value is:

$$137.9 \times \$650 = \$89,635$$

See also *appraised value; market value; rental value.*

Gross Rent Multiplier (GRM)

$$\frac{\text{sales price}}{\text{rent}}$$

$$\frac{\$90,000}{\$700} = 128.6$$

ground lease a form of net lease in which the tenant agrees to construct a building and occupy it for a number of years (often 50 years or longer). See also *net lease; percentage lease; variable lease.*

Growing Equity Mortgage (GEM) a form of mortgage in which monthly payments are increased periodically, with the additional portion being paid toward reduction of the principal balance. The GEM reduces the term required for full amortization of the loan. This form of financing may be arranged with either a fixed or variable rate of interest. See also *amortization; creative financing; full amortization; mortgage acceleration.*

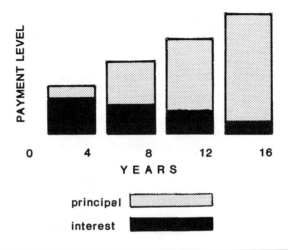

Guaranteed Mortgage Certificate (GMC) a security of the Federal Home Loan Mortgage Corporation (FHLMC) similar to a Participation Certificate (PC). However, interest is paid on the GMC semiannually rather than each month. See also *debt instrument; Federal Home Loan Mortgage Corporation (FHLMC); Freddie Mac; investment program; Participation Certificate (PC).*

H

hard money cash transferred or offered on the spot, as in the case of a good faith deposit. This contrasts with "soft" money, such as payments on a debt that are to be made in the future. See also *down payment; earnest money; good faith deposit.*

hazard insurance term describing homeowner's policies, providing casualty and liability protection to the homeowner. See also *homeowner's insurance.*

high ratio financing descriptive of a loan secured by real estate, when a high percentage of the property's market value is loaned. See also *financing; leverage.*

highest and best use a theory in the valuation of land and property, that value or potential value is largely dependent on utility. A property will be worth more if utilized in the best possible way. For example, a lot is ideally located for a high-traffic commercial purpose. Building a shop in that location would *historical* 76

represent the highest and best use of the land. See also *anticipation; change; competition; conformity; contribution; diminishing returns; increasing returns; plottage; regression; substitution; supply and demand.*

historical yield   a record of yields over time, as in past or existing direct participation programs offered by a sponsor company. The historical yield may be quoted to convince investors to select a program; but if that yield is computed on market values that are estimated without benefit of an independent appraisal, it may be inaccurate. See also *direct participation program; risk factor; sponsor; yield.*

HO-1   one of seven types of homeowner's policies, called the basic policy. It provides coverage for casualties, but only to the extent of 11 named perils. Liability insurance is also included. See also *basic policy; casualty insurance; liability insurance.*

HO-2   the broad form, providing casualty protection against 18 named perils, in addition to liability coverage. The broad form gives more protection against loss than the basic policy. See also *broad form; casualty insurance; liability insurance.*

HO-3   the all-risk form, including casualty protection against all perils except specified exceptions (for losses in or to a dwelling). In this policy, personal possessions are covered only to the extent of 18 named perils. The policy also includes liability insurance. See also *all-risk form; casualty insurance; liability insurance.*

HO-4   the renter's policy, designed to provide insurance for 18 named perils on personal property only. The owner of an apartment building or rented home is responsible for protection against losses to the structure. Liability insurance is limited to the immediate unit, and excludes the wider responsibilities of the building's owner. See also *casualty insurance; liability insurance; renter's policy.*

HO-5   the comprehensive policy, including casualty protection against all casualties not named as exceptions, along with liability insurance. See also *casualty insurance; comprehensive; liability insurance.*

HO-6   the condominium policy, designed for individual owners of condominium units. It gives the owner casualty protection for 18 named perils, and all-risk coverage can be purchased for a higher premium. Liability protection is limited to those liabilities only on individual premises. The condominium association is responsible for casualty and liability protection on common areas. See also *casualty insurance; condominium policy; liability insurance.*

HO-8   the older homes policy, giving an owner casualty protection only against 11 named perils, and liability protection. This policy will return a damaged property to "serviceable" condition, but will not necessarily replace the same quality of materials or workmanship. See also *casualty insurance; liability insurance; older homes policy.*

holding period the length of time a property is owned, used most often to describe an investment interest in real estate. See also *investment property*.

holdover clause a provision in a listing agreement, specifying that the designated broker will be entitled to commissions in the event that the house is sold within a certain period. The clause would be applicable to prospective buyers to whom the house was shown by that broker. For example, a homeowner puts a residence up for sale and retains a broker. After two months as an exclusive listing, another broker shows the same house to one of the prospective buyers the original buyer brought in. The holdover clause would be in effect if the specified period of time had not expired. See also *broker; commission; exclusive listing*.

holdover tenant a tenancy at sufferance, when the tenant remains in possession of a property after expiration of the lease. See also *lease; possession; tenancy at sufferance*.

home inspection a service performed by a contractor or other expert, the purpose of which is to identify defects requiring repair. The home inspection is usually requested in anticipation of a pending sale. Recent court decisions have made real estate brokers responsible for disclosure to buyers of flaws that would be discovered with a "diligent" inspection. This has increased the popularity of home inspection services. A professional inspector will not, under any circumstances, solicit repair work discovered during an inspection, or refer homeowners to other contractors. The inspection should include a written report. Home buyers may specify a home inspection as a contingency in an offer to purchase a property. See also *American Society of Home Inspectors (ASHI); contingency; deferred maintenance; inspection clause*.

homeowner's insurance protection against casualty losses to dwellings and personal property, and liabilities arising from injuries to others or damage to the property of others. Homeowners may purchase varying levels of coverage, and should update their policies periodically as market value grows. A policy may reimburse for casualty losses on the basis of Actual Cash Value (ACV) or replacement cost. The ACV method includes a depreciation factor, so that the homeowner receives an estimated current value. Replacement cost coverage reimburses the actual current replacement cost, but is subject to certain limits. For example, one policy specifies that replacement cost will be paid to a maximum of 400% of ACV. If a stereo system originally costing $1,100 is stolen from a home, and the insurer calculates that ACV (depreciated value) is only $200, the maximum reimbursement will be $800 (400% of ACV), regardless of actual replacement cost. See also *Actual Cash Value (ACV); casualty insurance; fire insurance; hazard insurance; liability insurance; replacement cost*. [See overleaf.]

Homeowner's Land Corporation (HLC) a federal agency that issues government-guaranteed bonds for the exchange of defaulted mortgages. The HLC was founded in 1932. See also *default; mortgage*.

Homeowner's Warranty Program (HOW) a form of 10-year warranty offered on newly built homes, usually offered by a developer or builder. See also *builder warranty; development*.

homeowner's insurance

NUMBER	POLICY	COVERAGE PERSONAL PROPERTY	DWELLING
HO-1	basic	11 basic perils	11 basic perils
HO-2	broad	18 named perils	18 named perils
HO-3	all-risk	18 named perils	all perils except named exclusions
HO-4	renter's	18 named perils	no coverage
HO-5	comprehensive	all perils except named exclusions	all perils except named exclusions
HO-6	condominium	18 named perils	no coverage
HO-8	older home	11 basic perils	11 basic perils

- no coverage
- 11 basic perils
- 18 named perils
- all perils except named exclusions

---

homestead an exemption that can be filed by the homeowner, preventing seizure of a home to satisfy encumbrances. Each state sets a limit on the amount of the homestead exemption (some states have no limits). Homestead laws may specify that no creditor except a mortgage lender may force the sale of a home to repay a debt. See also *default; encumbrance; principal residence; residential property.*

homestead estate the land and building occupied by a homeowner. See also *principal residence.*

horizontal property laws the state laws concerned with property rights of condominiums. The ownership of a unit extends only to the air space within the walls, with common elements owned jointly by the individual and other unit owners. Thus, the rights generally held by homeowners do not apply to the same extent to condominium owners. See also *air rights; common elements; condominium; real law.*

hybrid REIT a Real Estate Investment Trust (REIT) that purchases land and

improved

buildings and takes equity positions, but also may loan money to owners of existing buildings, or to those developing land. The hybrid REIT includes features of equity and mortgage REIT's and may emphasize equity and debt positions in varying degrees. See also *equity REIT; mortgage REIT; Real Estate Investment Trust (REIT).*

hypothecation the pledge of property as collateral on a debt, without surrendering physical possession. See also *collateral; mortgage; possession; secured debt.*

I

illegal contract a contract that is unlawful or void by its nature. For example, use of property for an illegal purpose will nullify a lease. See also *contract; unenforceable contract; void contract.*

imperfect title a title that is incomplete or defective, that cannot be conveyed or insured. See also *clear title; cloud on the title; defective title; good title.*

implied contract a form of contract arising from the action or consent of the parties, without entering into an actual written or verbal agreement. See also *agreement; contract; meeting of the minds; statute of frauds.*

implied easement a form of easement created when an encroachment upon the land of another has continued over a period of time, and the owner has not disallowed or complained about the use. See also *easement by prescription; encroachment.*

implied warranty a concept of law, that a contract includes certain assumed rights. For example, a tenant may assume that the landlord will not disrupt the right to occupy a unit for the purpose intended. That assumption is reasonable, and is an implied warranty. See also *lease; right of occupancy; tenant.*

impound (1) the setting aside of funds, as during an escrow period. Money is collected from the buyer for a down payment and settlement of closing costs, and from the seller for inspections and repairs mandated in the contract. (2) an account created by a lending institution for the collection and payment of property taxes and insurance. The homeowner's payment includes principal, interest and impound payments adequate to make lump-sum payments at future due dates. See also *escrow; lending institution; Principal, Interest, Taxes and Insurance (PITI).*

improved land any change made to raw land to increase its value and use, such as a building, fence, utilities, roads, and landscaping. See also *raw land; real property.*

improvement

improvement any addition or structure placed upon land. As long as improvements add value to the land, increasing returns may be expected. See also *addition; increasing returns; market value; over-improvement.*

imputed interest a provision in tax law. When interest charged on a loan is below current market rates, the principal and interest may be adjusted for tax purposes, and restated on a more reasonable basis. For example, a homeowner wants to transfer real estate to his son. He enters into a contract and grants a 3% loan. However, the Internal Revenue Service imputes interest at 9% based on average rates charged by lending institutions at the time the contract was entered. This will affect interest income to the seller, interest expense to the buyer, and the calculation of the taxable portion of payments if arranged as an installment sale. See also *interest; principal; tax basis.*

income approach an appraisal method that involves computation of the present value of future interests in real estate income. This method is used for commercial property. On an annual basis, the gross income is estimated and then reduced for a reasonable vacancy factor. From this, operating expenses are deducted. The resulting net income is multiplied by a capitalization rate to arrive at appraised value. See also *appraisal method; capitalization rate; cost approach; gross income; market comparison approach; net income; vacancy rate.*

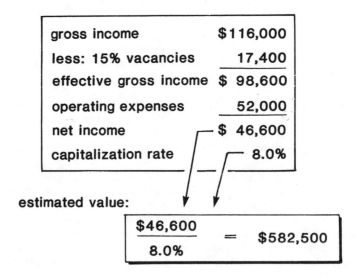

income participation a form of mortgage loan in which the lender shares in future profits. For example, a Shared Equity Mortgage (SEM) may be offered

increasing

when the borrower cannot qualify for a traditional mortgage. The borrower agrees that, upon sale of the property, a percentage of profits will be given to the lender, in addition to full payment of the mortgage. See also *creative financing; equity participation; lending institution; participation loan; Shared Appreciation Mortgage (SAM)*.

income property any real property that is used to generate income. For example, a homeowner buys a second home and moves to it, converting his previous residence into a rental. In that case, a previously residential property becomes an income property. See also *commercial property; residential property*.

income statement a financial statement that summarizes income, costs, expenses and net profits over a specified period of time, such as one year, a quarter, or a month. See also *balance sheet; financial statement*.

---

income statement

```
  revenues
−  costs
=  gross profit
−  expenses
=  operating profit
−  taxes
=  net profit
```

---

income tax federal, state or local taxes assessed on the basis of taxable income of individuals or companies. See also *net income; tax basis*.

incorporeal property non-physical value or rights. For example, a lending institution has an incorporeal right when it holds a mortgage on a property. And a homeowner whose property is more highly valued than neighboring homes because of an exceptional view has incorporeal value. See also *aesthetic value; future interest; intangible asset; lending institution; mortgage; tangible property*.

increasing returns a basic theory of valuation stating that improvements to property will increase market value, but only to an extent. At some point, improvements will no longer add to value, at which point the theory of diminishing returns takes effect. See also *anticipation; change; competition; conformity;*

incurable 82

contribution; diminishing returns; highest and best use; plottage; regression; substitution; supply and demand.

incurable depreciation a form of depreciation that cannot be reversed. For example, a building has deteriorated due to lack of care; repairing the property would cost more than could be recaptured in a sale. See also *curable depreciation; depreciation; physical depreciation.*

incurable title descriptive of title that cannot be conveyed due to a defect, such as an encumbrance that cannot be removed. See also *cloud on the title; defective title; encumbrance; title.*

index clause (1) a provision in a lease calling for periodic increases in rent level, based on an independent index (such as the Consumer Price Index). **(2)** the provision in a mortgage contract spelling out the terms for increasing interest rates in an Adjustable Rate Mortgage (ARM), including periodic and term caps and the index to be used in calculating changes in the rate. See also *Adjustable Rate Mortgage (ARM); cap; graduated lease; inflation; lease; mortgage.*

index loan a form of mortgage calling for a periodic adjustment in interest rate, based upon the movement in an independent index. The actual increase or decrease will usually be made based on the percentage change in the index, subject to caps on (a) the amount of increase that may be made per year and (b) the total increase that may be made for the entire term of the loan. For example, a loan is granted with a starting rate of 7.50%. At that point, the current value of an independent index is assumed to be 100.0%. The percentage change in the index each year is applied to the original interest rate. After five years, the effective rate of interest has grown to 8.26%. See also *Adjustable Rate Mortgage (ARM); cap; mortgage.*

industrial mortgage a mortgage on industrial property, used either to purchase land or replace corporate bonds. The industrial mortgage may be amortized over a shorter period than for other commercial properties, in as little as 10 years. See also *commercial property; full amortization; mortgage.*

inflation increases in prices resulting from excessive credit or money supply. Inflation is measured by the federal government through the Consumer Price Index (CPI), which measures the changes in a number of commodities. Housing plays a major role in the CPI. Between 1968 and 1984, housing values generally exceeded the average CPI. With a 1967 base of 100.0%, housing values grew to 361.7%, while the CPI overall grew to 311.1%. See also *deflation; market value.*

ingress the means of entering property, or a reference to the right of way onto a parcel of land. See also *easement; egress; right of way.*

inside lot a parcel of land situated between corner lots. See also *corner lot; parcel.*

index loan

YEAR	INDEX BASE	INDEX CHANGE	INTEREST RATE
	100.0		7.50%
1	103.4	+ 3.4%	7.76
2	105.8	+ 2.3	7.94
3	109.6	+ 3.6	8.23
4	107.3	− 2.1	8.06
5	110.0	+ 2.5	8.26

inflation

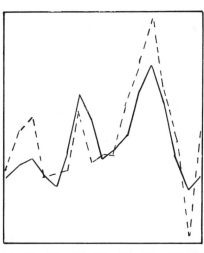

——— Consumer Price Index
− − − − − housing values

inspection 84

inspection clause a provision included in a contract for the purchase of property, specifying that the offer is made contingent upon completion of an inspection. Most contract provisions include a pest inspection contingency, and a general home inspection may be requested by a buyer. See also *contingency; home inspection; termite inspection.*

installment contract a form of purchase in which payments are made over a period of time. Title to the property remains with the seller until the entire purchase price has been paid. See also *conditional sale; contract; land contract.*

installment payment (1) a payment made as part of an installment contract. (2) regular monthly payments made by a homeowner to the lending institution in accordance with the terms of a mortgage. See also *amortization; interest; mortgage; principal.*

installment sale a form of sale in which title remains with the seller until the entire debt has been paid. For tax purposes, each payment is broken down into three parts:
    a. Interest, usually computed on a declining basis to achieve full amortization within a specified period of time.
    b. Principal, representing a return of the original owner's basis, which is not taxable.
    c. Principal, representing profit on the sale, which is taxable to the seller as it is received. When the loan is set up on a full amortization basis, the taxable payment will increase over time, as interest decreases. See also *basis; capital gain/loss; sale; tax basis.*

Institute of Real Estate Management (IREM) an organization affiliated with the National Association of Realtors (NAR), that awards the designation, Certified Property Manager (CPM) to qualified members. The Institute is located at 430 North Michigan Avenue, Chicago, IL 60611. See also *Certified Property Manager (CPM); National Association of Realtors (NAR); property manager.*

institutional lender the provider of a mortgage loan other than a relative, friend or other individual. Institutions may include banks, savings and loan institutions, savings banks, mutual banks, credit unions, insurance companies, or mortgage bankers. See also *conventional loan; financing; lending institution.*

instrument a legal form that establishes the existence of a contract, right, obligation, or transfer of property. See also *contract; deed; lease; mortgage.*

intangible asset value in property that is not physical. For example, an easement may add value to a property, even though it cannot be seen. And the right to possession granted under the terms of a long-term lease is a form of intangible value. See also *incorporeal property; tangible property; value.*

interest (1) the cost of borrowing money, charged as part of repayment on a compound or simple basis. For example, a borrower is charged 10% on a 15-year mortgage of $80,000. The total interest will be $74,744. (2) a right to present or future benefits of property ownership or investment. For example, an investor who owns units of a partnership or REIT has an interest in the program. See also *compound interest; investment property; simple interest.*

interest averaging a determination of the average rate of interest, when two or more loans are outstanding on one property. For example, a homeowner has two mortgages, one for $80,000 at 11.5% and another for $22,000 at 7.0%. The average interest must be weighted, because one loan represents a greater portion of the total. The average in this case is 10.53%. See also *mortgage; weighted average.*

---

interest averaging

$$\$80,000 \text{ at } 11.5\% \qquad \$22,000 \text{ at } 7.0\%$$

$$\left(\frac{80}{102} \times 11.5\right) + \left(\frac{22}{102} \times 7.0\right) =$$

$$9.0196 \quad + \quad 1.5098 = 10.53\%$$

---

interest only a type of loan requiring payment of interest, but no reduction of principal. In a balloon mortgage, full payment of the debt must be made at a specified date in the future, often requiring renegotiated terms or renewal. Such a loan may be granted to a borrower who cannot qualify for a traditional, fully amortized loan. See also *amortization; balloon mortgage; creative financing; principal; Renegotiated Rate Mortgage (RRM).*

interest rate a percentage charged to a borrower, or earned by a depositer. The rate is based on the principal amount. For example, a loan is granted at 11%, compounded monthly. Each month's payment will be broken down between interest on the outstanding loan balance, and principal. See also *compound interest; principal; simple interest.*

interim financing a temporary loan, granted to fund construction, or following payment of a previous loan but before a replacement loan is contracted. See also *bridge loan; gap financing; short-term loan.*

Internal Rate of Return (IRR) a calculation of yield based on recognition of the time value of money. Funds available for several years are assumed to be worth

International

more, because they could be reinvested to yield yet more profits; funds available for shorter periods of time have correspondingly lower value. For example, an investor deposits $10,000 in a program for five years. During that time, cash received totals $12,522. The average per year is $2,504, for an average annual yield of 25.0%. But most of that money is not received until liquidation of property in the last year. IRR is calculated on the assumption that money could earn 11% in another investment. With that assumed rate of return, the IRR is calculated based upon the year money is actually received. See also *cash flow; discounted cash flow; investment income; present value; rate of return; time value of money; yield.*

Internal Rate of Return (IRR)

YEAR	NET INCOME	PRESENT VALUE FACTOR (11%)	PRESENT VALUE AMOUNT
1	$ (839)	0.9009	$ (756)
2	214	0.8116	174
3	311	0.7312	227
4	1,486	0.6587	979
5	11,350	0.5935	6,736
total	$12,522		$ 7,360
average, 5 years			$ 1,472
initial investment			$10,000
Internal Rate of Return			14.72%

International Association of Assessing Officers (IAAO) an organization of professional tax assessors, located at 1313 East 60th Street, Chicago, IL 60637. See also *assessment; property taxes; tax basis.*

Interstate Land Sales Full Disclosure Act (ILSA) a consumer protection law designed to protect purchasers of land across state lines. The law requires anyone selling 100 or more parcels outside a domicile state, to file a statement of record. The purchaser has seven days from contract date to rescind the purchase. Rescission can be made within two years if a property report is not given to them at the time of sale. The ILSA is enforced by HUD. See also *Department of Housing and Urban Development (HUD); full disclosure; land; property report.*

intrinsic value   tangible, actual value above and beyond aesthetic or intangible value. See also *aesthetic value; intangible asset; tangible property; value.*

investment income   capital gains, interest and dividends, and rents received as a return of invested money. Investment income is contrasted with earned income (from salaries, for example) for tax purposes. See also *capital gain/loss; interest; net income; ordinary gain/loss; tax basis.*

investment interest   (1) interest earned on a deposit or other debt security. (2) a position in an investment program, such as the deposited capital in a partnership or REIT. See also *debt instrument; interest; net income; program.*

investment objective   the purpose an investor wants to achieve, or the stated intention of a program's management. For example, an investor may seek liquidity, protection from inflation, or shelter of income from taxation. And a program may state that its objective is to provide high current income or long-term growth. Every form of investment involves a risk factor, which must be considered when setting an investment objective. For example, aggressive high income investments call for greater risk than more conservative, defensive accounts. See also *inflation; liquidity; risk factor; tax shelter.*

investment program   any use of money for the purpose of generating income. These include direct participation programs such as limited partnerships; mortgage pools; or a Real Estate Investment Trust (REIT). In real estate programs, investors pool their money together and place it under professional management. See also *direct participation program; limited partnership; mortgage pool; program; Real Estate Investment Trust (REIT).*

investment property   any property held for the purpose of generating income from rent, reduction of taxes, and eventual capital gains. See also *capital gain/loss; net income; real property.*

investor basis   for tax purposes, the actual amount the investor has at risk. This amount consists of cash invested plus recourse loans and, with limits, certain nonrecourse loans. The investor cannot claim losses in excess of the basis. This provision was enacted into tax law and was modified to eliminate abusive tax shelters, particularly in the real estate industry. See also *at risk; basis; direct participation program; limited partnership; nonrecourse loan; recourse loan; tax shelter.*

involuntary alienation   a forced sale of real estate, brought about when a lien or mortgage is defaulted by the homeowner. See also *alienation; conveyance; forced sale; voluntary alienation.*

involuntary lien   a lien created and imposed upon real property without the permission or consent of the owner. There are two forms of involuntary lien: an equitable lien, usually a court judgement as satisfaction of a debt; and a statutory lien, such as a property tax assessment. See also *encumbrance; equitable lien; general lien; specific lien; statutory lien.*

J

joint and several liability an obligation or contingent debt shared by two or more tenants in severalty. For example, a mortgage contracted by a husband and wife creates a joint and several liability. See also *encumbrance; mortgage; tenancy in severalty.*

joint annuity an annuity that applies to two individuals rather than one. For example, a life insurance company agrees to make monthly payments to a married couple as long as either one is alive. See also *annuity.*

joint mortgage insurance a form of life insurance with a decreasing term benefit tied to the amount of an outstanding mortgage. The benefit is to be paid upon the death of either spouse. This form of life insurance is appropriate for a two-income family, when the economic consequences of the death of either spouse could mean becoming unable to afford mortgage payments. See also *life insurance; mortgage insurance.*

joint tenancy a unity of possession, or an estate held by two people. As an undivided interest, full ownership passes to the survivor upon the death of one tenant. See also *tenancy in common; undivided interest; unity of possession.*

Joint Tenants with Rights of Survivorship (JTWROS) an expanded description of a joint tenancy. As a form of registration of ownership, the entry "JTWROS" specifies the right of survivorship in ownership. See also *right of survivorship; tenancy in common.*

joint venture a form of organization in which two or more individuals or companies join to conduct business. The joint venture is applicable only for a specific project or property, whereas a partnership is a more permanent and broader ranging agreement. See also *partnership.*

judicial foreclosure the sale of property to satisfy a debt, as ordered by a court of law. This contrasts with a nonjudicial foreclosure that is spelled out in a contract. In that form, the lending institution is allowed to foreclose on a property as part of the agreement, and not requiring a finding by the court. See also *foreclosure; nonjudicial foreclosure.*

junior lien an encumbrance on property that is secondary to a previous lien. In the event of default, the senior lien holds priority of claim, and all junior liens are satisfied wholly or in part only after full settlement of the senior claim. See also *first lien; lien; priority; senior lien.*

junior mortgage a second mortgage or other form of mortgage taking secondary rights to settlement. The senior, or first mortgage has seniority over all junior mortgages. See also *first mortgage; mortgage; priority; second mortgage; senior mortgage.*

L

land the solid portion of the earth's crust. The definition includes both land and rights, unless otherwise specified, to minerals under a parcel of land. See also *improved land; raw land; real property.*

land certificate proof of title, including a legal description and the name of the owner. See also *certificate of title; legal description.*

land contract a method of purchasing property on the installment method. Title remains with the seller until all installment payments have been made. Some variations allow for conveyance of title after a specified portion of the total debt has been paid. See also *contract; installment sale; title.*

land purchase-leaseback the purchase of land but not improved real property on that land. The buyer leases the land back to the original owner, often under a contract providing for increased lease payments in the event that income from the improvements increases in the future. An owner may desire to sell and lease back land to raise capital without going into debt; to recognize a capital gain in a year when other losses offset that liability; or to take the profits from a land investment. See also *improved land; investment property; lease; tax basis.*

land residual technique a method for determining the value of land only. The appraiser must deduct the portion of estimated market value that is attributable to improvements and Net Operating Income (NOI) from that activity. The purpose is to isolate the value of land, assuming the highest and best use, similar to the income approach of appraisal. See also *appraisal method; highest and best use; income approach; Net Operating Income (NOI).*

landlord's warrant a provision included in some lease contracts, in which the tenant pledges personal property as collateral for obligations under the terms of the lease. In the event of default or late lease payments, the landlord may take possession of personal property and sell it to satisfy the debt. See also *collateral; default; lease; personal property; possession.*

landmark a familiar or prominent feature that is used to mark or indicate a boundary of property. It may be a feature of the landscape, a man-made structure, or any other permanent and recognizable point. See also *boundary rights; monument; property line.*

late charge a fee charged by a lender for late payment of an installment on a mortgage or other loan. Most mortgages specify two dates: a due date and a date after which a penalty will be assessed. For example, a homeowner's monthly bill states, "Due date: March 1. Penalty of $17.25 will be assessed if not paid by March 16." See also *finance charge; installment contract; lending institution; mortgage.*

latent defect bond a warranty on materials and workmanship, ensuring correction of defects discovered within a specified period of time following *lease*

construction, purchase or occupancy. HUD requires builders and developers to carry a form of one-year bonding for projects subsidized by that agency. See also *builder warranty; Department of Housing and Urban Development (HUD); home inspection.*

lease   a contract between a landlord (lessor) and tenant (lessee) granting the right of occupancy for a specified period of time and levels of payment. The level may be fixed or may vary on a prescribed formula, time or cost basis. See also *consideration; contract; right of possession; tenant.*

lease insurance   **(1)** a form of default insurance as part of a lease. In the event the lessee does not continue making payments as the lease requires, the lessor is insured for the amount due. **(2)** a form of decreasing term life insurance on a tenant's life, tied to the amount of payments due under a lease contract. See also *default insurance; life insurance; tenant.*

lease with option to buy   an agreement under which an eventual sales price is agreed to as part of a lease. The lessee has the option, at the expiration of the lease period, to purchase the property. This arrangement may include an additional payment, to be applied against a down payment on the property. Or it may be used as an incentive to tie a tenant into a lease, without requiring payments as part of the monthly agreement. See also *down payment; option; tenant.*

leasehold estate   a type of lease for a specific number of years, such as estates at will, at sufferance, or for years. The estate is held by the tenant, with all rights defined and limited by the terms of the agreement. See also *agreement; estate at sufferance; estate at will; estate for years; tenant.*

leasehold improvement   any additions, upgrades or other permanent changes that add value to property, that are made by the lessee. For example, a company holds a 99-year lease on a parcel of land, and constructs its offices on the site. See also *capital improvement; improvement.*

leasehold interest   any right to the use or possession of property, except the right of ownership. See also *interest; right of possession.*

leasehold mortgage   a mortgage loan secured by improvements and other interests in land. This form of mortgage will be junior to any mortgages previously granted on the same property. For example, a tenant who builds an office on leased land subsequently borrows money with that property as security. This mortgage is junior to all other liens that came about before that date. See also *junior mortgage; lien; mortgage; priority; senior mortgage.*

legal description   a precise and specific identification of the location of property, including the exact property line. References are made to plat maps, degrees, and the number of feet along the boundaries of a parcel. See also *lot and block description; metes and bounds description; parcel; platted land; property line.*

legal notice a form of notice recognized by law. For example, one party wishes to rescind an offer. This rescission can be made by letter, a form of actual notice. Or a lien is recorded in the county offices, a form of constructive notice. See also *actual notice; constructive notice; recording; rescission.*

legal opinion a statement or letter from an attorney, that the terms and conditions of an investment program are in compliance with the law, or that the program will or will not create a conflict for investors. For example, the prospectus of a limited partnership includes a section in which the legal opinion is given. It assures potential investors that, in the attorney's opinion, the specific activities and assumptions of the program are acceptable under the law. See also *investment program; limited partnership; prospectus; risk factor.*

legal owner the equitable owner, or owner of record to a property. The legal owner holds title but may have no rights beyond a lien on the property. See also *lien; title.*

legal rate the maximum interest rate that a lender can charge under the law. See also *financing; interest rate; usury.*

legal title good or equitable title, or title that has the appearance of being free of defects. See also *equitable title; good title; title.*

lender participation a form of creative financing in which the lending institution receives both interest on a mortgage, and a portion of profits from the use of the property. A form of creative financing, participation loans may be granted to borrowers who do not otherwise qualify for a traditional mortgage loan. The participation payments may be current or deferred. Example: a lender gives a participation loan to the purchaser of an apartment building. Each month, the payment to the lender includes principal, interest, and 15% of net profits from rentals. Example: a participation loan specifies that upon sale of the property, a portion of growth in market value will be paid to the lender. See also *creative financing; financing; mortgage; participation loan; Shared Appreciation Mortgage (SAM).*

lending institution the company that grants a loan to a borrower. Real estate mortgages are the business of savings and loan associations, banks, mortgage bankers, insurance companies, credit unions, and other conventional lenders; and of the Federal Housing Administration (FHA) and the Veteran's Administration (VA). Some lenders sell their mortgages in the secondary market, with organizations like the FNMA and GNMA picking up the loans and creating mortgage pools. See also *conventional loan; debt; Federal Housing Administration (FHA); Federal National Mortgage Association (FNMA); financing; Government National Mortgage Association (GNMA); secondary market; Veteran's Administration (VA).*

lessee the tenant in a lease agreement, who has been given the right of possession to property as specified in the contract. See also *right of possession; tenant.*

lessor

lessor the landlord in a lease agreement, who has granted the right of possession to property as specified in the contract. See also *right of possession; tenant.*

let (1) a synonym for lease, often used to describe available property, "to let." (2) the granting of a construction contract to the winner of a bid. See also *capital improvement; development; improvement; lease.*

letter of intent (1) an offer to enter into a contract, without actually making an offer. The letter expresses a willingness to contract with certain conditions and terms, but does not bind or commit either party. For example, one individual wants to purchase property held by another. A letter of intent is drafted and mailed, stating a desire to negotiate terms and stipulating that the seller would be asked to carry a loan. (2) often used to describe the document prepared at the time a deposit receipt is made. In this case, the letter of intent is an offer that, if accepted, is binding. The letter of intent spells out the major terms of the agreement, and serves as a temporary contract until a more permanent and detailed contract can be drawn. If the letter is signed by the seller, the offer is accepted. See also *agreement; contract; deposit receipt; memorandum of agreement; offer.*

level debt service descriptive of most mortgage loan arrangements. The same amount of payment is made each month, and is broken down between interest and principal. Because interest is based on the current outstanding loan balance, the relationship changes over time. During the early years of the loan, interest is the major portion of the payment. Toward the end of the term, interest is a minor part, and most of the payment is for principal. However, the amount of payment does not change throughout the life of the loan. The level debt payment can be accelerated, with extra payments applied toward principal. Mortgage acceleration has the effect of reducing the amount of time required for payoff, and of reducing total interest costs. See also *debt service; financing; full amortization; interest; mortgage acceleration; principal.*

level payments descriptive of payments required in most mortgage loans; payments made under a level debt service arrangement. See also *amortization; mortgage.*

leverage the use of money, especially borrowed money, to increase profits and interests in real estate and other investments. Homeowners make use of leverage when they borrow 80% of the home's sales price. However, the term usually refers to a wider application of the principal.
    Example: a homeowner borrows money based on the equity in a principal residence, and uses it to purchase two additional properties with minimum down payments.
    Example: an investor puts a minimum deposit into a program that, in turn, uses the combined deposits of investors to purchase property on a highly leveraged basis. Only a small portion of the total holdings are equity positions; the balance is borrowed.
    The principle behind leverage is that, by controlling a larger number of properties, potential profits will increase. There is considerable risk, however. Leverage places a greater demand on cash flow, and higher than expected

level debt service

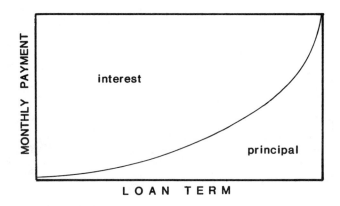

vacancies can mean an investor or program will be unable to make mortgage payments. And for leverage to be profitable, the market value of property must grow at a rate greater than the total interest paid over the same period of time.

In the past, a high volume of activity in leveraged investment programs was based on the desirability of purchasing properties while market values were growing rapidly, and when unlimited tax deductions were available. As the real estate cycle slowed, the market advantages of leverage disappeared. And as tax laws changed, investors were limited in the total amount of investment interest that could be deducted each year, and in the deduction of passive losses allowed under federal law.

Leverage is often referred to as the "effective" use of money, with the emphasis on borrowing as much as possible. A balanced approach should include an awareness of the risks. Leverage is appropriate when it is manageable and controlled, and when the homeowner or investor can afford added debt service without financial strain—assuming a high level of vacancy. See also *debt service; down payment; financing; investment program; limited partnership; mortgage; passive income; risk factor; tax basis.* [See overleaf.]

liability insurance protection against the loss that would result from injury to other people or their property, resulting from a homeowner's actions or caused by conditions on his property. For example, a neighbor's roof is damaged by a branch falling from a tree in the homeowner's yard. The cost of repairing the roof is covered under a homeowner's policy. Or, a visitor trips on a garden tool in the homeowner's yard, and fractures an ankle. The medical bills and any other damages will be paid by the insurance company under a liability provision. See also *casualty insurance; homeowner's insurance.*

lien an encumbrance or claim against real property, that may be voluntary. For example, a homeowner agrees to pledge real estate as collateral for a home

leverage

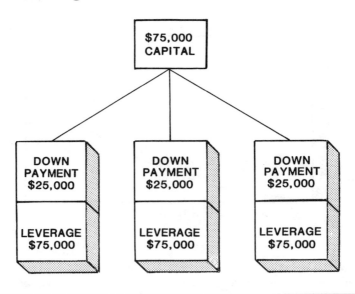

improvement being done by a contractor. A lien may also be involuntary. For example, a homeowner is delinquent in payment of a property tax bill. An involuntary lien is placed upon the property.

A lien may also be general or specific. A general lien refers to all properties owned by an individual, while a specific lien is placed on one property only. See also *encumbrance; general lien; involuntary lien; junior lien; Mechanic's Lien; secured debt; senior lien; specific lien; voluntary lien.*

lien affidavit a document certifying that (a) there are no liens or other encumbrances outstanding against a property, or (b) there are liens. In the latter case, each lien will be specified and described. See also *clear title; encumbrance; title report.*

lien in invitum (Lt.) an uninvited, or involuntary lien. See also *involuntary lien.*

lien release a cancellation or reconveyance of a lien. An unconditional lien release is used in some states to protect homeowners dealing with contractors for the construction or improvement of properties. The release ensures that the homeowner will not be responsible in the event the contractor fails to pay subcontractors or suppliers connected with a job. Without the release, the homeowner could be required to pay twice for work performed. For example, a contractor fails to pay a supplier. The supplier then exercises a lien and forces the homeowner to make payment, even though the contractor was already paid. See also *Mechanic's Lien; reconveyance; unconditional lien release.*

lien theory an interpretation of law in some states (lien theory states) that a lien does not give the lienholder the right of possession. So in the exercise of a lien, a foreclosure is mandated. In title theory states, the lienholder is allowed to take possession of foreclosed properties. See also *foreclosure; mortgage; real property; right of possession; title theory.*

life estate an estate involving real or personal property, that lasts for the duration of an owner's life, or until a specified event occurs (such as reaching the age of majority or becoming married). The recipient of property in a life estate is responsible for all property taxes and liens upon the real estate involved. See also *estate in land; personal property; real property.*

life insurance protection against the economic consequences of premature and unexpected death. The income earning head of a family may need life insurance to protect an investment in real estate. For example, a family depends upon income in order to make monthly mortgage payments. Life insurance is carried to pay off the mortgage and other debts, in the event that homeowner dies.

A form of life insurance designed specifically to pay off an outstanding mortgage debt is mortgage life. The face amount (death benefit) is tied to the balance outstanding on the mortgage loan, and will decline as equity builds up over the term of the loan. In the event of death, the insurance company will pay off the loan. This insurance can be purchased on a joint basis. For example, a family depends upon the income of both a husband and a wife. In the event either dies, a joint mortgage life insurance policy will pay off the entire balance of the mortgage.

Mortgage life is a form of decreasing term insurance. The premium is based upon the ages of the insured people, the mortgage balance, and the rate of interest. The premium remains level, while the actual death benefit declines over time. Decreasing time insurance not tied to a mortgage can be purchased from an insurance company, or may be provided on a group plan basis by an employer.

Level term insurance is granted for a specified period of years. The premium is based upon the age of the insured and the amount of insurance. After a specified period of years, the policy can be renewed for a higher premium. Most forms of level term include a guaranteed renewable clause, enabling an individual to renew the policy without evidence of insurance.

Whole life insurance provides both a death benefit and a cash value that increases over time. By a specified age or number of years (the policy term), the insurance portion of the whole life policy declines to zero, and the cash value represents 100% of the face amount.

Modern insurance products include variable and fixed rates of investment return, as well as flexibility in the amount of insurance and investment value carried. See also *face value; joint mortgage insurance; mortgage insurance; risk factor.* [See overleaf.]

like-kind property descriptive of a property of a similar nature, quality, or value, for the purpose of determining whether or not an exchange qualifies as tax-free. In an exchange, the Internal Revenue Service considers an exchange

life insurance

WHOLE LIFE

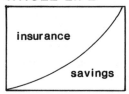

DECREASING TERM

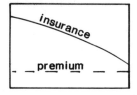

LEVEL TERM

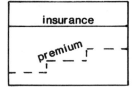

---

to be of like-kind based only on the similar nature of properties, regardless of quality or grade. See also *deferred gain; exchange; tax basis.*

limited partner an investor who has deposited a specified minimum of capital to purchase limited partnership units. This pooled fund is then managed by general partners, who invest the funds, borrow additional monies if the program is structured for leverage, and manage properties. The limited partner has no voice in management or selection of properties, but can be held liable only to the extent of money actually at risk. The general partner, in comparison, has unlimited liability. See also *at risk; direct participation program; investment program; passive income.*

limited partnership an investment program that includes both limited and general partners. The funds of many investors (limited partners) are pooled together and managed by the general partners, who are responsible for the selection and management of properties. A great amount of risk is associated with limited partnerships in the fact that invested funds are not liquid, except with certain publicly traded Master Limited Partnerships (MLP's). It is also difficult to identify experienced general partners without a thorough investigation of their background and track record. In the past, a large number of limited partnerships were structured to emphasize tax benefits, to the extent that they were considered abusive tax shelters. With changes in tax law, the traditional limited partnership is not as popular as MLP's, REIT's, and other, more economically motivated programs. See also *general partnership; passive income; Real Estate Limited Partnership (RELP); risk factor; Uniform Limited Partnership Act (ULPA).*

limited partnership

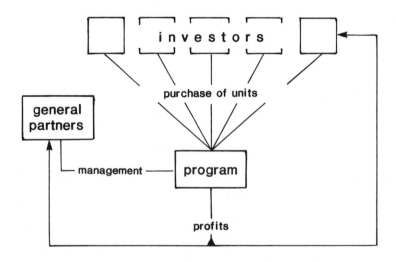

liquidation value   the total amount of money that is estimated to be available if sold at once. This estimate assumes a flexible sales price to encourage a quick sale. It is used for comparisons, especially in investment programs. The liquidation value does not consider the potential future value of income a property could earn if held for a number of years, nor does it allow for capital gains an investor is likely to realize by holding the property for a longer period of time. See also *capital gain/loss; cash value; future value; investment program.*

liquidity   the ready availability of cash. Assets are classified as liquid when they are held in readily accessible cash deposit accounts, or can be converted to cash quickly and without loss of value. Direct ownership of real estate is considered an illiquid investment, since the invested capital cannot be removed quickly or without selling the property. Investments such as stocks, mutual funds, and savings accounts, in comparison, are highly liquid.

There are two tests of liquidity. First is the ability to convert an asset into cash form. Second is the ability to obtain those funds quickly. The issue of liquidity is important to investors in balancing a portfolio. It is widely recognized that there is a higher degree of risk when too great a portion of investment capital is placed in illiquid accounts. See also *cash flow; conversion; investment objective; locked in; risk factor.*

lis pendens (Lt.) a reference to the constructive notice contained in a recorded document that could affect the status of title to property. See also *constructive notice; recording.*

listing **(1)** an agreement formed between a seller and a real estate broker, spelling out the terms of offering a property for sale. The listing agreement specifies what the broker will do to promote the sale of property, in exchange for which the seller agrees to pay a commission. It may also specify that the listing will be exclusive for a certain period of time, after which it will be made available to salespeople other than those employed by the listing broker. **(2)** a property for sale, that is listed in the newspaper, a Multiple Listing Service (MLS) publication, or with one broker exclusively. See also *agreement; exclusive listing; Multiple Listing Service (MLS); open listing.*

listing broker the broker with whom a seller of real estate first lists a property for sale. The listing broker may or may not ultimately sell the property, but will receive a partial commission if the property is sold through an open listing, by an agent of another firm. The listing broker may hold an exclusive on a property for a specified number of weeks before it is made available to other brokers. See also *broker; commission; exclusive listing; selling agent.*

listing contract an engagement contract or agreement between the seller and the broker, in which a rate of commission and other terms of listing a property for sale are spelled out. See also *commission; contract; exclusive listing; holdover clause.*

littoral rights the rights and privileges held by owners whose land borders on bodies of water, including the right of use, entry, and exit. See also *easement; egress; ingress; riparian rights.*

loan the granting of money from a lender to a borrower, usually for an agreed amount of interest and repayment schedule. A mortgage loan, for example, will specify the amount of payment, frequency, due dates, and the rate of interest charged. A loan may be secured by real or personal property, or unsecured. For example, a mortgage is a secured debt, as it is granted with real property as collateral, or protection, for the lender. In the event of default, the lender may sell the property to recover its loan. Investors may seek loans as a means of leveraging a limited amount of capital, with the idea of controlling a larger number of properties. The use of borrowed money also increases the investor's risk, as a high rate of vacancies will create a strain on cash flow, causing difficulties in maintaining debt service. See also *cash flow; debt service; financing; interest; leverage; mortgage; secured debt.*

loan application fee a charge assessed by a lender for the processing of a loan application. This includes the cost of investigating credit, checking on assets claimed, and verifying employment and personal references listing on an application form. See also *application fee; closing costs; lending institution.*

loan disclosure statement the specific terms of a loan, that a lending institution gives to the borrower. The statement includes the amount being borrowed, the Annual Percentage Rate (APR) of interest being charged, the total of payments with interest included, the due date of each payment, the total number of payments to be made, and the date that payments are to begin. See also *amortization; Annual Percentage Rate (APR); full disclosure; interest; principal.*

loan origination fee a form of closing cost charged by the lending institution. In some cases, this fee is another term for points (each point is equivalent to one percent of the amount borrowed, and acts as a form of additional interest the lender charges). In other cases, a lender may advertise that no points (or very low points) are charged for mortgage loans. However, a loan origination fee is assessed in place of what other lenders charge for borrowing money. See also *closing costs; lending institution; mortgage; origination fee; point.*

loan relief a reduction or suspension of loan payments, granted to a borrower by the lender. In cases where a temporary hardship (illness or loss of employment, for example) makes continuing payments a hardship, the lender may grant a form of loan relief. For example, a homeowner asks a lender to grant three months of loan relief. The balance outstanding at that point is $67,800, and the interest rate is 11%. The lender agrees to grant the three months, on the condition that the balance will be increased each month by 11% interest. At the end of three months, the loan balance will have grown to $69,681.65:

	interest	balance
Balance		$67,800.00
first month	$621.50	68,421.50
second month	627.20	69,048.70
third month	632.95	69,681.65

Loan relief may involve a reduction in the rate of interest charged to the borrower, granted in the interest of avoiding a foreclosure by reducing the required monthly payment. It may also refer to a compromised settlement of the entire debt. See also *foreclosure; interest; mortgage; principal; settlement.*

Loan-To-Value Ratio (LTV) a comparison between the outstanding balance of a loan and the current appraised value of the property. This ratio may be used to express a limit to which a lender will go on a mortgage loan. Or it may be used to estimate an owner's equity in property. For example, a homeowner owes $80,000 on an existing mortgage loan. The appraised value of the home is currently $107,000. The Loan-To-Value Ratio is 74.8%. See also *appraised value; financing; market value; value.* [See overleaf.]

loan value (1) the current balance of an outstanding loan. (2) the maximum amount or percentage of property value that a lender is willing to carry on a loan. (3) the value in negotiating the sale of property that is represented by an

Loan-To-Value Ratio (LTV)

$$\frac{\text{loan balance}}{\text{appraised value}}$$

$$\frac{\$80,000}{\$107,000} = 74.8\%$$

---

assumable loan at a lower than market rate. See also *assumable mortgage; down payment; financing; lending institution; leverage; mortgage.*

local assessment fees a fee charged to homeowners for local improvements, such as sidewalks or improved water facilities. The assessment is usually a one-time charge. See also *assessment; property taxes; tax basis.*

locational obsolescence a loss in property value, due to outside influences or structural conditions of the property itself, to the extent that the condition cannot be cured through improvement or renovation. For example, an industrial building is constructed in such a way that it cannot be converted to another use. See also *appraised value; economic obsolescence; incurable depreciation; market value; obsolescence.*

locked in (1) a situation in which an investor cannot sell interests in a program due to one of three causes:
    (a) to do so would produce undesired tax liabilities in the current year.
    (b) current market value has declined to unacceptable levels, and the investor believes it is necessary to hold in the hope that value will increase in the future.
    (c) there is no market for the asset. For example, an investor purchases units in a limited partnership. After several years, he desires to sell these units, but cannot locate another individual to buy; and the program does not offer to repurchase those interests.
    (2) a situation in which the owner of property or investments is unable to sell because an option to purchase has been given to someone else. For example, the owner of a rental house has granted an option to buy to the current tenant. See also *book value; investor basis; option; risk factor; tax basis.*

long-term lease a lease that is contracted for several years. On commercial property, long-term may refer to leases of 20 years or longer. For residential properties, any lease longer than three years is considered long-term. See also *lease; month to month; short-term lease; tenant.*

long-term loan any loan granted for longer than 20 years. For example, a 30-year mortgage would be considered as long-term, but a 15-year mortgage would not. See also *financing; mortgage; short-term loan.*

loop streets a variation in street pattern in which parcels face winding streets. This allows for a design in which a smaller number of properties face on streets with a high volume of traffic or noise, and also reduces the level of through traffic in a neighborhood. See also *cluster; curvilinear system; development; gridiron pattern; Radburn Plan; subdivision.*

loss the condition resulting from selling an asset for less than the purchase price, or when an asset currently held is valued less than at the time of purchase. A loss of a capital asset, such as real estate, is classified as a capital loss. Other asset losses are ordinary. See also *capital gain/loss; ordinary gain/loss; tax basis.*

lot and block description description of property in a plat book, or as recorded upon development. Each block is assigned a number within a subdivision, and within each block, lots are individually numbered for later reference in a legal description, or when a title search is performed. See also *legal description; parcel; plat book; recording; subdivision; title search.*

Low-Rate Mortgage (LRM) a form of creative financing in which the borrower is allowed to make a one-time interest payment, accompanied with a substantially larger than usual down payment. Principal is paid off in a short period of time, often as quickly as five years. Another variation involves a below-market interest rate in exchange for a large down payment, followed by amortization over a 10- or 15-year period. For example, a home costing $125,000 is purchased with a $62,500 down payment (50% of the cost). A one-time interest charge of $13,125 is added to the mortgage balance, bringing the total due to $75,625. Payments of $15,125 are made each year for five years. See also *creative financing; down payment; financing; mortgage; Zero Rate Mortgage (ZRM).* [See overleaf.]

M

mail box rule a rule regarding offer and acceptance of a contract. It states that an acceptance becomes effective at the time it is placed into the mail. The withdrawal of an offer must occur prior to acceptance. This rule applies only when the acceptance is actually mailed, and the time of mailing can be established. See also *acceptance; contract; offer.*

maintenance the care of a property, limited to repairs and general upkeep. Capital improvements, such as the addition of a new room, are not considered

Low-Rate Mortgage (LRM)

total cost	$125,000
less: down payment	62,500
balance	$ 62,500
interest charge	13,125
balance due	$ 75,625
payments per year	$ 15,125
years	5
total payments	$ 75,625

as maintenance expenditures, but must be added to the basis in property. Maintenance on a rental property is deductible for tax purposes. For homeowners, maintenance is necessary to create and improve market value. See also *deferred maintenance; market value; physical depreciation; tax basis; value.*

maintenance fee a monthly charge assessed to every unit owner in condominium and cooperative development, for the maintenance of common areas. See also *common area maintenance; condominium; cooperative housing; multiple dwelling.*

maintenance reserve a fund established to pay for future maintenance on property, commonly established by investment programs or owners of rental property. An amount of money is placed into a reserve account each month, to be used for periodic upkeep, so that future cash flow will not be adversely affected. For example, the owner of an apartment complex estimates that repaving, roof repairs, painting, and other maintenance expenses will average $12,000 per year. A maintenance reserve is established, and $1,000 per month is deposited into it. See also *cash flow; deferred maintenance; investment property; property manager.*

malfeasance commission of an illegal act; breaking the law. In comparison, misfeasance is an improper or inappropriate performance of a legal act, and nonfeasance is the failure to perform an act required by contract or law. See also *misfeasance; nonfeasance.*

manufactured home (1) a mobile home, which is not real estate but personal property. However, the tax laws include a special provision, allowing interest and tax charges on manufactured homes to be treated as principal residence deductions. **(2)** a permanent structure built directly on land, the components of which are prefabricated for quick construction, as opposed to the more traditional method of building homes on the site. See also *component building; mobile home; modular home; personal property; prefabricated housing.*

marginal land land that has minimal chances of producing profits for the owner, or of rising in value in the foreseeable future. Land may be considered marginal due to the terrain or location; or because development in nearby areas has stopped or appears to be moving in a different direction. See also *improved land; land; raw land.*

marginal tax rate the tax bracket, a percentage that will be assessed against taxable income. Rates change for defined ranges of income, based on whether a tax return is filed by a married couple, a married person filing separately, a single person, or a head of household. For example, a married couple reports taxable income of $35,000. Based on the 1988 rates published as part of the Tax Reform Act of 1986, they will be taxed at the rate of 15% on the first $29,750, and at 28% for income above that level. Their total tax liability is $5,932.50. (35% of $29,750 is $4,462.50; and 28% of $5,250 is $1,470.) See also *income tax; tax bracket.*

marginal tax rate

MARRIED, FILING JOINT RETURN	
MARGINAL RATE	TAXABLE INCOME
15%	$ 0–$ 29,750
28%	$ 29,751–$ 71,900
33%	$ 71,901–$149,250
28%	over $149,250

mark down a reduction or discount in the original asking price of a property. For example, a home is on the market with an asking price of $107,500. This is a mark down from the original asking price of $114,950. See also *asking price; discount, negotiation.*

mark

mark up an additional amount added to the price to compensate the seller for the real estate broker's commission and other closing costs. For example, a seller estimates his home is worth $100,000, but places it on the market for $107,000 to cover the costs of selling. See also *asking price; closing costs; commission; premium.*

market comparison approach an appraisal method under which estimates of market value are based on the prices of similar properties of the same type and in the same area. This is the favored method of real estate brokers when establishing an asking price on residential properties. Factors that influence this method include the time a property is on the market, location, special features and conditions of the property, and terms of the sale. See also *appraisal method; cost approach; income approach.*

market price the selling price of a property, as compared to market value. For example, a home is worth an estimated market value of $135,000. But the seller wants a fast sale, and it is offered and sold for $115,000. See also *basis; sale; value.*

market rent the economic rent of a unit, the amount that is reasonable based on rental rates for similar properties in the same area. See also *economic rent; rental value.*

market value the best price a property will bring on the market, assuming that buyers are available and there is a demand, and that the seller is not seeking a fast sale. The actual market value is the highest price a buyer will offer and the lowest price a seller will accept. See also *asking price; Fair Market Value (FMV); market price; ready, willing and able.*

marketability a condition of property that makes it ready for sale. Marketability may refer to condition of the property or title, price, desirability of location, or supply and demand. See also *asking price; salability; supply and demand; title.*

marketable title title that is clear, free of defects or unresolved disputes. A title may be marketable and have encumbrances at the same time. For example, a home is for sale with a first mortgage outstanding. However, there are no other liens or encumbrances, or questions about ownership. See also *clear title; encumbrance; good title; lien; mortgage; quiet enjoyment; title.*

mass appraisal the appraisal of a number of properties. See also *appraisal method; multiple dwelling.*

master lease the original, senior lease. A sublease may be entered, but all terms and conditions will be ruled and restricted by the terms of the master lease. For example, a master lease extends for 10 years, and specifies that no residential use may be made of property. A sublease cannot be legally entered that exceeds that term or establishes a residential unit on the premises. See also *lease; sublease.*

Master Limited Partnership (MLP) an investment program that adds a feature of liquidity to otherwise illiquid limited partnerships. Shares in an MLP are traded on public stock exchanges, so that investors may buy and sell interests at will. The MLP has been used to avoid double taxation of corporate dividends. For example, a corporation with large real estate holdings creates an MLP, which is an unincorporated form of organization. This "roll out" method gives corporate shareholders interests in the MLP without losing or selling their corporate shares. The MLP can also be created by revising the structure of one or more limited partnerships, in a "roll up" form. See also *investment program; limited partnership; liquidity; Real Estate Limited Partnership (RELP); risk factor.*

master plan a long-term development, growth or zoning plan for a city, county, or area. The plan is intended to control and coordinate growth and zoning, and includes maps, zoning proposals, and development ideas, concepts and limitations. See also *development; plan; subdivision; zoning map.*

maturity date (1) the date a debt security, such as a bond or certificate of deposit, matures. On that date, investors are entitled to a repayment of their principal. (2) the date used to calculate proportionate yield on a debt security, whether or not the investor will hold that security until actual maturity. For example, an investor owns a bond and plans to sell it within two years. To compare the value of the bond to other, similar investments, Yield to Maturity (YTM) is calculated. See also *debt instrument; investment program; loan; Yield to Maturity (YTM).*

Mechanic's Lien a statutory lien that establishes land or improvements as security for work performed. A provider of services, such as a contractor, can exercise the lien in order to force payment. See also *improvement; lien; lien release; secured debt; statutory lien.*

meeting of the minds one requirement for a legal and binding contract, that both parties must come to an agreement for the terms and conditions that are in force. No contract exists until a meeting of the minds occurs. The intentions of the parties and their purpose in entering a contract are tests of this standard. For example, an offer to buy or sell property cannot exist until price and other conditions—an offer and acceptance—have been made. See also *agreement; contract; express contract; implied contract; valid contract.*

Member Appraisal Institute (MAI) a nationally recognized designation for professional appraisers. The MAI is awarded by the American Institute of Real Estate Appraisers (AIREA) upon the successful completion of a series of examinations. See also *American Institute of Real Estate Appraisers (AIREA); appraiser.*

memorandum of agreement a preliminary agreement that serves as a binder, pending the signing of a more complete, detailed contract. This document is usually prepared and signed when a good faith deposit is made on property. As long as it meets the legal standards required, the agreement serves as a valid contract. See also *agreement; binder; contract; deposit receipt; good faith deposit; letter of intent; valid contract.*

metes

metes and bounds description   a precise way of describing property and its boundaries, used in legal descriptions. It specifies the exact length (metes) of property lines, and the direction the line runs, giving angles and terminal points on the basis of 360 degrees. See also *bounds; legal description; parcel; property line.*

mill   a standard used in assessing property taxes, based on assessed valuation of land and improvements. One mill is 1/10th of one cent. See also *assessed valuation; property taxes; tax basis.*

minimum rent   the amount of rent that is paid every month, regardless of other costs. For example, a percentage lease specifies that total rent may rise or fall based on the gross receipts of a retail tenant, but that a minimum, or base rent will always be paid. See also *base rent; lease; overage income; percentage lease; tenant; variable lease.*

misfeasance   the carrying out of a lawful act in an inappropriate or improper manner. In comparison, malfeasance is the committing of an unlawful act, and nonfeasance is a failure to perform in a prescribed manner. See also *malfeasance; nonfeasance.*

mobile home   a residential unit that is personal property rather than real property. The term is applied to a variety of structures, many of which never move from a lot. Owners may own the land on which a mobile home sits, or may pay monthly rent on a space in a mobile home park. See also *component building; manufactured home; modular home; personal property; prefabricated housing.*

mobile home certificate   a security issued by the Government National Mortgage Association (GNMA), which is secured by a mobile home rather than by real estate. The maturity period will generally be for fewer years than on a comparable real estate mortgage. See also *debt instrument; Government National Mortgage Association (GNMA); mortgage security.*

modular home   a home constructed of factory materials rather than built on the site. The term may apply to a range of structures, from mobile homes to permanent structures in modular developments. See also *component building; manufactured home; mobile home; personal property; prefabricated housing.*

month to month   a tenancy at will, an agreement between a landlord and a tenant on the terms and conditions of occupancy. In the absence of a lease, those terms may be modified or cancelled from one month to another. A month to month tenancy may come about at the inception of the agreement, or may be created when a lease expires and the tenant continues to occupy the unit. See also *lease; periodic tenancy; tenancy at will.*

monthly compounding   a method of calculating interest using 12 periods per year. Most fully amortized mortgage contracts are calculated on this basis. The outstanding balance at the beginning of each month is multiplied by the interest rate, and the sum is divided by 12. The result is the amount of that month's payment that will be applied to interest; the balance will reduce principal on the loan.

Monthly compounding is offered by many banks and savings and loans. For example, a time deposit pays 8%, compounded monthly. To calculate the first month's interest, divide the interest rate by 12:

$$\frac{8\%}{12} = .00667\%$$

The first month's interest on a $1,000 deposit would be $6.67. ($1,000 × .00667%)

Susequent months' interest is calculated by following these steps:

1. Add '1' to the monthly interest:
   .00667% + 1 = 1.00667
2. Multiply the sum by itself to calculate interest for the second month:
   1.00667 × 1.00667 = 1.01338
3. Multiply the sum by 1.00667 for subsequent months:
   1.01338 × 1.00667 = 1.02014 (third month)

See also *annual compounding; compound interest; daily compounding; interest; quarterly compounding; semiannual compounding.* [See overleaf.]

monument an object, landmark or point used to describe a boundary or property line. See also *landmark; legal description; metes and bounds description; parcel; property line.*

moral obligation an obligation based on what is fair or ethical, but not necessarily prescribed by the law. See also *good faith.*

mortgage **(1)** a document that establishes real estate as security for a loan. The borrower is allowed to occupy and use the property while the lien is in effect, but may not take actions that reduce market value and, thus, threaten the security of the lender. **(2)** as a verb, to mortgage is to pledge real estate as security for borrowed money. See also *collateral; hypothecation; lien; secured debt.*

mortgage acceleration paying off a loan at a rate above that required by the agreement, with the purpose of reducing total interest. The additional payments reduce principal; thus, subsequent calculations of interest are based on a lower outstanding balance.

A mortgage acceleration plan can be undertaken informally. For example, a homeowner adds $100 to payments each month, or makes a lump sum payment of $1,500 at the beginning of each year. The plan can also be put into effect at the time a loan is negotiated. For example, a homeowner agrees to repay a mortgage loan over a 15-year period rather than a 30-year period. A $90,000 loan at 11% interest will require payments of $857.10 per month to amortize the loan over 30 years; for an additional $165.84 per month, that same loan will be amortized over 15 years. The loan will be repaid in half the time, and with a total reduction in interest of $124,427.

An acceleration plan produces equity build-up at a greater rate. A homeowner planning to stay in a home for five years or less may consider a 15-year

monthly compounding

MONTH	8% FACTOR	BALANCE
		$1,000.00
1	1.00667	1,006.67
2	1.01338	1,013.38
3	1.02014	1,020.14
4	1.02695	1,026.95
5	1.03380	1,033.80
6	1.04069	1,040.69
7	1.04763	1,047.63
8	1.05462	1,054.62
9	1.06166	1,061.66
10	1.06874	1,068.74
11	1.07587	1,075.87
12	1.08303	1,083.04

repayment term rather than a longer one. For example, at 11%, a 30-year loan will have been reduced by only 2.8%; the majority of payments will be for interest, and very little equity build-up will occur. At 11% interest, a 15-year mortgage will have been 17.5% paid off after five years. See also *amortization; equity build-up; interest; principal.*

mortgage banker providers of funds for mortgage loans or refinancing plans. Some mortgage bankers specialize in short-term financing, or in commercial property lending; others deal only with loans that are insured or guaranteed by a federal government agency. See also *lending institution; secondary market.*

Mortgage Banker's Association (MBA) an organization offering educational programs for its members, including the designation Certified Mortgage Banker (CMB). The MBA is located at 1125 Fifteenth Street, N.W., Washington, DC 20005. See also *Certified Mortgage Banker (CMB).*

mortgage acceleration

YEAR	$90,000 loan, 11% LOAN BALANCE	
	30-YEAR TERM	15-YEAR TERM
5	$87,444	$74,259
10	83,034	47,052
15	75,411	0
20	62,217	
25	39,420	
30	0	
total interest	$218,556	$94,129

mortgage broker a go-between for lenders and borrowers. Services include fee-based mortgage lender locating, and completion of application forms, credit search, and rate shopping. See also *lending institution; loan; mortgage correspondent.*

mortgage certificate an instrument issued when more than one individual owns a part of a single mortgage. Terms of the mortgage are spelled out in the document; however, the certificate itself is not a note. See also *interest; mortgage pool.*

mortgage commitment a promise by a lender to grant a mortgage loan at a point in the future. The degree of commitment may extend only to the amount that will be loaned, or may also specify a rate of interest that will be charged. See also *agreement; commitment; financing; lending institution.*

mortgage constant a calculation of the relationship between annual debt service on a loan and the amount borrowed. This constant will be based upon the interest rate and repayment term. For example, a loan of $80,000, at 12% interest, to be repaid over a 30-year term, will require annual payments of $9,874.80. This amount, divided by the loan amount ($80,000) produces a mortgage constant of 12.3%. See also *debt service; interest; loan; principal.* [See overleaf.]

mortgage constant

$$\frac{\text{annual payments}}{\text{loan amount}}$$

$$\frac{\$9{,}874.80}{\$80{,}000} = 12.3\%$$

---

mortgage correspondent a company or individual who has been authorized by a lending institution to commit that institution to the lending of money. A ceiling is placed on the amount of a loan the correspondent is authorized to grant. Limited commitments of interest rates may be included in the agreement. See also *agent; lending institution; loan.*

Mortgage Guarantee Insurance Company (MGIC) a company that offers Private Mortgage Insurance (PMI) to borrowers, when required as a condition by the lending institution, to reduce the risks of default when the lender may be unable to recover its capital. For example, a lender is willing to grant a loan equal to 90% of a home's market value, on the condition that the homeowner will pay premiums for a PMI policy. The policy is to remain in effect until the loan has been reduced to at least 80% of the market value. Requiring PMI as part of a loan agreement reduces the lender's risks. See also *default insurance; equity build-up; foreclosure; Private Mortgage Insurance (PMI); risk factor.*

mortgage in possession a situation in which the lender has taken possession of property under a mortgage. Operation and maintenance of the property continues during the possession period. For example, a borrower is in default on a commercial building, and the lending institution takes possession. Tenants continue to offer goods and services, but make lease payments directly to the lender. At a point in the future, the original borrower may recover and have possession returned; or the property may continue to be operated by the lender or sold. See also *foreclosure; lending institution; possession.*

mortgage insurance (1) a term misleadingly applied to default insurance, a form of protection for the lender in the event of default. The premiums are paid by the borrower as a condition of the loan. (2) a form of life or disability insurance granted to a borrower, the benefits of which are based on the mortgage in effect.

Mortgage life insurance is protection on the life of the borrower, but the death benefit is a decreasing term policy based on the outstanding balance of the mortgage.

Joint mortgage insurance is issued on the lives of both spouses, and is appropriate when the family depends on two incomes. In the event of the death of either spouse, continuing to make mortgage payments would present an economic hardship. This insurance benefit pays off the entire mortgage balance.

Mortgage disability insurance protects a family in the event the income-earning spouse is totally disabled. If that occurs, the mortgage payments will be made by the insurance company for the duration of the disability. See also *default insurance; disability insurance; joint mortgage insurance; life insurance; Private Mortgage Insurance (PMI).*

mortgage lien descriptive of the right a lender has in granting a mortgage loan to a borrower. The lien exists on the property, and can be exercised in the event of default. See also *default; encumbrance; lien; secured debt.*

mortgage money the amount a lending institution has committed to mortgage loans. See also *financing; lending institution.*

mortgage pool an investment program in which a number of mortgages are purchased from a lender, by an agency, which subsequently sells shares in the pool to investors. Homeowners continue making payments to the original lender, which passes the funds to the agency. Interest is then distributed to the investors. This arrangement spreads the risks for investors, and provides them with liquidity, since shares can be bought and sold even while mortgages are still outstanding. See also *investment program; risk factor; secondary market.* [See overleaf.]

mortgage premium an added cost, charged by a lender for the origination of the loan. The premium may take the form of points or a flat origination fee. See also *closing costs; loan origination fee; origination fee; point.*

mortgage REIT a Real Estate Investment Trust (REIT) that specializes in lending money, either for the construction and development of new properties, or for loans on existing and occupied buildings. In comparison, an equity REIT limits activities to the ownership of properties; and a hybrid REIT combines equity and mortgage positions. See also *equity REIT; hybrid REIT; Real Estate Investment Trust (REIT).*

mortgage security any debt instrument purchased by an investor, either directly or through a pooled fund. See also *debt instrument; investment program; secondary market.*

mortgage value the value a lender sets on a property, for the purpose of determining the amount of money it will lend. This may be the same as market value, or a lender may appraise a property conservatively to reduce its risks. For example, a homeowner wants to take out a second mortgage and the lender appraiser the property. The homeowner believes the market value is higher than the lending institution concludes. In this instance, the mortgage value may be lower than actual or fair market value. See also *appraised value; Fair Market Value (FMV); market value.*

multiple

mortgage pool

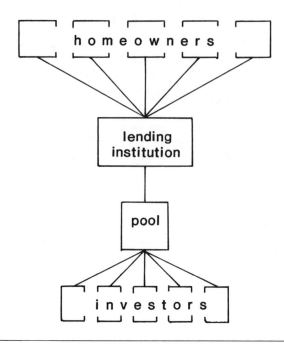

multiple dwelling a residential building designed to house more than one occupant, either owned or rented. See also *apartment; condominium; cooperative housing; duplex; residential property; triplex.*

Multiple Listing Service (MLS) an association that reports on open listings in a specific area. The member brokers and real estate firms submit listings to the service, and the MLS publishes a periodic directory for the members. Any member broker can sell the property, with commissions split between the original listing broker and the selling broker. See also *broker; commission; exclusive listing; listing; open listing.*

multiplier a calculated factor used for determining appraised value of income property. The annual income is multiplied by this factor to arrive at market value, and is developed based on the multipliers of similar properties in the same area. See also *appraised value; Gross Rent Multiplier (GRM); income approach; investment property; market value.*

municipal lien an assessment against property in one area, for the purpose of providing services or facilities. For example, a city applies a special assessment to install sidewalks on a street. See also *assessment; lien; local assessment fees; special assessment; tax basis.*

N

naked contract a contract that is unenforceable due to the lack of consideration in its terms. To be valid and legal, a contract must have three elements, without exception: offer, acceptance, and consideration. See also *consideration; illegal contract; unenforceable contract; void contract*.

National Association of Home Builders (NAHB) an organization providing educational, research and political services to member home builders. The association's address is 15th and M Streets, N.W., Washington, DC 20005. See also *residential property*.

National Association of Real Estate Brokers (NAREB) a trade association of brokers, appraisers, and other real estate professionals. NAREB awards the designation realist. See also *appraiser; broker; property manager; realist*.

National Association of Real Estate Investment Trusts (NAREIT) the national association of the REIT industry. The association publishes a newsletter and research services for member REIT organizations. The address of the association is 1101 Seventeenth St., N.W., Suite 700, Washington, DC 20036. See also *Real Estate Investment Trust (REIT)*.

National Association of Realtors (NAR) the largest association for professional real estate brokers, appraisers and counselors. NAR has over 600,000 members in the United States. The association was founded in 1908, and adopted its Code of Ethics in 1913. NAR members may belong to a number of affiliated associations, including the AIREA (which offers the MAI and RM designations); ASREC (and the CRE designation); IREM (the CPM); and RNMI (the CCIM and CRS designations). NAR's address is 430 North Michigan Avenue, Chicago, IL 60611. See also *American Institute of Real Estate Appraisers (AIREA); American Society of Real Estate Counselors (ASREC); Code of Ethics; Institute of Real Estate Management (IREM); Real Estate Securities and Syndication Institute (RESSI); Realtors National Marketing Institute (RNMI); Women's Council of Realtors (WCR)*.

natural financing an exchange or sale of real estate in which no financing is required beyond what the buyer and seller arrange between themselves. For example, a seller may carry a loan for a buyer; or properties are exchanged along with assumable mortgages. See also *exchange; financing; mortgage*.

natural person an individual, as distinguished from a corporation or other entity. In contractual matters, a corporation may assume many of the rights and duties of a natural person, without being exposed to personal liabilities. See also *contract*.

negative amortization a situation that can arise for the borrower in an Adjustable Rate Mortgage (ARM). If interest rates increase so that a fixed or limited monthly payment is not adequate to pay each month's interest, the outstanding balance of the loan will rise rather than fall.

This dilemma occurs only in ARM mortgages with payment caps rather than

negative

the more desirable rate caps. For example, a lending institution offers an ARM to a borrower for $80,000, at 9% interest. No discussion is made about limiting the increase in the interest rate; however, the promise is made that the monthly payment will never exceed $800 per month. Several years later, the rate has risen (based on growth in an outside index) to 14%, at a point that the loan balance is $78,450. The interest due on that balance at 14% is $915.25 per month. The borrower will have negative amortization (an increase in principal) of $115.25 with a payment capped at $800. The problem will grow worse each month as interest will be computed on a rising balance rather than a falling one. See also *Adjustable Rate Mortgage (ARM); amortization; cash flow; lending institution; payment cap.*

negative amortization

MONTH	PAYMENT	14% INTEREST	PRINCIPAL	BALANCE
				$78,450.00
1	$800.00	$915.25	$(115.25)	78,565.25
2	800.00	916.59	(116.59)	78,681.84
3	800.00	917.95	(117.95)	78,799.79

negative cash flow a situation when expenses and debt service on income property exceed income. For example, the owner of a rental property has a mortgage for $75,000, at 9%, with a 15-year term. Monthly payments are $760.70. Monthly rental income is $1,100 and expenses average $416, for an operating profit of $684. However, after making the mortgage payment, the negative cash flow is $76.70. See also *cash flow; debt service; Net Operating Income (NOI); risk factor.*

negative leverage a loss suffered when a leverage plan costs more in interest than the property yields to the investor. For example, a speculator purchases several rental properties and borrows money to do so. After selling all properties at a profit, the speculator suffers a loss, because interest exceeded capital gains. See also *capital gain/loss; leverage; risk factor; yield.*

negotiation an attempt to arrive at a meeting of the minds between a buyer and a seller, by determining the price and other terms of a contract. Negotiation may involve specific contingencies and adjustments for defects, responsibility for closing or inspection costs, and price. See also *acceptance; agreement; contract; counter-offer; meeting of the minds; offer.*

negative cash flow

rental income	$1,100.00
operating expenses	416.00
net operating income	$ 684.00
mortgage payment	760.70
negative cash flow	$ (76.70)

net income profit, the amount remaining after expenses are deducted from income. See also *capital gain/loss; cash flow; investment income; ordinary gain/loss; tax basis.*

net lease a lease in which the tenant is responsible for all expenses to maintain the property, including taxes, insurance, maintenance, and utilities. See also *gross lease; lease; net net lease; triple net lease.*

net listing a form of listing agreement in which the broker receives a commission based not on a percentage, but on the net sales price the seller will receive. For example, the seller agrees he will accept $110,000 on a net listing basis. If that home sells for $125,000, the broker receives the difference of $15,000. Net listings are not legal in many states. See also *broker; commission; listing contract.*

net net income usually a reference to actual cash flow, the amount left over after payment of all operating expenses as well as mortgage principal and interest. See also *cash flow; debt service; tax basis.*

net net lease a form of lease in which the owner pays none of the expenses. The tenant is responsible for rent payments as well as the costs of maintaining and insuring the property. See also *gross lease; net lease; triple net lease.*

Net Operating Income (NOI) the income from actual operation of the property. Not included are principal and interest payments or liabilities for income taxes. For example, gross income on a rental home is $11,400 for one year. Expenses are $2,011, for an NOI of $9,389. These proceeds are available for payments on a mortgage, and some portion may be paid in income taxes. See also *debt service; gross income; interest; principal; tax basis.*

Net Present Value (NPV) the present value of a future fund or asset, allowing for the holding period. If an investor wishes to accumulate equity over a specified number of years, the net present value is calculated by applying an assumed rate of interest to the target amount. For example, investment real estate is estimated to be worth a specific amount in 10 years. The present value *net*

of that estimate involves calculation of an assumed rate of return applied over the number of years estimated. See also *future value; holding period; Internal Rate of Return (IRR); present value; time value of money.*

net rent synonymous with Net Operating Income (NOI) in most common usage, or the amount of income remaining of rent, after operating expenses have been paid. See also *investment income; Net Operating Income (NOI).*

net spendable income cash flow; the money left after operating expenses, debt service, and income taxes are deducted from rental income. See also *cash flow; debt service; liquidity.*

net worth the equity of an individual or company. Net worth is the difference between all assets and all liabilities. See also *balance sheet; equity.*

net yield the profit, or return on an investment after deducting related expenses. For example, a rental property for sale for $500,000 produces $50,000 per year in rental income when fully occupied. This is a potential gross income of 10%. But from this, expenses, interest, and income taxes must be deducted. In addition, a reasonable vacancy rate should be applied to arrive at a realistic net yield. See also *current yield; gross income; vacancy rate; Yield to Maturity (YTM).*

new basis the basis in property after carrying over tax-deferred profits on a previous home. The federal tax laws allow a deferral of gains on the sale of a principal residence if another home costing as much or more as the sales price is purchased or built within two years. For example, a homeowner sells for $113,000 and gains $65,000 profit from the transaction. Within two years, a new home is purchased at a cost of $117,000. The new basis is $52,000 ($117,000 less deferred gain of $65,000). Upon sale of the new home, profit will be calculated using the new basis. See also *adjusted basis; basis; deferred gain; principal residence; tax basis; tax deferred.*

nonconforming use the use of property or land that is in variance with current zoning for the area, allowed to continue because that use preceded a zoning change. Nonconforming use ceases only when property is sold, destroyed, or the use changes. See also *improvement; zoning.*

noncontinuous easement a form of easement that must be renewed whenever property is sold. Most forms of easement accompany land and are continuous. See also *easement; right of way.*

nondisclosure the failure to report a material fact concerning a contract, property or transaction. For example, a seller is aware of severe structural problems in a house. The buyer does not ask questions about structural quality; however, the seller has misrepresented the facts by not disclosing them. See also *bad faith; full disclosure.*

nonearning investment an investment that is not producing income or profits, or one that is producing a drain on cash flow or a rate of return below that

new basis

OLD HOUSE
sale price	$113,000
basis	48,000
profit	$ 65,000

NEW HOUSE
basis	$117,000
deferred profit	65,000
new basis	$ 52,000

---

investors anticipated. See also *cash flow; interest; investment property; negative cash flow; rate of return; risk factor.*

nonfeasance a failure to perform a contracted or legal responsibility. In comparison, malfeasance is the commission of an illegal act and misfeasance is the improper completion or execution of a legal or contracted act. See also *malfeasance; misfeasance.*

noninvestment property reference to land and improvements intended for residential, vacation or public use. See also *residential property.*

nonjudicial foreclosure a form of foreclosure allowed by contract rather than ordered by a court of law. The loan agreement must include a power of sale clause for a nonjudicial foreclosure to take place, granting the lending institution those rights in the event of default. See also *default; foreclosure; judicial foreclosure; lending institution; power of sale.*

nonqualified REIT a real estate program that previously conducted activities as a Real Estate Investment Trust (REIT), that has either elected to be taxed as a corporation, or has lost the conduit tax treatment privilege due to violation of qualifying rules. See also *conduit tax treatment; Real Estate Investment Trust (REIT); tax basis.*

nonrecourse loan a loan in which the borrower may not be held liable in the event of nonpayment, beyond foreclosure on the subject property. For tax purposes, nonrecourse loans may be considered part of the taxable basis in a real estate program only to a limited extent. See also *at risk; default; investment program; limited partnership; recourse loan; tax basis.*

normal

normal sale   descriptive of a sale of property in which no unusual terms or conditions are imposed, and both buyer and seller execute their contractual duties. See also *abnormal sale; contract; sale.*

normal value   market value, the price a seller may expect to receive or a buyer must expect to pay under normal market conditions. See also *market value; value.*

notary fee   a charge for the notarization of documents in escrow, for the recording and transfer of real estate. See also *closing costs; recording.*

notice of completion   a recorded notice filed and published upon the completion of a home improvement. After the notice has been published, any subcontractors or suppliers must file applicable liens within a specified period of time (which depends upon the jurisdiction), or they will lose the right to attach property for non-payment. For example, a homeowner files a notice of completion, but one of the subcontractors on the job was not paid by the general contractor. If a lien is not filed within the jurisdictional period of time, that subcontractor cannot enforce a lien against the property. See also *improvement; lien; recording.*

notice of right of rescission   a disclosure required by federal law that must be given to a homeowner when a contract is entered for a home improvement. The notice discloses that the contract may be rescinded within three days of signing. Any deposits or down payments must be returned without further obligation if the right is exercised. See also *full disclosure; 3-day cancellation notice; voidable contract.*

notice of sale   a notice that a particular listing is no longer available, advising buyers, brokers, or sellers that the property has been sold. See also *acceptance; contract; sale.*

notice to owner   a written notice that must be given to homeowners when entering a contract for construction or improvement of property. It discloses the state's lien laws and advises the homeowner of possible liabilities to subcontractors in the event they are not paid by the contractor. See also *full disclosure; lien; Mechanic's Lien.*

notice to quit   a written document given to a tenant, demanding the vacancy of a unit. The notice must be given prior to the eviction date (the time varies by jurisdiction), and must be in compliance with the terms of a lease. See also *eviction; lease; right of occupancy; tenant.*

novation   the exchange of one liability or borrower for another. Novation may refer to the assumption of a loan, in which the original borrower is released from liability upon sale and transfer of property, and a new borrower is substituted; or when one loan is cancelled and another is contracted in its place. See also *substitution.*

O

obligation of contract the obligations under the terms of a contract; the actual performance specified and required of each party. See also *contract; performance; specific performance.*

obsolescence the loss of value due to economic, locational or functional changes. Economic obsolescence occurs when a property cannot be maintained or operated at a profit. For example, the style of a building makes it inefficient to heat or cool. With rising energy costs, the building loses market value. Functional obsolescence occurs when the cost to repair defects exceeds the potential income or profit from those repairs. And an example of locational obsolescence is the loss of value that occurs when income property is no longer profitable because a location no longer brings in traffic, or zoning ordinances change the character of an area. See also *economic obsolescence; functional obsolescence; locational obsolescence.*

occupancy rate (1) occupancy level; a ratio showing the comparison between units that are occupied, and total available units. For example, an apartment building contains 20 units, but only 17 are currently occupied. The occupancy rate is 85%. (2) rentable area; a ratio showing the actual rentable area of a building, in comparison with total area. For example, a building has 38,930 square feet of rentable space. But when service areas, stairwells, and hallways are included, the total area of the building is 42,000 square feet. The occupancy rate is 92.7%. See also *gross area; rentable area; vacancy rate.* [See overleaf.]

occupancy rate (level)

$$\frac{\text{occupied units}}{\text{total units}}$$

$$\frac{17}{20} = 85\%$$

offer a proposal for terms of a contract. The offer, to be valid, must specify all terms and conditions proposed. If accepted, a contract is formed. The other side

occupancy rate (area)

$$\frac{\text{rentable area}}{\text{total area}}$$

$$\frac{38{,}930}{42{,}000} = 92.7\%$$

---

may, however, make a counter-offer with modified terms and conditions. If the original offerer accepts those terms, a contract results. See also *acceptance; agreement; bilateral contract; contract; counter-offer; letter of intent; ready, willing and able; unilateral contract.*

offer to purchase an offer made by a potential buyer, in which the price and all other terms, conditions and contingencies are spelled out. If accepted by the seller, a contract is formed. See also *agreement; contract; counter-offer; purchase offer.*

offer to sell a listing of property. The seller advertises a price, with other terms to be disclosed when interested buyers are located. If a buyer accepts the price and other terms, a contract is formed. See also *agreement; contract; counter-offer; listing.*

Office of Equal Opportunity (OEO) an agency of the Department of Housing and Urban Development (HUD), responsible for enforcement and administration of the Fair Housing Act of 1968. See also *blockbusting; Department of Housing and Urban Development (HUD); Fair Housing Act of 1968; steering.*

Office of Interstate Land Sales Registration (OILSR) an agency of the Department of Housing and Urban Development (HUD) that oversees interstate land sales activities, and enforces the Interstate Land Sales Full Disclosure Act (ILSA). See also *Department of Housing and Urban Development (HUD); full disclosure; Interstate Land Sales Full Disclosure Act (ILSA); land; property report.*

older homes policy a homeowner's insurance policy designed to protect older homes. Under terms of this policy form, replacement is insured to serviceable condition. However, the materials and construction may not be of the same quality as in the original home. See also *fire insurance; HO-8; homeowner's insurance.*

open listing   a listing that is not exclusive with one broker, but is available to any qualified broker in the area. Open listings are offered through Multiple Listing Service (MLS) or other, similar sharing arrangements among member brokers. An exclusive listing may be in effect for a limited period of time, after which the property is opened to other brokers. See also *commission; exclusive listing; listing; Multiple Listing Service (MLS); selling agent.*

open mortgage   **(1)** a mortgage that can be paid in full at the discretion of the borrower, without a prepayment penalty. **(2)** a mortgage that is past due and may be foreclosed at any time. See also *default; foreclosure; mortgage acceleration; prepayment penalty.*

open-end mortgage   an arrangement under which the borrower may acquire additional funds at any time, up to a specified limit, or one allowing the borrower to borrow funds up to the original amount of the mortgage. See also *equity line of credit; mortgage.*

operating lease   a sublease, in which the sublessee physically occupies and uses the property. See also *lease; master lease; sublease.*

option   a right to property in the future. For example, a tenant is granted an option to buy a home, and makes monthly payments that are part rent and part down payment. In most options, the exact price and other terms are spelled out. In that instance, the option is an on-going offer with a deadline in the future. See also *agreement; down payment; lease with option to buy; offer; tenant.*

ordinary gain/loss   taxable profits and tax deductible losses that are not restricted, limited or subject to special rules. For example, some forms of investment income are subject to Alternative Minimum Tax (AMT). Limits are placed on loss deductions from investment activities. And passive income or losses are similarly restricted. See also *Alternative Minimum Tax (AMT); capital gain/loss; income tax; investment income; passive income; tax basis; Unrelated Business Income (UBI).*

original cost   the cost of land or improvements, before adjusting for additions after purchase, depreciation, and other changes to the original, adjusted basis. See also *adjusted basis; basis; tax basis.*

origination   the creation of a loan, including the lending institution's credit investigation, offer of terms and conditions, presentation of alternative loan plans, and final approval. See also *financing; lending institution; loan; mortgage.*

origination fee   a fee charged at the time a loan is granted, that may take one of two forms. In the first, the "origination fee" is a term meaning points charged, based on the amount being loaned. In the second, it is a flat fee in place of points, or charged in addition to points. See also *application fee; closing costs; loan origination fee; point.*

outbuilding

outbuilding an accessory structure on land, in addition to the main structure. See also *accessory structure; improvement*.

over-improvement an excessive investment in improvements, which will not produce an increase in market value. As a general rule, the market value of property is limited by the recent sale prices of similar properties in the same area. For example, a three-bedroom, two-bath home in a neighborhood may sell in a range between $95,000 and $110,000. One homeowner adds an additional bedroom, a fireplace, and a swimming pool. The total cost of improvements is $37,000. Upon sale, that homeowner should not expect to recover the investment, because the range of recent sales limits market value. And if that homeowner applies for an equity mortgage based upon the value of improvements, the maximum a lending institution will advance will be based on market value, not the cost of additions. See also *diminishing returns; improvement; market value; under-improvement*.

overage income the portion of rent paid in a lease agreement, above the minimum rent. In some forms of leases, particularly for retail space, the monthly rent contains a minimum, plus an overage based on the volume of gross sales. See also *lease; minimum rent; variable lease*.

P

package mortgage a mortgage on both real and personal property. Collateral for the mortgage loan includes the home and land, as well as appliances, fixtures or furniture included in the sale. For example, a seller includes in the price all fixtures and appliances. Rather than purchasing these separately, the buyer is granted a single loan for the entire purchase. See also *collateral; financing; mortgage; personal property; real property*.

paper reference to the acceptance of a note in lieu of cash. For example, a seller takes cash offered as a down payment and also carries a mortgage on a property, and is said to be taking a combination of cash and paper. See also *cash value; financing; mortgage; Purchase Money Mortgage (PMM)*.

paper street a street planned for development but still in the planning phase. See also *development; subdivision*.

paper title apparent title, that on paper appears to properly convey ownership, but may not. See also *conveyance; good title; title*.

par face value, or an equivalent. When a mortgage is valued at its outstanding balance, it is said to be at par. A lending institution might discount a mortgage or a series of mortgages if it believes some might default or become uncollectible. And when selling mortgages to a secondary buyer, fixed-rate contracts with higher than market value rates may be valued above par. The term is widely used to describe and compare the current market value of bonds and other debt instruments. Par is affected by the time until maturity date, and any premiums or discounts affect computation of actual interest yield. See also *debt instrument; face value; interest rate; maturity date.*

paramount title   title that takes priority over all other claims to title on a property, usually the original or established title. See also *priority; title.*

parcel   a lot within a tract of land, distinguished by specifically identified boundaries. See also *land; legal description; real property; tract.*

parity   equality in reference to the order of claims. For example, two liens exist against one piece of property. Neither is senior to the other, but are at parity. See also *equal dignity; priority.*

part performance   the status of a contract when performance is only partially satisfied. In such a contract, there remains something to be done. For example, a seller agrees to repair a damaged fence and a roof before the close of escrow. As of a specific date, only part of the work has been done. See also *contract; performance.*

partial eviction   constructive eviction that affects a portion of a property or only certain of the tenant's rights. For example, a lease specifies that the tenant has the right of possession to an apartment unit and to a storage area. The landlord subsequently remodels part of the complex, making the storage area inaccessible to the tenant. See also *constructive eviction; eviction; right of possession.*

Participation Certificate (PC)   evidence of part ownership in a mortgage security pool, similar to a stock certificate for stock market investors. See also *interest; investment program; mortgage security.*

participation loan   a form of creative financing in which the lender takes an equity position in the property securing the loan. For example, a borrower cannot qualify for a traditional loan, so the lender offers to grant the loan and take 10% of the profits from operating the property, and 10% of the profit upon sale. See also *creative financing; equity participation; mortgage; Shared Appreciation Mortgage (SAM).*

partition   the dividing of one piece of real estate between two or more owners. For example, three partners jointly own a six-acre tract of land. Upon dissolving the partnership, none of the individuals wants to sell the land, so it is partitioned equally, and ownership is changed to reflect separate title. See also *joint tenancy; tenancy in common; title; unity of possession.*

partnership   a form of organization designed for the convenience of the owners. The partnership itself does not pay taxes or assume liabilities; each partner is separately responsible, and the partnership is a means for reporting collectively.
   A general partnership can be formed among two or more individuals, corporations or other partnerships, for the purpose of conducting business

together. Each of the general partners is fully liable for debts of the entire partnership, and each must report a proportionate share of profits, or is entitled to a share of operating losses. The partnership exists to conduct business generally; in comparison, a joint venture is formed to conduct business for a limited project.

A limited partnership includes both general and limited partners. The general partners have personal liability for the debts of the organization, and will share in profits according to an agreed upon schedule. Limited partners have no direct voice in management of the organization, but are liable only to the extent of their investment. See also *general partnership; joint venture; limited partnership.*

partnership

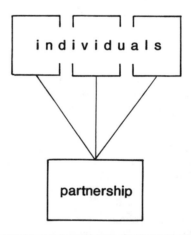

pass-through investment descriptive of the treatment of income in a mortgage pool. Mortgage payments are collected by a lending institution and passed on to the pool, which then distributes income and principal shares to investors. See also *Ginnie Mae pass-through; investment program; mortgage pool.*

passive income one of three types of income, as defined for federal tax purposes. Active income includes salaries and income from self-employment. Portfolio income includes interest, dividends and capital gains. And passive income includes any form of income from activities not involving the investor's direct control. For example, interests in a limited partnership (in which funds are managed and controlled by general partners) are passive. Under federal tax rules, passive losses cannot be deducted except to the extent that they offset passive gains in the same year. If no gains are made, losses can be carried forward to future years, or deducted against capital gains when interests are finally sold. See also *income tax; investment income; tax basis; tax shelter.*

personal

payment cap a contractual provision in an Adjustable Rate Mortgage (ARM), limiting the total monthly payment that the borrower will be required to make, regardless of the interest rate being charged. This limit may appear to be a positive feature in the contract, but can actually work against the borrower. If the level of interest rises to the point that the maximum payment cannot cover that month's interest charge, the loan balance will rise rather than fall, a condition called negative amortization. A more desirable cap is the rate cap, that limits the rate of interest the lender can charge. This prevents negative amortization and also places a ceiling on the monthly payment. See also *Adjustable Rate Mortgage (ARM); cap; negative amortization; rate cap.*

percentage lease a form of lease in which the monthly payments are based on the combination of a base rent and an overage. This provision is included in leases to retail stores. For example, a contract includes a provision specifying the minimum rent that will be paid each month, and in addition, an overage will be computed based on the gross receipts during the previous month. See also *base rent; lease; overage income; variable lease.*

perfect instrument a recorded instrument, one that is available for everyone to view. To achieve good title on a property, the complete chain of title must be identifiable through a review of recorded ownership and liens. See also *chain of title; constructive notice; good title; lien; recording.*

performance the completion of the agreed conditions in a contract. Performance includes all obligations of contract. For example, a buyer agrees to deposit a sum of money, obtain financing, and pay certain closing costs. And a seller agrees to convey title and pay for specified repairs. See also *contract; obligation of contract; part performance; specific performance.*

periodic estate an estate that does not specify a definite termination date, often created when a lease expires but a tenant continues to possess the property. Provisions remain in effect as long as the terms—such as monthly payments—continue with both tenant and landlord in agreement. The estate is automatically renewed from one period to another until actual termination or change of terms. See also *estate at will; holdover tenant; month to month; tenant.*

periodic tenancy a form of tenancy that proceeds from month to month, in the absence of a lease. See also *holdover tenant; lease; month to month.*

permanent mortgage REIT a form of Real Estate Investment Trust (REIT) that is formed to grant long-term mortgage loans to developers and builders, or on existing properties. See also *investment program; mortgage REIT; Real Estate Investment Trust (REIT).*

personal property any property other than real property, also called chattel. The term includes furniture, appliances, automobiles, and other possessions not permanently affixed to land and improvements to land. See also *chattel; real property.*

physical 126

physical depreciation deterioration of property through wear and tear or the effects of time. This is distinguished from depreciation allowed for tax purposes, which is a deduction based on value and possession rather than physical condition. For example, an investor owns real estate that is increasing in value, but is still allowed to deduct depreciation. In comparison, a homeowner fails to maintain a property, and it depreciates in value due to its actual condition. See also *assessed valuation; depreciation; market value; obsolescence; value.*

physical life the actual useful life of property, as opposed to a depreciable life. In tax law, each property can be depreciated over a specified number of years. However, that property may be physically sound for a number of years that are shorter or longer than the depreciable life. See also *depreciation; economic life; obsolescence; useful life.*

piggyback loan a form of financing in which one or more lenders subordinate their interests in loans to another lender. The term may also be applied to the combining of gap financing with a permanent mortgage loan. See also *financing; gap financing; lending institution; mortgage; subordination.*

piggyback loan

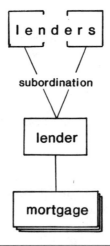

plan a drawing or blueprint of a property or an area, showing the proposed layout. See also *development; subdivision; tract.*

Planned Unit Development (PUD) a comprehensive form of land use that carefully plans an entire area's zoning, access and traffic patterns. It includes distinct residential and commercial districts; clustering of streets in consideration of density, noise factors, and traffic; convenience of shopping centers, recreational, and other facilities; and open space. See also *density; development; tract; zoning.*

plat book a collection of tract maps, identifying individual parcels. The plat book is used in lot and block descriptions, with each parcel referenced by its assigned number and page. See also *bounds; lot and block description; subdivision.*

platted land an area that has been surveyed and divided into specific lots. See also *legal description; subdivision; tract.*

Pledged Account Mortgage (PAM) a form of mortgage in which a sum of money is deposited as an initial pledge of security, in addition to the real estate itself. The account is drawn down during the early years of the mortgage, with the effect of accelerating amortization. Once the fund has been depleted, the monthly payment either increases or remains at the same level as before. See also *collateral; Graduated Payment Mortgage (GPM); mortgage acceleration.*

Pledged Account Mortgage (PAM)

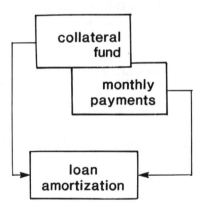

plottage a theory of valuation, stating that land values are increased when adjacent, singularly owned lots are combined into single ownership, and put to a common use. This increases the value of the land to a greater degree than would be possible if each parcel had been left under separate ownership. See also *anticipation; change; competition; conformity; contribution; diminishing returns; highest and best use; increasing returns; regression; substitution; supply and demand.*

pocket

pocket listing a listing that should be open, but is kept, or pocketed, by a broker. Hiding a listing from other brokers is considered unethical and not in the best interests of the seller. See also *exclusive listing; listing; open listing.*

point a fee paid to a lender for obtaining a loan. One point equals one percent of the loan's original balance. Points are used by institutions to increase income from lending activities, and may be increased or decreased depending upon the demand for mortgage loans and the supply of money. For example, a lender advertises that mortgage loans are available at a lower than market rate, thus attracting borrowers. However, that institution charges higher points than the competitor. See also *basis point; mortgage premium; origination fee; premium; principal.*

point

LOAN AMOUNT	1 POINT	2 POINTS	3 POINTS
$ 80,000	$ 800	$1,600	$2,400
90,000	900	1,800	2,700
100,000	1,000	2,000	3,000

point of beginning a starting point in a land survey, used in metes and bounds descriptions. The measurement of a parcel proceeds from the point of beginning, identifies the boundary lines, and returns to the same point. See also *legal description; metes and bounds description; parcel; survey.*

police power the control that governments have to zone, restrict, control or seize land. These powers include the right to create and enforce building codes or ordinances, rent controls, and other regulations in the public interest. See also *allodial system; building code; zoning.*

pool insurance a form of insurance on a portfolio of mortgages held in a mortgage pool. The insurance reduces the risk of losses not covered by individual homeowner's insurance policies on the properties within the pool. See also *homeowner's insurance; investment program; mortgage insurance; mortgage pool; risk factor.*

possession the holding of or physical control over property, either by ownership of title or occupancy by a tenant. See also *actual possession; adverse possession; constructive possession; right of possession.*

power of attorney authorization granted to an individual to act in behalf of another as agent or representative. The limits to that power are specified in the document. See also *agency; attorney in fact; proxy.*

power of sale **(1)** the right granted in a mortgage contract, enabling the lending institution to sell the property in the event of default, without resorting to the courts, also known as a nonjudicial foreclosure. **(2)** authorization given to an agent to sell a property. For example, a homeowner places a property on the market in another state, and cannot be present to negotiate a contract. He assigns a power of sale to a broker or other representative. See also *agency; attorney in fact; default; foreclosure; lending institution; mortgage; nonjudicial foreclosure.*

prefabricated housing a structure manufactured from component, factory-made parts that are delivered to a site and assembled. See also *component building; manufactured home; mobile home; modular home.*

preferred debt a debt that has seniority over all other debts in the event of sale of a secured property. See also *debt; first mortgage; priority; senior mortgage.*

preliminary lien notice a disclosure given by contractors when a home improvement begins, notifying the owner of the rights to enforce debts with liens on the property. See also *full disclosure; improvement; lien; Mechanic's Lien.*

preliminary prospectus an advance copy of an investment prospectus, given to investors in anticipation of completing registration of the program with the Securities and Exchange Commission. It is also referred to as a "red herring" because disclosures on the cover are made in red ink. See also *investment program; prospectus; red herring; SEC Rule 430.*

preliminary title report a summary of the condition of title, published prior to the closing date of a sale. A final title report is prepared after a final check for claims or liens, at the closing date. See also *abstract of title; good title; title report.*

premium **(1)** the cost of an insurance policy, to be paid monthly, quarterly, semiannually, or annually. **(2)** costs above face value. For example, a loan is granted for a specified amount and at a rate of interest. Points are also charged, representing a premium on the loan's face value. **(3)** value above the face value of a security. For example, a bond has an interest rate above current market rates, and thus has a current market value that is at a premium in comparison to its face value. See also *discount; face value; homeowner's insurance; life insurance; mark up; mortgage; point.*

pre-offering questionnaire a form that is completed by an investor in a private partnership, prior to being accepted as a suitable, qualified participant. Private placements are offered to a limited number of people, and generally require higher initial deposits than required by comparable public programs. Suitability may refer to income, net worth, or liquid assets. See also *investment program; limited partnership; private placement; risk factor; suitability; tax shelter.*

prepaid

prepaid interest interest paid in advance of the due date. For tax purposes, interest is not deductible until actually due, regardless of when it is paid. However, some investment programs have been structured to prepay interest, supposedly offering investors an immediate tax deduction in excess of the amount of cash deposited. See also *interest; mortgage; tax shelter.*

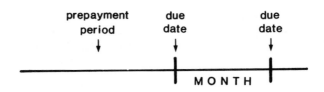

prepaid taxes taxes paid in advance. In the federal and state income tax systems, individuals and companies are required to pay taxes during the year, either through payroll withholding or tax deposits. Prepaid state income taxes are deductible as itemized deductions on federal tax returns.

Property taxes are prepaid, usually for six-month periods. When a property is sold, the buyer is required to reimburse the seller for that portion of property taxes that has been prepaid. This adjustment is made as part of the closing costs. For example, the seller has prepaid $510 of property taxes, covering 180 days. The buyer purchases property when 33 days remain in that period. The property tax assigned to the buyer is computed as 33/180ths of the total, or 18.33%:

$$18.33\% \times \$510 = \$93.48$$

See also *income tax; property tax; proration; tax basis.*

prepayment clause a provision in a mortgage loan contract spelling out the terms under which the loan may or may not be prepaid. It specifies the amount of the loan that can be prepaid each year without a prepayment penalty. See also *debt service; interest; mortgage acceleration.*

prepayment penalty an assessment made by a lending institution against a borrower who pays a loan before the due date. For example, a homeowner has an existing loan for 12.5%; however, a new loan can be obtained for 9% at a different institution. To prepay the existing loan, the borrower is charged a prepayment penalty. See also *financing; interest; refinancing.*

present value the amount of money required today to create a sum of money in the future, assuming a rate of interest and the effects of compounding. Present value is computed in one of two ways. First, of a single sum of money to be deposited now (present value of 1); second, of a series of deposits required to reach a target amount (present value of 1 per period).

For example, an investor wants to accumulate $18,000 within five years. If interest can be earned at the rate of 9%, compounded annually, how much will be needed to place in an account today? Referring to an amortization table for the "present value of 1," the factor listed is 0.6499 313. This factor is multiplied by the desired sum to arrive at the present value:

$$0.6499\ 313 \times \$18,000 = \$11,698.76$$

By depositing this amount today and compounding it at 9%, the fund will be worth $18,000 in five years.

To create the same fund with a series of annual deposits, the investor would refer to an amortization table giving factors for a "sinking fund," or "periodic payments." At 9% compounded annually, the factor is 0.1670 924. This factor is multiplied by the desired sum to arrive at the present value:

$$0.1670\ 924 \times \$18,000 = \$3,007.66$$

By depositing this amount at the beginning of each year (and assuming that interest is payable at the end of each year), the fund will be worth $18,000 in five years. See also *compound interest; future value; interest; time value of money.* [See overleaf.]

present value (of 1)

YEAR	INTEREST	BALANCE
		$11,698.76
1	$1,052.89	12,751.65
2	1,147.65	13,899.30
3	1,250.93	15,150.23
4	1,363.52	16,513.75
5	1,486.25	18,000.00
	$6,301.24	

presumptive title the belief that title is held to land, based on the possession and occupation of that land, when actual title may be held by someone else. See also *possession; title.*

pre-tax profit the net profits from operation, including deduction of interest and depreciation, before taxes are computed. For example, an investor holds

prime

present value (of 1 per period)

YEAR	DEPOSIT	INTEREST	BALANCE
1	$ 3,007.66	$ 0	$ 3,007.66
2	3,007.66	270.69	6,286.01
3	3,007.66	565.74	9,859.41
4	3,007.66	887.35	13,754.42
5	3,007.66	1,237.92	18,000.00
	$15,038.30	$ 2,961.70	

a rental property and produces a net profit of $11,433 in one year. However, this profit does not reflect a tax liability on those profits of $3,201. See also *after-tax profit; income statement; net income; tax basis.*

pre-tax profit

rent receipts		$75,000
operating expenses	$19,240	
interest	36,145	
depreciation	8,182	
total expenses		$63,567
pre-tax profit		$11,433

prime location a highly desirable location of property, due to economic or aesthetic advantages. For example, an ideally situated retail space or a home with an exceptional view would be described as prime locations. These factors affect market value. See also *aesthetic value; appraised value; market value; value.*

prime rate   a rate used to judge interest rate movements and the demand for money. It is the lowest rate a commercial lender charges for short-term loans to its preferred customers. Long-term mortgage rates will be directly affected by changes in the prime rate. See also *financing; interest; lending institution; long-term loan.*

principal   (1) an individual who appoints an agent to represent interest, such as a broker who contracts with real estate agents. (2) an individual who currently owns property, referred to as a "principal" in a sales contract. (3) the face amount of a loan, the amount due. See also *agent; financing; interest; loan value; mortgage.*

Principal, Interest, Taxes and Insurance (PITI)   the total monthly payment made by a borrower when a portion of that payment is for impounds. Those portions assignable to taxes and insurance are later paid by the lending institution in behalf of the homeowner. The term "PITI" refers to a loan that includes such impounds. See also *impound; interest; level payments; property taxes.*

principal residence   the primary home, one in which the homeowner resides for a majority of the time. The distinction between a principal and second home is used for determining qualification for deferral of gain upon sale. The deferral is available only on property used as a principal residence for no less than three of the previous five years preceding the sale date. See also *deferred gain; noninvestment property; tax basis.*

prior lien   a lien that has priority of claim in the event of default of a property offered as security, a first or senior lien. See also *default; first lien; lien; senior lien.*

priority   (1) the seniority of one lien over another. In most cases, liens have priority based on the order in which they are filed and recorded. An exception is a tax lien, which takes priority over all other liens on a property. (2) the promotional interests specified in some limited partnership agreements. Under a priority clause, the general partners are ensured a profit before limited partners receive their shares. See also *default; limited partnership; promotional interest; recording; senior lien; subordination; tax lien.*

private lender   an individual who arranges financing for a borrower, as opposed to an institutional lender. See also *conventional loan; financing; institutional lender; lending institution.*

Private Mortgage Insurance (PMI)   default insurance, protecting lending institutions in the event a borrower is unable to continue payments. PMI premiums are paid by the borrower as a requirement of the contract, even though it insures the lender. The contract specifies that PMI premiums must continue to be paid until a specified level of equity has been built up (usually 20%). This insurance

private

reduces the risk that a lending institution will be forced to foreclose on properties in which title or no equity exists for the borrower. See also *conventional loan; default insurance; equity build-up; foreclosure; mortgage insurance.*

private placement a limited partnership that is not made available to the general public, but is funded by a small number of investors, each depositing a substantial sum of money (often in staged payments over a period of years). See also *limited partnership; public offering; risk factor; Securities Act of 1933; staged payment; tax shelter.*

private property all property not owned publicly, which is subject to rights under the allodial system of ownership. See also *allodial system; property; residential property.*

pro forma a projection of future earnings, profits or market value in an investment program, presented to induce investors to purchase interests. See also *financial statement; investment program; market value; net income; tax basis.*

production rate the current yield on Ginnie Mae pass-through securities, set according to the prevailing FHA mortgage rate. See also *current yield; Ginnie Mae pass-through; mortgage pool; pass-through investment; residential mortgage; yield.*

profit and loss statement a summary of income, costs and expenses, and profits or losses from operation of income property or an organization. For example, the owner of a rental house receives $11,465 in rent, and has $3,215 in operating expenses. A profit and loss statement would list each expense and show a net profit of $8,250. See also *income statement.*

---

profit and loss statement

```
  revenues
- costs and expenses
= profit (loss)
```

```
   $11,465
 -   3,215
 =$  8,250
```

property

program general reference to a limited partnership, whether public or private; or to any investment entered into or anticipated by an individual. See also *direct participation program; investment program; limited partnership; Real Estate Limited Partnership (RELP).*

progress payment a payment made to a contractor during the course of an improvement or construction project. The payment is based upon the percentage of completion as dictated by the contract schedule. See also *addition; improvement.*

progression the increase in value of a property due to the existence of a similar property of higher quality. See also *appraised value; market value; regression.*

promissory note a debt instrument or note signed by the borrower, promising to repay a loan of a specified amount, in periodic payments or with a lump sum, at a stated rate of interest, and by an identified due date. See also *debt instrument; loan.*

promotional interest income to be earned by the promoter or general partner in a direct participation program. A subordinated interest gives other, limited partners a priority of payment of future profits, while an unsubordinated interest grants the promoter a percentage of profits or a stated amount of cash upon sale, regardless of whether or not the sale is profitable. See also *direct participation program; interest; priority; subordination.*

property an asset and related rights, in land and improvements (real property) or furnishings, equipment, and personal items (personal property). See also *chattel; interest; personal property; real property; title.*

property line the boundary of a parcel of land. See also *bounds; legal description; parcel.*

property manager a person or firm responsible for physical management of investment properties. The manager may reside on the site, or manage a property without a physical presence. The terms of property management are critical in evaluating limited partnerships and other investment programs, as the quality of care and maintenance will affect future market value. See also *Certified Property Manager (CPM); investment program; limited partnership; market value.*

property report a disclosure report prepared by developers and made available to purchasers whenever 50 or more lots are sold. The report spells out everything that is included with the purchase, including paved streets, utilities, and other basic services; value and location of parcels of land for sale; and all features included in or excluded from the price. See also *full disclosure; Interstate Land Sales Full Disclosure Act (ILSA); land; Office of Interstate Land Sales Registration (OILSR); parcel; subdivision; tract.*

property residual technique an appraisal method in which value is estimated on the basis of estimated future income, also known as the income approach.

property

See also *appraisal method; future value; income approach; market value; reversionary interest.*

property taxes a tax on property based on an assessed valuation, the proceeds of which are used to fund local services (schools, utilities, streets and roads, and fire services, for example). See also *ad valorem tax; assessed valuation; tax basis.*

proration the division of an expense between the buyer and the seller, or assessment of costs for a partial month. For example, a property tax bill of $710 is prepaid by the seller for 180 days, from July 1 to December 31. But on July 21, the house is sold. In this instance, 21 of the 180 days are assigned to the seller, and 159 days to the buyer. On the closing statement, the buyer will be charged for the applicable portion of prepaid property taxes:

$$159/180 \times \$710 = \$627.17$$

Interest expense is prorated from the sale date until the first loan payment date. For example, a home purchase closes on July 21. Interest on the loan balance is $600, and the first payment will be due on August 1. The 10 days between closing and the payment date are prorated to the buyer:

$$10/31 \times \$600 = \$193.55$$

See also *closing date; interest; property taxes.*

proration

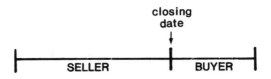

prospect an individual who may become a buyer, who is viewed as being serious and sincere about purchasing a home on the market. See also *broker; listing; purchase offer.*

prospectus a statement disclosing the terms, conditions, risks, and use of funds in an investment program. The prospectus includes descriptions of the investment objectives, the experience of management, conflicts of interest, a tax and legal opinion, audited financial statements, fees that will be charged to investors, and other important information needed to make an informed decision. In the legal sense, any communication intended to promote investment in a program is considered a prospectus. In practice, however, it refers to a printed document that must be given to prospective buyers at the time an offer to sell is made. See also *direct participation program; full disclosure; investment program; limited partnership; preliminary prospectus; risk factor.*

proprietary interest the interest of an owner or anyone holding partial equity in a property. See also *equity; interest; title.*

proprietary lease a lease for a cooperative unit, in which the tenant of a unit is also an investor in the cooperative. See also *cooperative housing; lease; operating lease; tenant.*

proxy a right assigned to another person to represent the interests of the principal. See also *agency; attorney in fact; power of attorney.*

public offering a limited partnership that is made available to the general public, subject to meeting of suitability standards. These standards will not be as strict as for investment in a private partnership in most cases. A public offering can be made only following registration of the program with the Securities and Exchange Commission, and publication of a prospectus that must be given to each person who is solicited. See also *direct participation program; investment program; limited partnership; private placement; suitability.*

public sale an auction of property that has been foreclosed, and is offered by the lending institution or holder of a lien. See also *foreclosure; lien; sale.*

purchase-leaseback a technique of investing in real estate, in which the buyer leases property back to the seller. This provides the seller with a cash settlement but continuing occupancy; and the buyer acquires property already occupied by a tenant, thus ensuring relatively safe and continued cash flow under a lease created at the time the sale occurs. See also *cash flow; investment program; land purchase-leaseback; lease; possession.*

Purchase Money Mortgage (PMM) a mortgage granted as partial payment for property, rather than cash. For example, a seller agrees to carry part of the financing for a buyer. See also *consideration; down payment; hard money; mortgage; paper.*

purchase offer a unilateral contract, in which one individual specifies the terms under which he will be willing to purchase a property from the seller. The seller is not required to respond, and a contract is created only if the terms are accepted. See also *acceptance; contract; offer to purchase; unilateral contract.*

purchase price the price actually paid for a property, assumed to be the Fair Market Value (FMV), or the highest amount the purchaser was willing to pay and the lowest amount the seller was willing to accept. See also *asking price; Fair Market Value (FMV); market value.*

pyramiding a technique of leveraging, in which the equity in one property is used to finance the purchase of additional properties. In theory, pyramiding can be used indefinitely to build substantial investment value. In practice, the demands of debt service or maintenance, combined with unexpected vacancies or non-payment of rents, may create an excessive drain on cash flow. As a result, the risks of pyramiding are substantial. See also *cash flow; debt service; down payment; equity; investor basis; leverage; risk factor; vacancy rate.* [See overleaf.]

pyramiding

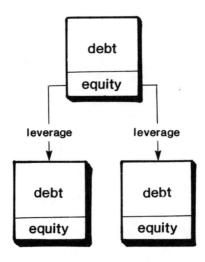

Q

qualified asset a term used to describe assets that a Real Estate Investment Trust (REIT) may hold to continue qualifying for conduit tax treatment (when all profits are passed through to investors, and the REIT itself is not liable for taxes). The REIT must hold no less than 75% of total assets in the form of real property equity or mortgage interests. See also *conduit tax treatment; investment program; Real Estate Investment Trust (REIT); real property.*

quantity-survey method an appraisal method in which value is estimated based on the material and labor cost to replace an existing building. See also *appraisal method; market value; replacement cost; reproduction cost.*

quarterly compounding a method of computing interest based on four periods per year. The stated annual rate is divided by four (quarters), and interest is calculated using that rate for each of the quarters in the year. For example, an investor deposits $1,000 in an account yielding 9%, compounded quarterly. This produces a quarterly rate of 2.25%, and an annual rate of 9.31%. After one year, the $1,000 deposit has grown to $1,093.08. See also *annual compounding; compound interest; daily compounding; monthly compounding; semiannual compounding.*

quiet enjoyment **(1)** freedom from defects in title, a reference to the security of ownership without the fear of title defects. **(2)** the right of a tenant to privacy and freedom from unnecessary disturbances while occupying the premises. See also *clear title; good title; right of occupancy; tenant; title.*

quarterly compounding

QUARTER	9% INTEREST	BALANCE
		$1,000.00
1	$ 22.50	1,022.50
2	23.01	1,045.51
3	23.52	1,069.03
4	24.05	1,093.08

quitclaim deed a form of deed that provides the least amount of protection of ownership, and includes no warranties of title. It is an instrument used to release property from claims so that title can be conveyed quickly. See also *cloud on the title; conveyance; deed*.

R

Radburn Plan a pattern of lots in a subdivision, consisting of adjacent groupings of cul-de-sacs. This design minimizes traffic and allows for open space planning. The name is derived from the town of the same name in New Jersey, where it was first used. See also *cluster; curvilinear system; development; gridiron pattern; loop streets; subdivision*.

Rapid Payoff Mortgage (RPM) a form of mortgage consisting of a fixed rate of interest, and principal payments that increase over time. The effect is that the loan is repaid more rapidly than with a level-payment plan. It is ideally suited for borrowers who expect higher income in the future, and who want to reduce total interest cost and the number of years a loan will be outstanding, but who cannot afford higher payments today. For example, an $80,000 loan is established at 9% interest with a 30-year amortization. Payments are $644 per month. But the contract calls for increases of $100 per month every three years. See also *creative financing; financing; Growing Equity Mortgage (GEM); mortgage acceleration*. [See overleaf.]

rate cap a clause included in an Adjustable Rate Mortgage (ARM) limiting the interest rate the lending institution can charge. The cap has two parts. First, a contract provides for the maximum increase allowable per period (usually six or 12 months). Second, a maximum is placed on the level that can be charged for the entire contract. For example, an ARM's current rate is 7.5%. The lender

Rapid Payoff Mortgage (RPM)

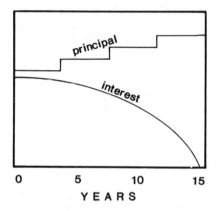

may increase this level by no more than one point per year, and by no more than six points for the entire contract. The maximum the borrower will be required to pay during the term of the loan is 13.5%. A lender may include a clause for a holdover of a higher rate to absorb differences when the indexed rate exceeds the maximum. In that case, the lender will pay the maximum rate even after the indexed rate falls below that maximum. See also *Adjustable Rate Mortgage (ARM); cap; mortgage; payment cap.*

rate cap

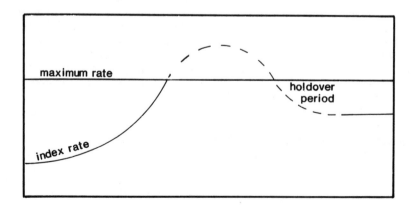

rate of return in most common use, the percentage yield of total annual earnings to the original cost of an investment. However, the term is loosely used to describe yield calculated by a variety of methods. In comparing different investments, it is necessary to first determine that the rate of return is calculated on the same basis. See also *investment income; total return; yield.*

rate of return

$$\frac{\text{annual earnings}}{\text{cost}}$$

$$\frac{\$14{,}935}{\$175{,}000} = 8.5\%$$

raw land land without improvements, either structural or basic services (streets, utilities, or drainage). See also *improved land; land.*

ready, willing and able term used to describe a viable buyer. That buyer is ready in the sense that the timing is right, willing to enter a contract at this time, and able to fulfill the financial obligations involved. See also *agreement; contract.*

real estate land, tangible features on the land, and permanent improvements added to it. The rights to real estate may extend downward into the earth and upward into the air. For example, the owner of a condominium on the second floor owns the air space within the walls, even though not attached to the ground; and a shared portion of the land itself. The value of real estate may be increased by intangible features, such as an exceptionally good view or attractive retail location. See also *air rights; improvement; intangible asset; personal property; real property; tangible property.*

real estate cycle the relationship between supply and demand, which affects the current market value of property. The cycle follows a predictable course over time. Demand for property rises, causing an increase in construction of new retail or commercial sites. As the demand is met and exceeded, development continues to the point that supply is greater than demand. The level of construction activity declines in response to vacancies and lower profits, so that demand eventually increases and the cycle begins again. The cycle is distorted by outside factors, such as excessive investment money being put into the market for tax write-offs, or legislated tax incentives or disincentives. See also *appreciation; buyer's market; market value; seller's market; supply and demand; value.*

real estate cycle

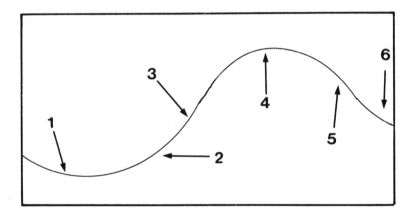

1 demand rises
2 construction increases
3 demand falls
4 supply exceeds demand
5 construction decreases
6 demand rises

Real Estate Investment Act of 1961 designed to encourage investment in real estate, this legislation set rules for operation of Real Estate Investment Trust (REIT) programs. See also *investment program*.

Real Estate Investment Trust (REIT) a form of pooled investment that combines diversification with liquidity. Investors purchase shares of the trust, which in turn becomes involved in real estate investment in one of several forms. An equity REIT purchases real estate directly; a mortgage REIT lends money, either for the development of new properties, or on existing and occupied structures; and a hybrid REIT combines debt and equity positions. Shares of REIT programs are traded over exchanges like stock of publicly traded corporations. See also *equity REIT; hybrid REIT; mortgage REIT*.

Real Estate Limited Partnership (RELP) a form of limited partnership specifically designed to purchase real estate. In the past, a large number of RELP programs were designed to provide investors with tax shelter. However, a series of tax laws passed since 1982 have eliminated most of these benefits, notably the Tax Reform Act of 1986. RELP programs may be blind pools (identifying the general intent of the program, but without a specific property in mind), or specified programs (organized to buy one or more specific properties). See also *blind pool; direct participation program; investment program; limited partnership; risk factor; specified program; Tax Reform Act of 1986.*

Real Estate Mortgage Investment Company (REMIC) a form of pooled investment created as part of the Tax Reform Act of 1986. The pool offers multiple classes of interests in mortgage-backed securities, from the fixed pool of mortgages it holds. See also *investment program; mortgage pool; mortgage security; Tax Reform Act of 1986.*

Real Estate Securities and Syndication Institute (RESSI) an organization established in 1972 to provide information to the real estate syndication industry. RESSI is an affiliate of the National Association of Realtors (NAR). Its address is 430 North Michigan Avenue, Chicago, IL 60611. See also *investment program; limited partnership; National Association of Realtors (NAR); syndicate.*

Real Estate Settlement Procedures Act (RESPA) a 1974 law requiring lenders to follow certain standards in the collection of money and estimates of closing costs, applicable to federally insured or guaranteed loans. Lenders are required to estimate total closing costs within three business days after filing for a loan. They are also restricted in the amount that can be held in escrow for insurance or taxes, and must report all settlement costs to both the buyer and the seller at least one day prior to closing. And a uniform settlement statement must be supplied to the buyer. See also *closing costs; Department of Housing and Urban Development (HUD); settlement; uniform settlement statement.*

real estate stock corporation a corporation involved directly in the ownership and management of real estate. Individual investors may purchase and sell shares on the open market, thus enjoying a higher level of liquidity and diversification than is possible through direct purchase of property. See also *interest; investment program; liquidity.*

real law the area of law concerned with rights of real estate owners, landlords and tenants. See also *allodial system; contract.*

real property real estate; land and improvements and the rights of ownership, use or possession in it. Real property is distinguished from personal property in its permanent, affixed nature. See also *improvement; land; personal property; real estate.*

realist designation granted to members of the National Association of Real Estate Brokers (NAREB). See also *broker; National Association of Real Estate Brokers (NAREB).*

realized gain the amount of money paid to equalize value in an exchange of property, that is usually subject to income tax, also called the boot. See also *boot; exchange; income tax; recognized gain.*

realtor 144

realtor designation granted to qualified professional members of the National Association of Realtors (NAR). See also *broker; Code of Ethics; National Association of Realtors (NAR)*.

realtor-associate a designation granted by the National Association of Realtors (NAR) to salesperson members. See also *National Association of Realtors (NAR); salesperson*.

Realtors National Marketing Institute (RNMI) an organization affiliated with the National Association of Realtors (NAR), that produces educational material for members and grants several designations, including the CCIM and CRS. See also *Certified Commercial Investment Member (CCIM); National Association of Realtors (NAR)*.

reappraised lease also called reappraisal lease, a lease that includes a provision for periodic changes in monthly payments. The increase or decrease is to be based upon changes in market value of the property. This provision is usually found in long-term lease agreements. For example, a 20-year lease includes a provision that an independent appraisal will be performed at five-year intervals, and that the percentage of increase in market value will be applied to the lease agreement. Monthly payments are to be increased at the same rate as growth in market value, but are limited to 5% per period. See also *lease; long-term lease; market value; variable lease*.

reappraised lease

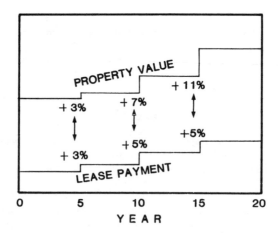

recapture clause **(1)** a provision in a lease contract, giving the landlord the right to cancel the lease if a specified event occurs, or if a condition is not maintained. This clause is often found in percentage leases. The contract specifies that if a certain level of monthly gross receipts is not maintained over the period of the lease, the agreement can be cancelled. **(2)** a provision in a ground lease allowing the tenant to purchase the property at a specified time in the future, and for a specified price. See also *ground lease; lease; percentage lease.*

recognized gain a portion of proceeds from the sale or exchange of property that is subject to income tax. See also *capital gain/loss; exchange; income tax; tax basis.*

reconciliation the last step carried out during an appraisal of property, in which the appraiser establishes an estimate of current value. This process involves combining estimates arrived at by the application of different appraisal methods applied to compute value, and allowances for any special circumstances of the subject property. See also *appraisal; market value; valuation.*

reconveyance the release of an encumbrance upon full satisfaction of debt. A deed of reconveyance is recorded to release title to the equitable owner. See also *conveyance; debt; encumbrance; title.*

recording a notice filed in the record of a county, documenting the creation or satisfaction of all encumbrances affecting property ownership, purchase or sale. See also *encumbrance; lien; mortgage; title.*

recording fee a closing cost charged for the documentation of ownership transfer. See also *closing costs; mortgage.*

recourse loan a loan for which an investor is considered liable. The recourse loan is included for tax purposes as part of the basis in a property. For example, an investor places $5,000 in cash in a program, and signs a recourse note for an additional $5,000. His basis is $10,000. See also *direct participation program; investment program; limited partnership; nonrecourse loan; tax basis.*

recovery period the number of years required to fully depreciate an asset under the Accelerated Cost Recovery System (ACRS). This was first introduced as part of the Economic Recovery Tax Act of 1981 (ERTA), and amended by subsequent tax legislation. See also *Accelerated Cost Recovery System (ACRS); depreciation; Economic Recovery Tax Act of 1981 (ERTA); tax basis.*

red herring a preliminary prospectus, so called in reference to the red ink used to state caveats on the cover of the document. It discloses the terms of an offering, but is subject to the completion of registration with the Securities and Exchange Commission. See also *full disclosure; investment program; preliminary prospectus; SEC Rule 430.*

redemption period a period of time allowed in some states, during which owners of foreclosed property may redeem their ownership by payment of past due debt, interest, and accrued costs. See also *default; foreclosure; right of redemption.*

redlining

redlining the illegal practice of restricting the amount of money at risk, or of refusing to grant mortgage loans in one area, due to a decline in market values in that area. See also *Department of Housing and Urban Development (HUD); Office of Equal Opportunity (OEO).*

re-entry the contractual right of a landlord to take possession of leased property in the event the conditions of the lease are not met. See also *eviction; lease; right of possession; tenant.*

refinancing the replacement of one or more existing loans with a new loan. Refinancing is justified when a fixed-rate loan can be replaced by a current loan at a lower rate, or when the homeowner wants to combine two older loans into a single mortgage agreement. Refinancing will involve a title search, appraisal, and other closing costs, and the homeowner may be required to pay a prepayment penalty on the old loan. To justify the refinance, the total cost should be divided by the amount of monthly savings. This will produce the number of months required to absorb the cost.

For example, a homeowner originally borrowed $80,000 at 12%, to be repaid over a 30-year term. The current balance of the loan is $64,500, and monthly payments are $823. That loan can be refinanced at 8.5%. However, closing costs will be approximately $2,190 and a prepayment penalty of $1,860 will be assessed. The homeowner borrows $68,550 (the combination of the balance on the old loan, closing costs, and prepayment penalty). Monthly payments with a 15-year amortization will be $675, or $148 less than payments on the old loan. It will take 27 months to absorb the cost of refinancing ($4,050 divided by $148). See also *financing; loan; mortgage.*

reformation the modification of an original contract, undertaken upon discovery of fraud, error, misrepresentation, or a failure to define the true and intended agreement. See also *agreement; contract.*

registration statement a document filed with the Securities and Exchange Commission by the sponsor organization offering securities for public sale. The details of the program are fully disclosed and explained, and are the same as disclosures made in a prospectus for investors. See also *full disclosure; investment program; prospectus; risk factor.*

regression a valuation theory stating that a property will decline in value when it is situated near other properties that are of lower quality, or that are not maintained to the same degree. The theory is based on limitations in market value set by neighborhood average values. See also *anticipation; change; competition; conformity; contribution; diminishing returns; highest and best use; increasing returns; plottage; substitution; supply and demand.*

Regulation A a section of the Securities Act of 1933, spelling out the limits under which an offer of securities can be made, without the requirement that a registration statement must be filed. See also *full disclosure; investment program; prospectus; public offering; registration statement; SEC Rule 254.*

Regulation Z better known as the Truth in Lending Act, a federal regulation

refinancing

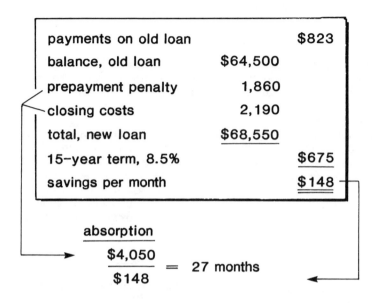

requiring full disclosure by lenders of the terms and conditions of a loan. These include advising the borrower of the amount and frequency of payments, total interest cost, and the Annual Percentage Rate (APR) being assessed. See also *Annual Percentage Rate (APR); full disclosure; interest rate; loan.*

release clause   a provision in a contract that provides for rescission or cancellation of the agreement, in the event that contingencies occur or that performance is not completed, or consideration is withdrawn. The released party to the contract, upon exercise of the release clause, may be fully excused from any obligations; or may be excused from performance of a portion of the agreement. See also *contingency; contract; escape clause; mortgage.*

remainder interest   a future interest in a life estate. Title to property will pass to the named individual upon the death of the estater owner. See also *fee simple; future interest; life estate; reversionary interest.*

remaining balance table   a table showing the percentage of a loan outstanding at the end of each year in the term, based on the applicable interest rate. For example, for a 12% loan with a 30-year term, a remaining balance table will show the following percentages of the original loan outstanding:

Renegotiated 148

after year	percentage
5	97.7%
10	93.4
15	85.7
20	71.7
25	46.2

Homeowners can refer to remaining balance tables to calculate equity build-up based on loan payments, or to estimate the value of mortgage acceleration. See also *equity build-up; full amortization; interest; mortgage acceleration; principal.*

Renegotiated Rate Mortgage (RRM) also known as a Rollover Mortgage (RM), a form of financing in which the interest rate and other terms are to be recalculated on specified dates. For example, a homeowner has an RRM for 9.5%, to be amortized over a 30-year term. However, the contract specified that the loan is callable (due) in five years. At that point, the homeowner must renegotiate, and the lending institution will either renew the loan under the same terms, or modify terms based on current interest rates. See also *creative financing; financing; lending institution; long-term loan; Rollover Mortgage (RM).*

Renegotiated Rate Mortgage (RRM)

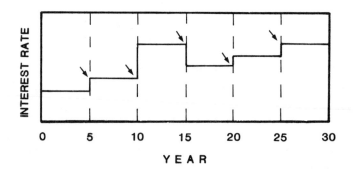

↘ **Renegotiation dates**

rent insurance a form of protection that reduces a landlord's risk in the event of a fire or other casualty. If rental income is lost as the result of a casualty, the insurance company will reimburse the landlord until the building is restored to habitable condition. See also *casualty insurance; fire insurance; risk factor.*

rent option a form of lease in which a part of the payment is assigned to rent, and part to be applied as a down payment on purchase of the property. The option contract should specify the price and purchase date. It should also require that a separate fund be established to deposit the funds representing a future down payment, and should state the terms under which those funds will be returned if the option is not exercised. See also *down payment; lease with option to buy; option.*

rentable area that portion of a building that is to be rented out to tenants, excluding access areas and other non-rentable space. See also *area; Floor-Area Ratio (FAR); occupancy rate.*

rentable area

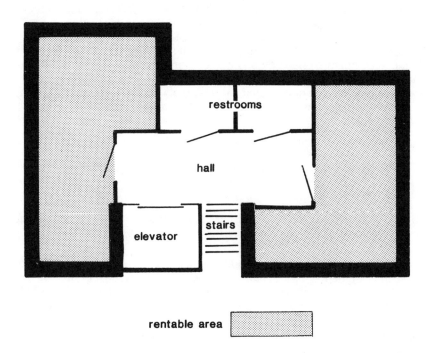

rental pool descriptive of a program that invests the capital of a number of investors or limited partners in rental property, manages property in behalf of investors, and distributes net profits proportionately. See also *direct participation program; limited partnership; mortgage pool.*

rental value the estimated value of income property calculated by multiplying rental income by a factor, called the Gross Rent Multiplier (GRM). See also *appraisal method; Gross Rent Multiplier (GRM); income approach; valuation.*

renter's

renter's policy a homeowner's insurance form, also referred to as HO-4. It covers personal property of the tenant, but not the structure itself. The landlord is responsible for insuring the building against losses. See also *fire insurance; HO-4; homeowner's insurance.*

replacement cost an appraisal method in which value is based upon the cost to reconstruct a building, given current labor and material rates. "Replacement" for this purpose refers to returning a building to the same functional purpose, but not necessarily an exact duplicate. See also *appraisal method; cost approach; reproduction cost; value.*

replacement value a type of homeowner's insurance coverage, under which losses will be paid based on their current replacement value, rather than original cost. The other method, Actual Cash Value (ACV), insures property for its original cost, minus depreciation. Most replacement value provisions limit the total amount that will be paid, usually as a factor of the ACV value.

For example, a homeowner is the victim of a theft. Two items are taken: a stereo originally costing $1,100, with depreciated value of $200 (based on the insurance company's estimate); and a television originally costing $750, with a current depreciated value of $300. Under an ACV policy, the homeowner will receive only $500, the depreciated value. A replacement value policy specifying maximum payment equal to 400% of ACV would pay $1,550:

> stereo— original cost $1,100
> ACV value $200
> maximum reimbursement, 400% of ACV, $800
> television— original cost $750
> ACV value $300
> reimbursement, total replacement value, $750

See also *Actual Cash Value (ACV); casualty insurance; depreciation; homeowner's insurance.*

reproduction cost the value of a building based upon an estimate of the cost to construct in the event of a total loss, given the current cost of material and labor. The appraisal is based on the premise that an exact duplicate would be built. See also *appraisal method; cost approach; replacement cost; value.*

rescission the cancellation of a contract, based on the discovery of fraud, misrepresentation, or illegality. Rescission may be exercised at any time by an individual who is party to a voidable contract. For example, a minor contracting for a non-necessity may rescind the contract, or may allow it to remain in force. Rescission may also occur if a disclosure required by law is not made. For example, a lender does not report the terms of interest and payments as required by the Truth in Lending Act. See also *cancellation; contract; illegal contract; unenforceable contract; voidable contract.*

resident manager an individual who works or resides on the property under management. See also *Certified Property Manager (CPM); investment program; property manager; risk factor.*

Residential Member (RM) a designation awarded to qualified members of the AIREA. See also *American Institute of Real Estate Appraisers (AIREA); appraiser.*

residential mortgage a mortgage secured by residential property, usually occupied by the owner. See also *financing; mortgage; secured debt.*

residential property housing occupied by the owner as a principal residence, including houses, condominiums, cooperatives, mobile homes, and other forms of property designed and used for non-commercial purposes. See also *commercial property; principal residence; real property.*

restrictive covenant a limitation placed upon the use of property, either by contract or through local zoning regulations. For example, a city places a density restriction on development of tract homes; or a condominium association does not allow owners to use their units for manufacturing, retail, or other commercial purposes. See also *agreement; density; zoning.*

retainage a portion of a total contract withheld pending satisfactory completion. A homeowner, for example, withholds 10% of the total agreed price for a home improvement, until the work has been completed, inspected and approved. A contractor may also withhold a percentage of payments due to subcontractors for the same reason. See also *contract; improvement.*

return on equity a calculation of yield in which annual net income is divided by the equity investment in the property. For example, an investor buys a four-unit apartment house for $155,000, and earns $9,407 in net profit the first year. Return on equity is 6.1%. See also *equity; investor basis; net income; yield.*

return on equity

$$\frac{\text{annual net income}}{\text{equity}}$$

$$\frac{\$9,407}{\$155,000} = 6.1\%$$

Reverse Annuity Mortgage (RAM) a method of equity conversion entered into by agreement between a homeowner and an insurance company. The RAM is suited for individuals who have a high level of equity, but are in need of regular *reversionary*

monthly income. The insurer offers annuity payments, either for a specified period of years or for the remainder of the homeowner's life. In return, the home equity is pledged as collateral and the annuity payments, plus interest, accumulate as a mortgage. Upon expiration of the annuity period or death of the homeowner, the insurer is repaid its annuity. A limited number of insurers offer such programs, and only to individuals above a specified age (usually 62 or higher). See also *annuity; collateral; equity conversion; loan; mortgage.*

reversionary factor the factor from an amortization table used to compute the present value of 1. This factor, multiplied by a sum of money desired in the future, tells how much must be place on deposit at the beginning of the period, assuming a given rate of interest and method of compounding. See also *compound interest; interest rate; present value.*

reversionary factor

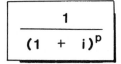

$$\frac{1}{(1 + i)^p}$$

i   interest rate
p   number of periods

reversionary interest **(1)** a future interest in a life estate. Title to property is not conveyed in the terms of a will, so that ownership of assets reverts to the original owner or that owner's heirs. **(2)** a provision included in the terms of some limited partnership agreements, entitling the sponsor to a share of future profits. These amounts are often to be paid before limited partners receive their share of profits, if any. See also *direct participation program; fee simple; future interest; investment program; life estate; limited partnership; remainder interest.*

right of first refusal the right to purchase property owned by another person, before it can be offered to an outsider. The provision is often included in the regulations of cooperative housing developments. For example, a shareholder/tenant desires to sell his rights. The cooperative has a contractual right to offer to buy that interest, if it chooses, before it can be offered to a new investor. See also *cooperative housing.*

right of occupancy the legal right of a tenant who has complied with the terms of a lease to occupy and use the premises, or the right of a legal owner to use real estate for its intended purpose. See also *lease; quiet enjoyment; tenant.*

right of possession the legal right of an owner to possess or control land and improvements, or of a tenant in compliance with the terms of a lease to occupy and use the premises. Possession is distinguished from legal title, and may be granted by contract. Actual possession refers to the physical presence and control of property; and constructive possession is the direct control over the occupancy and use of premises, whether physically occupied or not. See also *actual possession; constructive possession; possession.*

right of redemption a right granted in some states, allowing owners of properties in foreclosure to reclaim all rights to the property. It can be achieved by paying the amount in arrears plus all fees accrued until that point. The redemption period is limited, and the right exists only until expiration of that time. See also *default; encumbrance; foreclosure; redemption period.*

right of survivorship the right of a surviving joint tenant to claim sole ownership of property. See also *Joint Tenants with Rights of Survivorship (JTWROS); tenancy by the entirety; title.*

right of way the legal right to pass over or through the property of another to enter or leave land, either granted by the owner of an adjacent parcel or existing as a public right of way. See also *access right; easement; egress; ingress.*

riparian rights rights to the use of waterways for access to and from property, more often referred to in the Eastern portion of the United States. See also *access right; littoral rights.*

risk factor the conditions of an investment or contract that threaten the security, profits or cash flow of an investor or owner. Lending institutions assume risks in lending money to borrowers. Investors assume risk of inadequate cash flow, liquidity, or casualty losses. And landlords take the risk of high vacancies. An investor in tax shelters assumes a tax risk. Risk can be reduced through limits on leverage, avoidance of excessive leverage, diversification, the purchase of insurance, or pooling investment funds with those of other investors. See also *cash flow; investment objective; leverage; liquidity; tax basis.*

Rollover Mortgage (RM) a form of financing in which the interest rate, payment term and other conditions are renegotiated periodically. Also called a Renegotiated Rate Mortgage (RRM), the rollover protects the lending institution in the event that current interest rates and other market conditions change drastically after the contract is entered.

The rollover provision might specify amortization at a long-term rate, while the entire loan balance is callable within a short period of years. For example, a homeowner contracts for a mortgage to be repaid on a 30-year amortization schedule. However, the agreement specifies that the entire balance is due in five years. At that point, terms are to be renegotiated, and the remaining debt rolled over into a new loan. See also *creative financing; financing; lending institution; Renegotiated Rate Mortgage (RRM).* [See overleaf.]

Rollover Mortgage (RM)

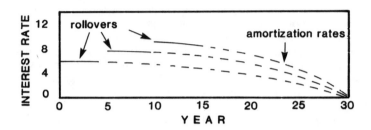

rule of 72 a calculation that gives an approximation of the time required to double an amount of money on deposit. To calculate, 72 is divided by the amount of interest. For example, an individual purchases an investment guaranteeing a 9.5% annual rate of return. The rule of 72 reveals it will take about 7.6 years to double that investment. The calculation is only an estimate, and will be distorted slightly if the compound method is not known or is not taken into account. See also *compound interest; interest rate.*

rule of 72

$$\frac{72}{\text{interest rate}}$$

$$\frac{72}{9.5\%} = 7.6 \text{ years}$$

S

safety the condition of risk associated with a particular investment, or an objective an investor holds. For example, an investor may be willing to accept a low yield in return for a high level of safety in an insured account. And another investor will seek the highest possible yield, reducing the safety factor. In its extreme form, this becomes speculation. See also *investment objective; risk factor; speculation; yield.*

salability   marketability; descriptive of a property that can be sold at or near the asking price, without delay. Salability varies with the level of demand, location, and other influences. See also *marketability.*

sale   the conveyance of title to property, from the buyer to the seller at an agreed upon price. See also *conveyance; offer to sell; title.*

sale contract   the document signed by buyer and seller once a meeting of the minds has been reached. All terms and conditions are specified in the contract, including the price, a description of the property being conveyed, and all contingencies. See also *agreement; contract; conveyance; meeting of the minds.*

sale-leaseback   the technique of selling property and continuing to occupy it. However, the past owner becomes a tenant, and the buyer assumes the role of landlord. The strategy is employed by owners of property who desire capital, but continue to need the facility. See also *land purchase-leaseback; tenant.*

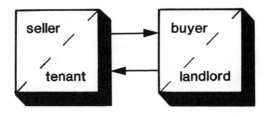

sale-leaseback

salesperson   an individual employed by or associated with a real estate broker, who brings together a buyer and a seller. Most states require a salesperson to be licensed and under the supervision of the broker before entering into sales activities. The salesperson is normally compensated by way of a commission based on the final sales price of the property. See also *agent; commission.*

salvage value   **(1)** the value of property at the time it is traded in or sold, assuming full depreciation has been claimed. Before the Accelerated Cost Recovery System (ACRS) was used, salvage value was figured prior to establishing the amount of annual depreciation to be claimed. **(2)** the tangible value of property received upon sale, or estimated market value at the time of abandonment of property. See also *abandonment; Accelerated Cost Recovery System (ACRS); depreciation; tangible property; value.*

Schedule 156

Schedule K-1 a tax information form completed as part of a partnership tax return (form 1065) and sent to each partner. The Schedule advises partners of their proportionate share of income, interest, depreciation, and other items affecting taxable income. See also *general partnership; investment program; limited partnership; tax basis.*

Schedule K-1

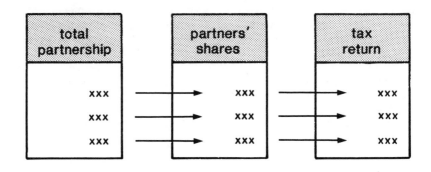

seasoned mortgage a mortgage that has been outstanding for a number of years, usually on properties with substantial equity build-up resulting from the duration of ownership. See also *debt service; equity build-up; mortgage.*

SEC Rule 10b-6 a rule of the Securities and Exchange Commission, establishing standards for direct participation program sponsors. The rule limits claims that can be made to the general public. See also *direct participation program; full disclosure; investment program; limited partnership; sponsor.*

SEC Rule 147 also known as the intrastate exemption, a rule allowing a direct participation program to forego registration with the Securities and Exchange Commission. To qualify, the program must offer interests in one state only. See also *direct participation program; limited partnership; registration statement.*

SEC Rule 254 a rule of the Securities and Exchange Commission setting limits on the sale of securities that are not registered. An offering circular, a document similar to a prospectus, must be given to investors prior to a solicitation. See also *direct participation program; full disclosure; limited partnership; prospectus; registration statement; Regulation A.*

SEC Rule 430 a Securities and Exchange Commission rule specifying that a preliminary prospectus must be given to customers at the time an initial solicitation is made. See also *full disclosure; investment program; preliminary prospectus; red herring.*

second mortgage a subordinated debt, one that has lower priority than a first lien. In the event of default, the first (senior) lien is satisfied first, before junior mortgages and other liens. See also *junior mortgage; mortgage; subordinated debt*.

secondary location property located in less desirable spots. A prime location, in comparison, is ideally situated for its purpose. For example, two retail shops of approximately the same size are compared to one another. The first has ample visibility, exposure to traffic and parking, and is considered a prime location. The second is not as visible, and is not exposed to as much traffic. It is a secondary location. See also *prime location*.

secondary market descriptive of the industry that specializes in buying and selling of existing mortgages. An agency purchases first mortgages from savings and loans and other lenders, and creates a mortgage pool. The borrower continues making payments to the original lender, who then submits proceeds to the pool. Investors buy shares in the pool and receive monthly payments for principal and interest. See also *debt instrument; investment program; mortgage pool; mortgage security*.

secured debt a debt for which tangible property is pledged as collateral, such as a mortgage secured by real estate. In the event of default on the loan, the lender may seize and sell the secured property to satisfy the obligation. See also *collateral; debt; default; mortgage*.

Securities Act of 1933 legislation governing activities in the investment industry. Provisions include ensuring full disclosure to customers of all material risks in publicly offered securities; the requirement that a prospectus be written and given to customers before a solicitation is made; and the requirement that publicly offered securities must be registered with the Securities and Exchange Commission. See also *full disclosure; prospectus; registration statement; risk factor*.

security (1) collateral pledged as a promise to repay a debt. For example, real estate serves as the security in a real estate mortgage loan. (2) an investment objective. For example, an investor requires that accounts are insured, or that return of principal is guaranteed. (3) an investment as defined by the Securities and Exchange Commission. Included are stocks, bonds, and interests in limited partnerships. See also *collateral; investment objective; investment program; performance*.

security deposit a sum of money paid by the tenant in a rental or lease agreement, that ensures the premises will not be damaged during the tenancy. The deposit is returned when the tenant vacates, assuming no damage has been done. See also *deposit; lease; tenant*.

security interest an interest in property that protects the lender against nonpayment. For example, a mortgage is a security interest of the lender. See also *collateral; interest; investment program; mortgage*.

self-liquidating

self-liquidating program an investment program designed for the return of capital to investors, either on a periodic repayment schedule, or through full liquidation of holdings at a specified date in the future. For example, some forms of Real Estate Investment Trust (REIT) programs include a finite-life provision, often 10 years from the formation date. See also *investment program; Real Estate Investment Trust (REIT)*.

seller take-back a condition in which the seller of real estate agrees to help finance the purchase. The seller may finance all or part of the purchase price, and might have to offer take-back in order to help a buyer who cannot otherwise qualify for a conventional loan. See also *financing; mortgage*.

seller's lien a lien on property held by the seller who has agreed to carry part of the financing. It ensures payment of the debt and, in the event of default, allows the seller to sell the property to pay the obligation. See also *collateral; default; lien; mortgage; Purchase Money Mortgage (PMM)*.

seller's market a market in which there are more buyers requiring properties than there are properties available. In those conditions, the seller is likely to receive the full asking price, and market value is probably higher, in response to the demand. See also *buyer's market; real estate cycle; supply and demand*.

selling agent the broker or agent that finds a buyer for the property. The selling agent receives a portion of the commission, in a split with the listing broker. See also *agent; broker; commission; listing broker*.

semiannual compounding a method of computing interest, using two periods per year. For example, an investor receives 8% interest on $1,000 in an account at the local bank, with compounding computed on the semiannual basis. Interest will be 4% (one-half of the annual rate), or 8.16% per year. To compute semiannual compound interest, divide the annual rate by two:

$$8\%/2 = 4\%$$

To compute the annual rate, convert the semiannual rate to decimal form, add one, and multiply it by itself:

a) $4\% = .04$
b) $.04 + 1 = 1.04$
c) $1.04 \times 1.04 = 1.0816$
d) $1.0816 = 8.16\%$ APR

See also *annual compounding; compound interest; daily compounding; monthly compounding; quarterly compounding; simple interest*.

senior lien a lien that has a priority of claim in the event of default. Such a lien will be satisfied before all other liens. See also *default; junior lien; lien; priority*.

senior mortgage a first mortgage, one that has priority of claim over all other liens. See also *first mortgage; junior mortgage; mortgage*.

semiannual compounding

MONTH	8% INTEREST	BALANCE
		$1,000.00
6	$ 40.00	1,040.00
12	41.60	1,081.60
18	43.26	1,124.86
24	44.99	1,169.85
30	46.79	1,216.64
36	48.67	1,265.31

Senior Real Estate Analyst (SREA) a professional designation awarded to qualified members of the Society of Real Estate Appraisers (SREA). See also *appraiser; Society of Real Estate Appraisers (SREA)*.

Senior Residential Appraiser (SRA) a designation of the Society of Real Estate Appraisers (SREA), granted to members upon the completion of qualifying study courses. See also *appraiser; Society of Real Estate Appraisers (SREA)*.

separate property property owned and held by a husband or wife, that is not considered to be jointly owned. It must be owned prior to the marriage, purchased with separate funds, or acquired by gift or inheritance. See also *community property; property*.

septic system a tank for the holding of sewage until solids convert to liquids or gases and release into the ground. See also *improvement*.

settlement the final transfer of title in a real estate sale, following satisfaction of all terms and conditions of the contract and final resolution of all contingencies. See also *closing date; conveyance; title*.

sewer a system for the disposal of wastes, that transports material from properties to a disposal site. See also *improvement*.

Shared Appreciation Mortgage (SAM) a form of creative financing in which the lender grants a loan, usually with a below market fixed rate of interest. In exchange, the lender is entitled to a share of the appreciation in the property's value, to be paid upon sale or after a stated number of years. For example, a buyer cannot qualify for a conventional loan. The lender agrees to provide financing above the down payment, on the condition that, upon sale, 20% of the profits go to the lender. The contract further states that if the property has not been sold after 15 years, the appreciation will be due, and will be based on an appraisal at that time. See also *creative financing; equity participation; mortgage.*

Shared Appreciation Mortgage (SAM)

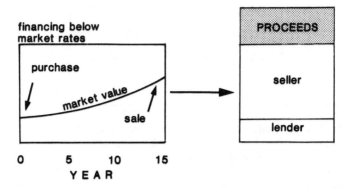

Shared Equity Mortgage (SEM) **(1)** sometimes used to describe a Shared Appreciation Mortgage (SAM). **(2)** a form of purchase involving two or more part owners. Each is responsible for an agreed upon share of the down payment, and is entitled to occupy a portion of the property. They are equally responsible for the full obligation under the terms of the mortgage, however, as the lender will consider this a form of tenancy in common or a joint tenancy. **(3)** a mortgage granted to a buyer, when an investor has supplied a portion of the down payment. That investor is entitled to an agreed upon share of profits upon sale. If a rental property, the agreement should also specify whether or not the investor is entitled to a share of profits from rental income. For example, an individual is buying a rental property, and is required by the lender to make a 20% down payment, but the buyer has only 10%. A relative invests the difference. They agree that the relative will receive 10% of the monthly net operating profit (and will also be responsible for 10% of the loss in case of vacancy); and that, upon sale, the relative will be paid 30% of the net proceeds. See also *creative financing; joint tenancy; mortgage; tenancy in common.*

shares of beneficial interest interests held in a Real Estate Investment Trust (REIT), similar to stock of a corporation. Investors do not own proportionate shares of properties the trust buys, but do own shares in the trust itself. Those shares can be bought and sold on public exchanges, like corporate stock.

Shared Equity Mortgage (SEM)

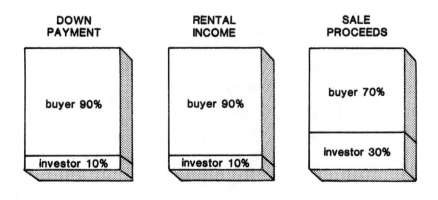

See also *investment program; liquidity; Real Estate Investment Trust (REIT)*.

short-term lease a lease that runs for a relatively short term. In the residential market, short-term is one year or less. Commercial leases are considered short-term if established for periods less than five years. See also *lease; long-term lease*.

short-term loan a loan that is scheduled to be repaid in ten years or less, generally. The exact definition varies by institution, and by the lending policies, limits and purposes of loans. See also *loan; long-term loan*.

silent partner one that has no control over the policies or operation, management, buying or selling of properties. For example, a limited partner is silent in the operation of the partnership. See also *direct participation program; investment program; limited partner*.

simple contract an agreement or contract that is either preliminary to a more complete contract, or one that is entered informally. See also *agreement; binder; contract; meeting of the minds*.

simple interest interest that is not compounded. It is paid based on the principal amount only. For example, 8% simple interest paid on a $100 deposit will be $8.00 per year. See also *compound interest; interest*.

single family dwelling a private residence, designed for occupancy by one family. See also *multiple dwelling; residential property*.

sinking find an accumulation of money, at interest, to be used for future payments on an obligation. Periodic payments are made, calculated to provide an adequate fund at a given rate of interest that will be compounded at a

simple interest

YEAR	8% INTEREST ON $100	
	simple	quarterly compounding
1	$ 8.00	$ 8.24
2	8.00	8.93
3	8.00	9.65
4	8.00	10.46
5	8.00	11.31

specified rate. See also *accumulated value; future value; time value of money.*

Society of Real Estate Appraisers (SREA)   a professional trade association of professional appraisers, that grants the SRA and SREA designations. The society's address is 645 North Michigan Avenue, Chicago, IL 60611. See also *appraiser; Senior Real Estate Analyst (SREA); Senior Residential Appraiser (SRA).*

special agent   an individual given the authority to represent a principal in one, specified matter or activity. For example, a broker is a special agent for the seller, responsible for locating buyers. In comparison, a general agent represents a principal in a range of matters; and a universal agent acts for the principal in all matters. See also *agent; general agent; principal; universal agent.*

special assessment   a levy on real property for the funding of public conveniences, such as lighting, sewers or sidewalks. The assessment is a form of tax lien against each parcel in the area that benefits from the improvement. See also *assessment; improvement; lien; tax lien.*

special hazard insurance   insurance used in mortgage pools, protecting investors against losses not usually included in standard homeowner's policies, related either to property or the security of the debt itself in relation to the level of equity. See also *hazard insurance; mortgage pool; Private Mortgage Insurance (PMI).*

special lien   a term sometimes used to describe a specific lien. See also *specific lien.*

special warranty deed a deed that warrants title only for the period of ownership and not before that time. See also *cloud on the title; deed; title; warranty deed.*

specific lien also called a special lien, one that applies to one property only. For example, a Mechanic's Lien protects a contractor in the event the homeowner does not pay for a completed improvement. See also *collateral; general lien; lien; Mechanic's Lien; special lien; tax lien.*

specific performance fulfillment of the terms of a contract, either exactly as promised or in essence. When one party fails to perform under the agreement, the other will sue. For example, defaulting on a commitment to make monthly mortgage payments will result in a suit for specific performance. See also *part performance; performance; substantial performance; suit for specific performance.*

specified program a form of real estate limited partnership in which the general partners have identified actual properties they intend to purchase. Investors' money will be used only for that specified purpose. In comparison, the more common blind pool program identifies only the general purpose and investment policy of the partnership, but does not identify a location or specific property. See also *blind pool; direct participation program; investment program; limited partnership; risk factor.*

speculation the acceptance of high risks in an attempt to realize substantial profits in the short term. For example, an individual purchases real estate in the belief that it can be resold within one year or less at a profit, anticipating an increase in demand. If right, the speculator will make a fast profit. If wrong, the property might decline in value.

As an investment objective, speculation is a strategy requiring the shortest possible holding period and fast turnaround, with little or no concern for safety. A key element for the speculator is supply and demand. If demand does increase for an asset the speculator holds, while supply is limited, the strategy will be profitable. See also *investment objective; risk factor; safety; supply and demand.*

sponsor the person, persons, or company responsible for organizing a selling group in a limited partnership program. The sponsor also serves as general partner, purchasing, managing and selling properties in behalf of investors, and reporting to them. See also *direct participation program; investment program; limited partnership.*

spread (1) the difference between the asking price of a property, and the final selling price. As a method for judging the condition of the market, a potential buyer or seller can examine the spread in one area for the past one to two years. A growing percentage spread indicates weakness in the market for the seller, while a narrowing percentage indicates improvement in prices and growing demand for properties. For example, average asking prices during the past six months were $95,000, while average sales prices were $89,500. The spread has averaged 5.8% of asking prices. However, one year ago, the average asking *spreading*

price ws $93,000 and the average sale went for $85,000, or a spread of 8.6%. **(2)** for a lending institution, the difference between the rate money earns and the cost of that money. For example, a lender charges an average rate to borrowers of 9.1%. It costs the lender 6% to obtain those funds from depositers and other lenders. The spread is 3.1%. See also *asking price; bid; interest; lending institution.*

spread

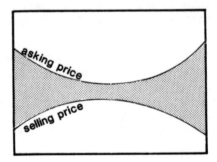

spreading agreement the extension of security for a loan, beyond an original property to other properties owned by the borrower. This reduces the risk for the lending institution, as a greater level of security is attached to the outstanding balance. See also *collateral; lending institution; lien; mortgage; security.*

square-foot method a method of appraising a property based on the cost per square foot of a recently constructed building. The building used must be of comparable quality and use for the method to be valid. That cost is multiplied by the total square feet in the building being appraised. See also *appraisal method; cost approach; replacement cost; reproduction cost.*

staged payment a method of purchasing units in a limited partnership. An initial investment is followed by periodic additions with the amounts and dates of staged payments identified at the time the investor enters the program. This technique is most often seen in private placement programs, when investors might be unwilling or financially unable to commit the entire amount at the start of the program. See also *investor basis; limited partnership; private placement.*

stand-by commitment a promise to lend money. A contractor or developer obtains the commitment from a lender while financing a project with a short-term loan. The stand-by may become permanent mortgage financing in the future, or might serve as a contingent promise, pending a different commitment for a permanent loan. See also *commitment; financing; long-term loan; mortgage; short-term loan.*

staged payment

YEAR	INVESTMENT
initial	$30,000
1	15,000
2	15,000
3	15,000
total	$75,000

standing loan a loan that is not being amortized, pending the location of permanent financing. This occurs when a project has been completed, but a permanent mortgage has not yet been finalized. The standing loan will be repaid in full upon obtaining the permanent mortgage. See also *amortization; bridge loan; gap financing; mortgage.*

statute of frauds a generally accepted policy in law that certain contracts and other instruments must be in writing in order to be enforceable, such as contracts or deeds in real estate. While a buyer and a seller may reach a general agreement or preliminary contract, either verbal or written, the final sale must be in written form. See also *agreement; contract; deed; mortgage; unenforceable contract.*

statutory deed a form of deed in which some of the usual and customary provisions are not written out in full, but are included in abbreviated form. These provisions are implied in a statutory deed, and the document is enforceable to the same degree as one in which the provisions are written out in full. See also *contract; deed.*

statutory lien a lien that derives from statute rather than from a voluntary act of an owner. For example, a tax lien or assessment is applied to all properties in the affected area. See also *equitable lien; involuntary lien; lien; voluntary lien.*

statutory mortgage any mortgage that is in compliance with the laws of the jurisdiction. See also *mortgage.*

steering the illegal act of showing a buyer homes only in a specific area, or directing them away from a neighborhood, on the basis of racial or religious discrimination. Another form of steering involves purposely offering properties

stepped-up

for sale to an individual to pressure other owners to sell, creating potential profits for a speculator. For example, a speculator advises owners that minority families are moving to the area, and states that this will drive market values downward. The speculator offers to purchase their homes at prices below current market value, with the intention of later reselling those properties at a profit. See also *blockbusting; Department of Housing and Urban Development (HUD); Fair Housing Act of 1968.*

stepped-up basis the establishment of a current market value of property for tax purposes. This occurs when a property is inherited or acquired through a tax-free exchange. For example, a home originally costing $28,000 is inherited many years later. At the time of the inheritance, the market value is estimated at $75,000. This becomes the stepped-up basis for income tax purposes. See also *adjusted basis; basis; exchange; market value; tax basis.*

straight lease also called a flat lease, one in which monthly payments are unchanging over the full term of the lease. See also *flat lease; lease; percentage lease; variable lease.*

straight-line depreciation a method of recovering the cost of a capital asset, in which the same amount of depreciation is claimed each year. For example, an investor purchases a rental house for $95,000. The value of land is $27,000, and that portion is not depreciable. However, the balance of $68,000 must be depreciated over 27.5 years. The annual depreciation will be $2,473 ($68,000 divided by 27.5 years). Under current tax rules, real estate must be depreciated on the straight-line basis. Other types of property may be recovered on an accelerated basis, or under an election to use alternative straight-line methods. See also *declining balance depreciation; depreciation; recovery period.*

straight-line depreciation

YEAR	DEPRECIATION	NET BASIS
		$68,000
1	$2,473	65,527
2	2,473	63,054
3	2,473	60,581
4	2,473	58,108
5	2,473	55,635

straight loan a term sometimes used to describe a balloon mortgage. The borrower makes interest only payments over a specified period of time, and the entire balance becomes payable at the end of the term. See also *balloon mortgage; interest only; loan; mortgage.*

subdivision a tract originally owned by one individual or company, that is broken down into parcels, with the intention of building homes and selling the land and improvements in the future. See also *development; land; parcel; tract.*

sublease a lease entered into between an original tenant and another tenant. For example, the landlord signs a lease for 10 years with the primary tenant. Three years later, that tenant moves to larger quarters, and subleases to another tenant for the remaining seven years of the original, or master lease. See also *assignment; lease; master lease; tenant.*

sublease

```
┌──────────┐
│ landlord │──┐
└──────────┘  │
           lease
              │
┌──────────┐  │
│  tenant  │◄─┘
└──────────┘──┐
          sublease
              │
┌──────────┐  │
│  tenant  │◄─┘
└──────────┘
```

subordinated debt a debt that has lower priority than another lien secured by the same property. See also *debt; junior lien.*

subordination the assignment of a lien to junior status of priority. This occurs, for example, when land is sold. In order to facilitate the sale, the original land owner agrees to subordinate the mortgage to a construction loan. See also *junior lien; lien; priority.*

substantial performance virtual satisfaction of the agreed upon terms in a contract. Some minor or technical omissions may remain outstanding; however, the requirements of the contract have been met. See also *part performance; performance; specific performance.*

substitution a theory in valuation, stating that a property's best possible market price will be limited by the market value of other, similar properties. If two similar homes are for sale, the one that is priced lower will be likely to sell first. And the remaining property's market value may be lowered as a result of that sale. See also *anticipation; change; competition; conformity; contribution; diminishing returns; highest and best use; increasing returns; plottage; regression; supply and demand.*

suit for specific performance a suit filed in response to default or another breach of contract, to force performance. See also *breach of contract; default; performance; specific performance.*

suitability descriptive of the attributes of an investor, to judge his or her qualification to invest in a particular program. The concept applies to all investments, but is most often associated with direct participation programs. Suitability refers to sophistication; experience as an investor; total assets or net worth; available cash; and tax bracket.

For example, an individual desiring to buy and sell a large number of properties as a speculator will be judged to be making a suitable investment based on experience in real estate trading; knowledge or sophistication in that field; available cash and other property; and cash available to purchase and pay loans on real estate. Direct participation programs state suitability requirements. For example, a program might state that a suitable investor must possess either $100,000 in liquid assets or total net worth of $250,000. See also *direct participation program; investment objective; net worth; risk factor; tax bracket.*

supply and demand a theory of valuation stating that market prices rise and fall depending upon the current availability of properties, and the need for those properties. For example, there are more buyers in need of homes than there are homes for sale in one area. Prices will rise in response to the demand. And when an excess of properties is available, prices will fall in response to a limit in the demand. See also *anticipation; change; competition; conformity; contribution; diminishing returns; highest and best use; increasing returns; plottage; regression; substitution.*

supply and demand

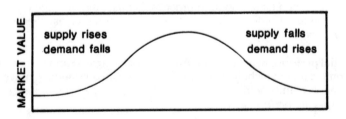

surrender of lease   an agreement between a landlord and a tenant to end a lease prior to the scheduled term. The tenant is released from further obligation, and the landlord is free to lease to another individual, or to dispose of the property. See also *lease; tenant; voidable contract.*

survey   the measurement of land in order to identify exact bounds, often undertaken in anticipation of a sale. See also *bounds; legal description; metes and bounds description.*

survey fee   the fee charged for completion of a survey, at the time of closing. See also *bounds; closing costs.*

swap program   (1) the payment of shares in a program, in lieu of cash. Several construction REIT programs used this technique to satisfy debts between 1972 and 1974, when cash was not available to pay mortgages and other obligations. (2) a form of limited partnership allowing investors to trade their shares for interests in different programs offered by the same general partner. At the time of exchange, profits on the prior program are taxable to the investor, as the two transactions are considered as separate investments. See also *investment program; limited partnership; Real Estate Investment Trust (REIT); tax basis.*

sweat equity   that portion of equity in a property that derives from the owner's own efforts. For example, a homeowner constructs an addition that adds market value, or renovates a run-down home to marketable condition. See also *equity build-up; market value; value.*

syndicate   also called an underwriter, a company or collective grouping of companies that agrees to purchase the units in a limited partnership for resale to investors. A selling group is formed among securities broker-dealers, and units are then offered to investors through sales representatives. See also *direct participation program; investment program; limited partnership.* [See overleaf.]

T

take-out commitment   a promise by a lender to provide financing, usually to a developer who is underway on a project. The actual permanent mortgage may later be placed with the lender providing the commitment, or with another lender. See also *commitment; lending institution; stand-by commitment.*

tangible property   assets with physical form such as land and improvements (real property) or furniture and appliances (personal property). See also *intangible asset; personal property; property; real property.*

tax basis   (1) for income tax purposes, the amount of income or the value of assets on which a tax liability is based. For example, an individual sells a security for $2,000, or a profit of $1,200. The basis in that security was the original cost, $800. (2) in the sale or exchange of real estate, the original purchase

syndicate

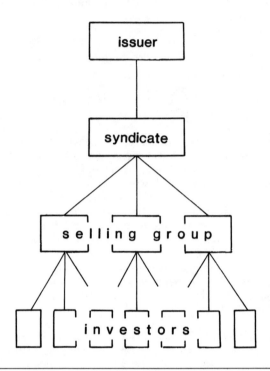

price, plus closing costs and improvements, and less allowable depreciation. **(3)** the assessed valuation of real estate, for the purpose of computing local or state property taxes. See also *adjusted tax basis; assessed valuation; basis; capital gain/loss; income tax; property taxes; stepped-up basis.*

tax bracket the range of taxable income on which a given rate of income tax is due. For example, a married couple earning less than $29,751 per year is said to be in the 15% bracket (federal taxes, 1988 rates). All taxable income above that level falls into the next bracket. See also *after-tax profit; income tax; marginal tax rate.*

tax deduction an expense that can be claimed on a business or individual tax return, to reduce gross income. For example, an individual runs a business and is self-employed. He may reduce gross income for salaries and wages, office supplies, travel, utilities, and all other ordinary, reasonable and necessary business expenses. However, capital assets must be depreciated over a number of years, and cannot be deducted in the year purchased.

Individuals may claim itemized deductions to reduce adjusted gross income, as part of the process of arriving at taxable income (income is also reduced by allowances for personal exemptions). An investor is allowed to claim

tax bracket

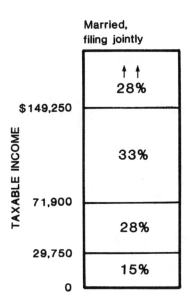

deductions for all expenses incurred in that connection. A real estate investor can claim deductions for property taxes, mortgage interest, advertising, maintenance, insurance, and other usual expenses. See also *income tax; net income.*

tax deferred the status of income on which taxes are not paid until a later date. For example, earnings in qualified retirement plans are not taxed until money is withdrawn. In the case of real estate, gains on a sale are deferred on a principal residence when a new house is built or purchased within two years from the date of sale. See also *basis; deferred gain; exchange; principal residence.*

Tax Equity and Fiscal Responsibility Act of 1982 (TEFRA) a federal tax law that reduced the advantages of investing in tax shelter programs. The law established a system of penalties for false or misleading statements or claims made by promoters or sponsors regarding the tax benefits of investing in their programs. See also *direct participation program; limited partnership; sponsor; tax shelter.*

Tax-Exempt Investor Program (TEIP) a form of limited partnership especially suited for individual retirement accounts and other structures under which taxes are deferred. Such programs emphasize income rather than current tax benefits. For example, a partnership may be structured to avoid leverage or the purchase of highly depreciable property, as interest and depreciation expenses are not advantageous in a tax deferral situation. See also *investment program; limited partnership; Real Estate Limited Partnership (RELP).*

tax 172

tax lien a lien imposed on property by state or local governments, to raise revenues through property taxes. This form of lien has priority over all other liens in most instances. See also *involuntary lien; lien; priority; property taxes; senior lien; statutory lien.*

tax participation a clause included in a lease that specifies the tenant will be responsible for higher monthly payments when property taxes are increased during the lease term. See also *graduated lease; lease; property taxes; tenant; variable lease.*

Tax Reform Act of 1969 a federal tax law that established rules for minimum tax, and that set standards for recapture of depreciation expenses. See also *Alternative Minimum Tax (AMT); depreciation; investor basis.*

Tax Reform Act of 1976 a federal law that set limitations of losses, and introduced the concept of at risk. With certain exceptions (notably for real estate programs), investors could claim losses only to the extent of their cash and recourse investment basis. See also *at risk; investor basis; limited partnership; recourse loan; tax shelter.*

Tax Reform Act of 1978 a federal law that modified rules for investors in tax shelter programs. At risk rules were tightened, but real estate programs were excluded from many of the restrictive provisions. See also *at risk; investor basis; limited partnership; tax shelter.*

Tax Reform of 1984 a federal tax law that changed the rules for depreciation and capital gains, and introduced new reporting rules for tax shelters. See also *capital gain/loss; depreciation; tax shelter.*

Tax Reform Act of 1986 a federal tax law that changed individual and corporate tax rates and brackets; eliminated favorable tax treatment for long-term capital gains; and eliminated the tax advantages of investing for passive losses. See also *capital gain/loss; investor basis; passive income; tax bracket.*

tax service fee a charge assessed either at closing in a real estate transaction, or by a lending institution, for the collection and payment of property taxes. See also *closing costs; lending institution; property taxes.*

tax shelter (1) a program that legally defers taxes on income, or a strategy of tax avoidance that reduces the amount of current tax liability. An individual retirement account or a Keogh plan are examples of legal tax shelters. (2) a program, especially a limited partnership, that is designed to emphasize tax advantages to investors as a primary goal, with economic benefits either secondary or nonexistent. (3) a term generally used to describe all limited partnerships, due to the widespread identification of many such programs with tax abuse during the 1970's and early 1980's. See also *direct participation program; income tax; limited partnership; tax basis.*

teaser an unusually low rate offered by lending institutions. To promote Adjustable Rate Mortgage (ARM) selection, the institution advertises the rate (also called the 'today rate'). However, it is removed six to 24 months later, and replaced with a higher rate that more closely resembles the current market rate. See also *Adjustable Rate Mortgage (ARM); financing; interest; today rate.*

teaser

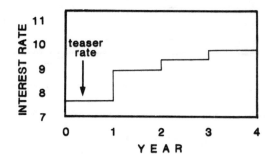

tenancy at sufferance the condition that is created when a tenant remains in possession of property after expiration of the lease. See also *holdover tenant; lease; possession; right of possession.*

tenancy at will a periodic tenancy, in which the agreement is renewed on a month to month basis but can be terminated or changed by mutual agreement at any time. See also *month to month; periodic tenancy; right of possession.*

tenancy by the entirety an estate held jointly by husband and wife. A feature of this form of ownership is unity of possession. In the event of the death of one individual, all rights pass to the survivor. See also *joint tenancy; right of survivorship; unity of ownership.*

tenancy in common an undivided interest in property, when two or more individuals own a property together. The property cannot be subdivided or specific parts identified as belonging to one or the owner. See also *joint tenancy; right of survivorship; undivided interest; unity of ownership.*

tenancy in severalty sole ownership of property and property rights, by an individual or organization. See also *legal owner; right of possession.*

tenant an individual occupying real property under a rental or lease contract. See also *lease; right of occupancy.*

term mortgage a mortgage calling for regular payments of interest only, with the entire balance due at the end of a specified term, usually granted for a limited number of years. See also *balloon mortgage; interest only; mortgage.* [See overleaf.]

term mortgage

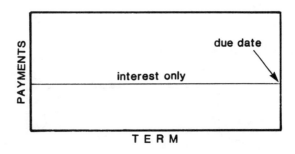

termite inspection a service provided to homeowners to discover the presence of subterranean termites and other destructive pests. The inspection is required in most jurisdictions at the time a home is offered for sale, and is usually paid for by the seller. Most states require the report as a means for disclosing potential problems, and the inspection should be called for in a real estate contract. Property owners should contract for termite inspections periodically to prevent extensive damage over time. The U.S. Department of Agriculture estimates that $250 million is spent each year for pest control, one-third for damage repairs and two-thirds for chemical treatment. Infestation is especially common in the southeast, moderate in the central area, and lower in the northernmost states and Canada. Besides the subterranean termite, other pests can cause damage to wood-constructed homes, and will be included in a termite inspection. Other pests include drywood termites, powder-post beetles and carpenter ants. See also *full disclosure; inspection clause.*

third party an individual involved in a contract, other than the buyer and seller. For example, a broker is a third party in a real estate contract. See also *broker; contract; principal.*

3-day cancellation notice a notice given to the homeowner when a home improvement contract is signed, advising that the agreement can be cancelled within three working days without obligation. See also *contract; improvement; voidable contract.*

time share a part ownership in property. The arrangement is popular for vacation homes. For example, an individual purchases a one-week interest in a vacation home. He is entitled to occupy that home for one week of the year. A time share interest could be difficult to sell. The owner must locate another owner interested in acquiring a larger interest in the property, or locate an outside buyer. See also *multiple dwelling; right of possession; unity of ownership.*

time value of money reference to the way that money will accumulate over time when interest is compounded. For example, a $1,000 deposit will grow to

$10,892.50 in 20 years when interest is compounded monthly. In comparison, when interest is 6%, the same deposit will grow to only $3,310.20. The lower rate of interest produces a lower time value. See also *compound interest; future value; interest; present value.*

time value of money

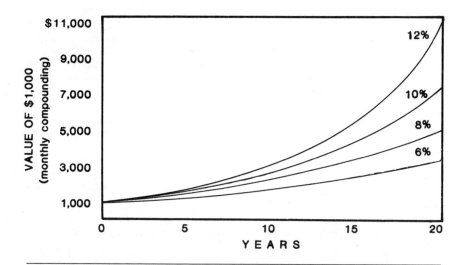

title the lawful ownership of real property, or evidence of clear and legal ownership. See also *allodial system; clear title; evidence of title; legal title; right of possession.*

title company an insurance company that grants title insurance on real property. This protects the owner against any undiscovered encumbrances on that property that existed before the date of purchase. In the event that a lien was recorded and not discovered by the title company, the lien will be paid as a claim of the policy. See also *abstract of title; clear title; cloud on the title.*

title insurance binder a form of temporary title insurance, issued near to the actual closing date. It protects the new owner immediately, and will be replaced by a permanent policy after closing. The title insurance company performs a final investigation to ensure that no liens were placed on the property immediately prior to closing. See also *binder; closing date; settlement.*

title insurance policy a form of protection for either the homeowner or the lender. The company investigates all recordings related to the property, and identifies all liens and encumbrances in existence. The title search may uncover unknown encumbrances. In the event a lien exists that was filed prior to the

title 176

conveyance of title, and the title insurance company did not discover it, the lien will be paid by the company. This policy remains in effect for the entire duration of ownership. See also *chain of title; defective title; encumbrance; risk factor.*

title plant the accumulated information on all properties in a given area, owned by a title insurance company. All liens, encumbrances, mortgages, and reconveyances recorded are listed in the plant in order of properties. The plant serves as a record of the chain of title, for the purpose of issuing an abstract of title and title insurance policy. The insurer risks missing a filed lien, in which case a policy will be issued ensuring clear title. In that instance, the title company will be liable for satisfaction of the undiscovered lien. See also *chain of title; encumbrance; lien; mortgage; real property; recording.*

title report a report completed by the title insurance company, reporting on the status of title to a specific property. Any outstanding liens or defects in title will be pointed out in the report. See also *abstract of title; clear title; defective title; encumbrance; legal title.*

title search an investigation of the status of title and related liens on properties. It is undertaken by a title company or, in some states, by an attorney. See also *color of title; encumbrance; legal title; real property.*

title theory the theory followed in some states that a mortgage holder is the legal owner of property, and remains so until the obligation has been eliminated. In a title theory state, the lender may take possession in cases of default. In lien theory states, possession can come about not by right, but by either a court order or by specific contractual provisions. See also *default; lien theory; mortgage; real property; right of possession.*

today rate also called the teaser, the initial rate of interest charged on an Adjustable Rate Mortgage (ARM). Its purpose is to attract buyers and make the ARM appear more desirable than the rates charged by competitors. However, the rate is removed within six to 24 months, and replaced by a much higher rate. See also *Adjustable Rate Mortgage (ARM); interest; rate cap; teaser.*

Torrens certificate a document stating the condition of title, without the need for a more extensive title search. The certificate is issued by a court, after publishing a notice and deadline for all claimants that might hold liens. After the deadline, any discovered liens are dismissed. See also *clear title; encumbrance; title search.*

total return a computation of the rate of return on an investment, including net income during the holding period, gain upon sale, and any tax savings resulting from ownership. For example, an individual earns $29,600 upon sale, after holding a property for 7 years; had $18,400 in net profits from rental income; and reduced income taxes by $6,000 during the holding period. If the property originally cost $125,000, the total return is 43.2%. The average annual total return (total return divided by the 7-year holding period) is 6.2%. See also *after-tax profit; capital gain/loss; Internal Rate of Return (IRR); net income; tax basis; yield.*

total return

sales price	$154,600
purchase price	125,000
capital gain	$ 29,600
net rental income	18,400
tax benefits	6,000
total profit	$ 54,000
total return	43.2%
years held	7
annual return	6.2%

townhouse an apartment, condominium or individually owned unit containing two or more stories. The unit is attached on one or both sides to other townhouses, sharing a common wall. See also *apartment; condominium; multiple dwelling; Planned Unit Development (PUD)*.

track record the historical performance of the limited partners in a direct participation program. The track record is often included in the prospectus and in sales literature to convince new investors to purchase interests.

A track record showing consistent high returns to investors is one method for evaluating and comparing one program to another, and for choosing experienced management. However, the track record can also be deceiving, for a number of reasons:

— If the record was achieved in unrelated programs, the record does not indicate how well the same individuals will be able to perform in real estate.

— If the track record occurred during a period of growing values in real estate, and the future will be recessionary, the investor has no way to tell how well management will perform.

— High returns might have been achieved by selling existing interests to investors in subsequent programs, and for inflated values. Thus, the track record is manufactured and does not indicate good management skills.

— Prior programs still in existence might be evaluated based on an appraisal that is not entirely independent. In that case, the track record is distorted. See also *direct participation program; expected return; historical yield; investment program; limited partnership; risk factor*.

tract an area of land intended for subdivision into lots for future home sites, or the description of a completed residential development. See also *land; parcel; subdivision*.

tract house   a home in a tract, built on a floor plan that is identical or similar to the other homes in the same tract. See also *residential property; subdivision*.

transfer clause   a conditional provision in a lease contract allowing the tenant to cancel the agreement in the event of transfer to another location. The provision might specify that in order to take effect, the transfer must be for a specified number of miles away from the property under lease; and that notice of 30 days or more must be given to the owner. See also *cancellation; escape clause; lease; voidable contract*.

transfer fee   a charge assessed against the buyer, seller, or both, by a lending institution, for transferring a mortgage at the time of sale. See also *closing costs; lending institution*.

transfer tax   a tax imposed on property at the time of sale, exchange or inheritance, usually included as a closing cost and payable at settlement. See also *closing costs; settlement*.

triple net lease   also called net net net lease, a form of agreement in which the tenant is responsible for payment of all expenses, including maintenance, insurance, and property taxes, in addition to the payment of monthly rent. See also *lease; net lease; tenant; variable lease*.

triplex   a three-unit home or apartment building, sharing common walls. See also *apartment; duplex; multiple dwelling*.

true value   the estimated Fair Market Value (FMV) of property that can be realized when the seller is willing to sell within a reasonable period of time. See also *Fair Market Value (FMV); market value*.

trust deed   alternate term for a deed of trust, an instrument that creates a lien, used instead of a mortgage in some states. See also *deed of trust; mortgage*.

turnover   the amount of time, on average, for a single property to be sold; for mortgages to be paid off or replaced; for the sale of a number of properties in one area; or for occupancy by tenants in a lease agreement. See also *lease; mortgage; real estate cycle; supply and demand*.

20-day notice   a provision in a contract for a home improvement, stipulating that the contractor must begin work within 20 days. Failure to comply is a violation of contractor licensing regulations in some states, and serves as a means for preventing delay. See also *contract; improvement; performance*.

U

unbalanced improvement   the status of land that is either over-improved or under-improved. The land is not being utilized to its highest and best use, and has too much or too little invested in it to produce what would otherwise be a reasonable level of income or, upon sale, of profit. See also *highest and best use; improvement; over-improvement; under-improvement.*

unconditional lien release a release signed by a contractor, releasing the homeowner from all future liabilities that might arise due to nonpayment of subcontractors or suppliers. For example, a contractor is paid in full for work performed, but fails to compensate a subcontractor. The unpaid person can exercise a lien on the homeowner's property to force payment. The unconditional lien release places the liability back on the contractor. See also *improvement; lien release; Mechanic's Lien.*

under-improvement a failure to maximize the potential of a property, or to invest funds to put that property to its highest and best use. This will hold down market value and inhibit appreciation. It may also hold back the potential appreciation of other, similar properties in the same area. See also *highest and best use; improvement; over-improvement.*

undivided interest a proportionate interest in real property that cannot be specifically identified or separated from the rights of fellow owners. For example, the owner of a condominium has an undivided interest in common elements of the development. The owner may not claim a specific portion of those elements as being individually owned or possessed. See also *common elements; condominium; cooperative housing; interest; partition; right of possession.*

unearned increment the increase in market value of property due to conditions beyond the owner's direct efforts. For example, property values rise in a neighborhood because demand has grown and the supply of housing has decreased. See also *earned increment; market value; supply and demand.*

unencumbered property real estate that is completely free and clear of any liens or mortgages, assessments, or unpaid encumbrances of any kind. See also *clear title; encumbrance; free and clear; title.*

unenforceable contract a contract that is outside of the law, or that contains elements making it invalid. For example, it may contain unequal consideration; it may be of a nature requiring a written document, but the contract was entered orally; or one of the parties is a minor or is otherwise not legally able to enter a binding contract. See also *consideration; contract; performance; void contract.*

Uniform Limited Partnership Act (ULPA) a law intended to oversee the formation, structure and practices of limited partnerships. See also *direct participation program; investment program; limited partnership.*

Uniform Partnership Act (UPA) a law that defines the qualifications of businesses operating as general partnerships. The law specifies the standards of operation and reporting for such businesses. See also *general partnership; partnership; tax basis.*

uniform

uniform settlement statement a statement that summarizes and discloses all transactions of money at settlement in a real estate sale, both for the buyer and the seller. The standardized form is a requirement on all transactions financed by lenders that are federally regulated. The statement identifies the buyer, seller and lender; the purchase price, prorations, down payment, and net amount due from the buyer; the selling price, closing costs, outstanding mortgages and liens, and net amount payable to the seller; and all closing costs due from buyer and seller at settlement. See also *closing costs; Department of Housing and Urban Development (HUD); lending institution; proration; Real Estate Settlement Procedures Act (RESPA); settlement.*

unilateral contract a form of contingent contract, in which a specific offer to perform is made by one party. It becomes a legal contract only if the second party responds by agreeing to perform; however, the unilateral contract does not obligate nor bind the second party.

For example, one individual signs an offer to purchase and submits it to the seller. The seller may enter into a binding contract by agreeing to the terms offered; may make a counter-offer with modified terms; or may reject the unilateral contract without response.

In comparison, a bilateral contract is one in which both sides are bound by mutual agreement. The distinction is in having reached a meeting of the minds. A unilateral contract lacks this element until the second party agrees to stated terms. See also *bilateral contract; contract; counter-offer; letter of intent; meeting of the minds; offer to purchase; performance.*

unilateral listing an open listing, one in which no one broker has the exclusive right to show the property or solicit offers. In this arrangement, the broker is not specifically obligated to take any special measures to advertise the availability of the property. See also *commission; Multiple Listing Service (MLS); open listing.*

unimproved property raw land, property that does not involve any structures, utilities or other forms of improvement. See also *improved land; land; raw land.*

uninsurable title descriptive of title in such condition that a title insurance company is unwilling to underwrite the risk. Either a cloud on the title makes it an unacceptable risk, or uncertainties about encumbrances against the property bring the identification of legal ownership into question. See also *cloud on the title; defective title; title.*

unit **(1)** an apartment or singularly owned condominium or cooperative in a building with multiple and separate divisions of living space. **(2)** ownership in a limited partnership, the equivalent of shares in a corporation. The total of outstanding units represents limited partners' equity positions in the program. See also *apartment; condominium; cooperative housing; direct participation program; equity; investment program; limited partnership; multiple dwelling.*

unit-in-place method an appraisal method involving estimates of the reproduction cost, not of the entire structure, but of its individual components. See also *appraisal method; cost approach; reproduction cost.*

unit value ratio a method of estimating total value of a condominium or cooperative unit, based on a comparison between the initial appraised value of an individual unit, and the value of the entire development. For example, a condominium unit is for sale. The approximate value of the entire complex is already known. To arrive at the current market value of the unit, the original cost of $85,000 is divided by the original value of the development, which was $1,450,000. The result is 5.9%. The appraiser will use the unit value ratio to assume that the total value of the unit should include 5.9% of common elements. See also *appraised value; common elements; condominium; cooperative housing; market value.*

unit value ratio

$$\frac{\text{appraised unit value}}{\text{appraised value of all units}}$$

$$\frac{\$85,000}{\$1,450,000} = 5.9\%$$

unity of ownership the status of a joint tenancy in property. The total value belongs to both individual owners in whole, and rights to tangible and identified areas cannot be divided between them. For example, a husband and wife own a home in joint tenancy. Each has full rights and obligations as an owner. And in the event of the death of either, the surviving spouse will become sole owner. See also *joint tenancy; right of survivorship; tenancy in common.*

unity of possession the shared right in a tenancy in common. Neither of the owners has a distinguishable seniority of rights; the possession is indivisible except through disposal of the property. See also *joint tenancy; right of possession; tenancy in common.*

universal agent an agent who has the right to represent a principal in all matters. This agent is distinguished from a general agent, who has the right to act in behalf of the principal only in a defined range of matters; and from a special agent, who can act for the principal only in one, specified contract or other transaction. See also *agent; general agent; power of attorney; principal; special agent.*

Unrelated Business Income (UBI) for tax purposes, income derived from any activity that is not the primary, intended purpose of the program or business organization. For example, an investor purchases units in a real estate partnership. During the first year, uninvested funds are placed into an interest-bearing account. The primary purpose of the program is to purchase, manage and sell real estate. Interest income is unrelated to that purpose.

UBI from a program designed to provide tax-free or tax-deferred income may be deemed taxable to the investor in the year earned. See also *direct participation program; investment program; limited partnership; tax basis.*

use density   the ratio of land that can be improved, compared to total square feet of land. For example, a developer plans to construct 10 homes on 33,000 acres of land. Local zoning laws specify that no less than 12% of the total land area must be left for open space. The developer plans homes that will build up to 28,500 square feet, or 86.4% of the total. See also *area; density; subdivision; zoning.*

use density

$$\frac{\text{allowable square feet}}{\text{total square feet}}$$

$$\frac{28{,}500}{33{,}000} = 86.4\%$$

use value   a factor in developing the appraised value of property, that allows for the use to which a building is put. For example, a large house is located in an area where zoning allows conversion of homes to rental units. The home could be improved and broken up into several units, increasing its market value by generating income. However, the owner wants to preserve the house as a single family residence. That use value factor will affect the estimated market value. See also *appraised value; highest and best use; market value; value.*

useful life   **(1)** the number of years that a specific property will serve its intended purpose, given the factors of physical depreciation. **(2)** a concept in tax law prior to 1981, when assets were depreciated over a useful life, which was an estimate of the economic life of that property. The determination of a reasonable useful life was used as the basis for a depreciation period. Under current methods, the useful life concept has been replaced by the establishment of uniform recovery periods. See also *depreciation; economic life; physical life; recovery period.*

usury the practice of charging a rate of interest that exceeds limits set by law. Depending upon the state where a loan is granted, the degree of usury, and the scope of violations, lenders charging usurious rates may be allowed to continue collecting interest, but only to the level of a legal rate; they may lose the right to collect interest on the loan; or they may be barred from recovering any portion of the outstanding loan. See also *interest rate; legal rate; lending institution*.

V

VA mortgage a mortgage guaranteed by the Veteran's Administration (VA). The loan is granted by a conventional lending institution, with the guarantee of repayment an added feature. See also *conventional loan; lending institution; mortgage; Veteran's Administration (VA)*.

vacancy rate **(1)** the degree of vacancies in a rental property, measured by the number of units that are unoccupied. For example, a building with 84 units has eight vacancies. The vacancy rate is 9.5%. **(2)** the degree of vacancies measured in the lost income from vacant units, compared to total potential income in the property. In an apartment containing 84 units, eight vacancies account for a higher average rent than the property generates. Those vacancies account for rental income of $5,350, while total potential income is $42,800. In this example, the vacancy rate is 12.5%. **(3)** vacancies as measured by the amount of time a rental property is not occupied. For example, an investor purchases a home and rents it out. During the first year, it is vacant for two of 12 months. The vacancy rate is 16.7%. See also *cash flow; gross income; occupancy rate*. [See overleaf.]

vacant land raw land, in its natural state and without any improvements. See also *raw land*.

valid contract a contract that is both lawful and enforceable. See also *consideration; contract; performance*.

valuation **(1)** the estimated market value of property, developed during an appraisal. **(2)** an estimate of value for the purpose of calculating an assessment or property tax. See also *appraised value; assessed valuation; market value*.

value the monetary worth of property under present market conditions. Value varies with supply and demand and the economic state of the market. See also *Fair Market Value (FMV); market value; supply and demand*.

variable lease a lease including a provision for increases in monthly rent payments. The increase is calculated on the basis of correspondingly higher expenses of the property, inflation, or on an agreed upon schedule.

For example, a lease specifies that monthly payments will change according to increases in property taxes on the property. Another lease is scheduled to change in accordance with movements in the Consumer Price Index. And another includes a schedule for specific increases every three years during a 15-year lease term.

vacancy rate

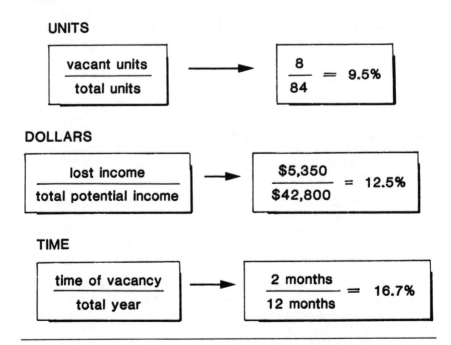

A percentage lease is a variable form used in retail location leases, calling for payments above a base rent based on the level of gross income. See also *base rent; ground lease; lease; net lease; percentage lease.*

Variable Rate Mortgage (VRM) a mortgage in which the interest rate is changed periodically, in accordance with movements in an outside index of inflation or interest costs. This loan, also known as an Adjustable Rate Mortgage (ARM) or Flexible Rate Mortgage (FRM), usually includes provisions for either a rate or payment cap. Rate caps limit the increase in the rate of interest per period and for the entire loan term. A payment cap limits the amount of monthly payment that will be made. See also *Adjustable Rate Mortgage (ARM); Flexible Rate Mortgage (FRM); interest; mortgage; payment cap; rate cap.*

variance an exception made to prevailing zoning regulations. The variance must be requested, and is granted when the current rules create a hardship or when compliance is not possible. See also *zoning.*

verbal contract a contract entered into without an accompanying written summary. Such a contract is legal and enforceable, although specific terms of the agreement will be difficult to prove in case of a dispute. A written contract documents the intended terms and can establish a meeting of the minds; a verbal contract depends upon the memories of both parties only. Certain types of transactions, such as the conveyance of real estate, must be contracted in written form in order to be valid. See also *agreement; contract; meeting of the minds; sale contract; statute of frauds.*

Veteran's Administration (VA) a federal government agency formed in 1930 to administer benefits granted to veterans and their families. The VA guarantees mortgage loans for qualified individuals, made through a conventional lending institution. The VA's address is 810 Vermont Avenue, Washington, DC 20420. See also *conventional loan; lending institution; VA mortgage.*

visual rights the rights to a view, or to prevent construction that will obstruct that view. See also *aesthetic value; air rights; zoning.*

void contract a contract lacking elements required by law, including consideration and a meeting of the minds of both parties. A contract is also void when one or both parties cannot legally be bound by the agreement. See also *agreement; consideration; contract; meeting of the minds; unenforceable contract.*

voidable contract a contract that can be nullified by one or both parties. The contract remains in effect as long as both individuals agree to continue its terms. A minor may void a contract at will except for certain necessities of life. Or the voidability may be built into a contract itself by way of an escape clause or contingencies. See also *agreement; contingency; contract; escape clause.*

voluntary alienation the disposal of property by sale, gift or surrender. The conveyance is made by actions of the owner. In comparison, an involuntary alienation occurs when property is taken from the owner due to default, or by condemnation. See also *alienation; conveyance; involuntary alienation.*

voluntary conveyance a surrender of title, made by the owner to a lender or other lien holder. This action releases the owner from the obligation and avoids the foreclosure process when default is otherwise unavoidable. See also *conveyance; foreclosure; title.*

voluntary lien a lien created by the owner's action, such as the commitment to a mortgage, a home improvement loan, a home equity loan, or another form of lien. An involuntary lien arises without any action by the owner. For example, a tax lien is created from the authority of a state or local government to assess and collect property taxes. See also *equitable lien; involuntary lien; lien; statutory lien.*

W

want of consideration the absence of consideration in a contract, or the failure to perform as promised and agreed. See also *consideration; contract; performance.*

warranty deed a deed fully warranted by the grantor, ensuring clear title and promising to defend that title against any encumbrance that might exist at the time of transfer. See also *clear title; deed; good title; quiet enjoyment; special warranty deed.*

wasting property a type of property that may be depleted over time, so that value diminishes. For example, mineral or timber value declines as resources are removed from the land. See also *depletion; depreciation; land; value.*

weighted average the total rate being paid when two or more loans are outstanding. When loan balances are not identical, the true average will be closer to the rate of the higher balance loan. For example, a homeowner has two mortgages. One is for $70,000, and carries a rate of 11%. The other is for $30,000, with a rate of 9%. The average rate being paid is 10% (11% plus 9%, divided by 2). However, because the balances are different, the average must be weighted. Compute the balances of the loans as a fraction of the total debt, and multiply by the interest rates:

a) $70,000/$100,000 × 11% = 7.7%
b) $30,000/$100,000 × 9% = 2.7%
c) 7.7% + 2.7% = 10.4% weighted average

The computation of the total rate is important when refinancing is being considered. For example, the homeowner paying on two mortgages must determine the weighted average to decide whether the offered refinance rate is lower than the current cost of the loans. See also *debt service; interest averaging; refinancing.*

weighted average

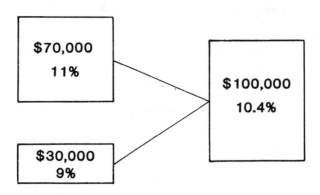

Women's Council of Realtors (WCR) an organization affiliated with the National Association of Realtors (NAR), for women who are realtors. Their address is 430 North Michigan Avenue, Chicago, IL 60611. See also *National Assocation of Realtors (NAR); realtor.*

work out an agreement reached between a lending institution and a borrower to modify the terms of an existing loan. This occurs when there is a possibility of default under the original terms, and both parties wish to avoid a foreclosure. Work out may take one of several forms. The interest rate and required payment can be lowered temporarily or permanently; the repayment schedule can be revised and lengthened, also resulting in lower payments; or the payments can be suspended for an agreed period of time. See also *debt service; default; foreclosure; lending institution.*

working capital the difference between current assets and current liabilities, calculated as a measure of cash flow for an individual or company. Current assets include cash and assets that are convertible to cash within one year or less. And current liabilities are debts payable within one year (incuding 12 months' payments due on a mortgage or other long-term debt). For example, an investor has current assets valued at $42,650 and current liabilities of $19,310. His working capital is the difference, or $23,340. See also *cash flow; liquidity.*

working capital

```
  current assets
− current liabilities
= working capital
```

```
    $42,650
−   $19,310
=   $23,340
```

wraparound an arrangement for financing a purchase, by combining an existing loan with a new loan. The lending institution granting the new loan collects the total payment, and agrees to make payments due on the original loan. The new loan is junior in priority to the existing one. The arrangement enables the buyer to make a single payment, and the new lender often earns a profit in the difference between rates of the two loans. See also *junior mortgage; lending institution; loan; mortgage.*

Y

year to year a periodic tenancy in which the terms of the agreement are extended annually. This is similar to a month to month arrangement, with the distinction usually being the frequency of payments. For example, an agreement calls for annual rent payments. Once the rent is paid, the tenant has the right to occupy the premises for the full year. The agreement may be cancelled at the end of the year, or extended through mutual agreement. See also *month to month; periodic tenancy; right of occupancy.*

yield the return on an investment, usually computed by dividing annual net income by the original cost or amount invested. For example, an individual purchases a rental property for $150,000, and earns a net profit of $14,600 the first year. The yield is 9.7%. See also *interest; investment income; net income; rate of return; return on equity.*

yield

$$\frac{\text{annual net income}}{\text{cost}}$$

$$\frac{\$14,600}{\$150,000} = 9.7\%$$

Yield to Average Life (YAL) the estimated compound interest an investor will earn in a GNMA mortgage pool, assuming all income is reinvested. This calculation is useful when comparing one investment program to another. See also *compound interest; Ginnie Mae pass-through; Government National Mortgage Association (GNMA); investor basis; mortgage pool.*

Yield To Maturity (YTM) the total rate of return on an investment, considering current income plus capital gains. For example, a real estate investor realizes approximately 8% per year in net rental income. But after 10 years, the property is sold at a substantial gain. The combined profit, divided by the number of years held, is the total yield to maturity. The yield is also adjusted to allow for the holding period and timing of gains, so that an exact calculation considers the time value of money. See also *interest; Internal Rate of Return (IRR); rate of return; return on equity; time value of money.*

Z

Zero Rate Mortgage (ZRM) a form of mortgage calling for a one-time payment of interest or a finance charge, accompanied by a substantial down payment. Following this, principal-only payments are made over a short term. For example, a home is valued at $110,000. The buyer makes a down payment of $60,000 and pays a one-time finance charge of $5,000. The balance of $50,000 is repaid in five annual installments of $10,000 each. See also *creative financing; down payment; mortgage.*

zoning the rules in effect in one area for the nature of property that can be constructed and the use or limits on use. For example, industrial activities cannot be undertaken in residential areas. Zoning controls traffic, noise, hazards, safety and density. See also *commercial property; density; real property; residential property; use density; variance.*

zoning map the division of a city, county or other areas into zones. Each type of zone is reserved for specific uses, such as residential, commercial or industrial. See also *density; use density.*

Checklists

Neighborhood Checklist

Neighborhoods should be evaluated before a home is purchased. Sellers or agents should have answers ready for buyers in the following subjects:

Area services
- maintenance of public facilities
- social service outlets
- volunteer programs

Child care
- availability
- reputation

Churches
- availability
- location

Climate
- average highs, lows
- droughts
- extremes

Crime
- area safety
- neighborhood watch programs
- statistics and trends

Cultural facilities
- location
- museums, libraries, theater

Employment
- opportunities
- trends
- volume

Fire service
- distance
- fire statistics
- quality

Hazards
- industrial sites
- pollution

Health care
- distance
- hospitals and doctors
- insurance coverages accepted
- paramedic service

Home maintenance level
- care other homeowners take
- level of on-going improvements
- quality in the area

Noise level
- airport or train facilities
- traffic noise level

Other residents
- children
- family ages
- neighborhood associations

Parking
- convenience
- restrictions
- street parking

Planning
- buffers to commercial areas
- future plans
- moratoriums
- street arrangements
- zoning mixture

Police and sheriff
- community involvement
- location of stations
- neighborhood patrols
- reputation

Privacy
- arrangement of homes
- neighborhood landscaping
- size of lots

Recreation
- location
- number of outlets
- quality

Sales statistics
- homes for sale in area
- months on the market
- swing (asking to sales price)
- trends over two years

Schools
- location
- quality
- transportation provided

Shopping
- location
- shopping centers

Street lighting
- adequacy
- future plans

Terrain
- effects of weather
- flooding
- land grading
- planning
- slides or erosion

Traffic
- commute conditions
- level
- trends

Transportation
- cost
- distance to work
- public systems
- quality

Utilities
- refuse collection
- water quality

Zoning
- classifications (zoning map)
- enforcement
- special assessments

Home Inspection Checklist

Buyers should inspect homes inside and out to determine condition and identify any defects. Some aspects of this inspection, particularly systems behind the wall (plumbing and electrical, for example) may require the advice of a contractor or other expert. An independent home inspection can be required as a contingency in an offer, or the buyer can pay to have a complete inspection performed.

The following list summarizes the major parts of the house that should be inspected. The buyer should find out the last time a system or component was replaced or repaired, and should determine the current condition.

Air conditioning system
- age
- capacity
- condition
- cost of use
- noise level

- warranty

Appliances
- age
- maintenance record

Real Estate Dictionary

Attic
- dampness
- insulation
- rodent infestation

Basement
- dampness
- flooding
- lighting
- termite or rodent infestation

Brickwork
- cracks
- loose mortar

Ceilings
- cracking
- holes
- peeling
- water stains

Chimney
- construction
- loose bricks
- tilting

Doors
- alignment
- locks
- opening and closing

Drainage (gutters and downspouts)
- broken sections
- condition
- leaks
- rotting (wood gutters)

Driveway
- cracks
- grading

Electrical
- adequacy
- building code compliance
- exposed wires
- fuse box or circuit breakers
- outlets
- 220-volt wiring

Fences
- condition
- property line

Floors
- condition
- materials
- levelness
- sags

Foundation
- cracks
- evenness

Garage
- capacity
- construction

Heating system
- age
- capacity
- efficiency
- maintenance

Hot water system
- age
- type (circulating or free-standing)

Insulation
- amount and type
- caulking
- efficiency
- weatherstripping

Landscaping
- appearance
- cost of upkeep
- maintenance time required
- soil type

Paint (Exterior and interior)
- age and condition
- appearance
- quality

Plumbing
- leaking
- rusting
- type of piping
- water pressure

Porches and decks
- condition
- material

Roof
- age
- bare spots
- condition
- curling tiles
- materials
- warranty

Screens
- hinges
- holes or tears

Sidewalks
- cracks
- holes
- unsafe features

Siding
- lifting
- loose pieces
- warping

Stairs
- loose handrails
- loose treads

Walls
- cracks
- holes
- visible seams
- water stains

Waste disposal
- maintenance
- septic system location

Water supply
- adequacy of supply
- quality test

Windows
- alignment
- condition
- cracks or breaks
- rotting
- screens
- self-insulated windows
- storm windows

Home Layout Checklist

A home should be suited to a family's size and lifestyle. The right property depends upon current needs, future plans, and the length of time a buyer intends to stay in the house. The following points of evaluation should be checked:

Bathrooms
- adequate size
- number of baths

Closet size
- convenience
- space
- type of closets

Energy efficiency
- age of systems
- design of rooms

Expansion potential
- lot size
- structural design

Fireplace
- age and condition
- type

Improvements
- compatibility with design
- planning
- quality of construction

Kitchen
- age and condition
- appliances
- lighting
- size
- storage space

Real Estate Dictionary

Lighting
- adequacy
- electrical system limitations
- expansion potential

Living room
- location in the house
- size

Planning
- general layout
- practicality
- style

Privacy

- number of windows
- proximity to other homes

Room size
- ceiling height
- floor space

Storage space
- attic and basement space
- garage space

Utility room
- appliances included
- location in the house
- size

Mortgage Checklist

Every lender has different terms and policies, and may offer a variety of different loans. Buyers should get answers to the following questions:

What type of loans do you offer?
- Fixed Rate Mortgages
- Adjustable Rate Mortgages
- Fully amortized or add-on interest
- FHA or VA loans
- Other financing arrangements

What are your interest rate policies?
- Differences for each type of loan
- Lower rates for higher down payments
- Lower rates for shorter loan terms

What are your minimum down payments?
- For older homes
- For newer homes

What are the criteria for qualifying?
- Income level
- Employment
- Years in the area
- Credit history
- Amount of down payment

What other requirements are there?
- Private mortgage insurance
- Default insurance (terms)
- Co-signers or guarantors

What are your terms on ARM loans?
- Rate caps per period and entire loan
- Payment cap
- Carryover of excess rates
- Voluntary acceleration payments
- Refinancing

How can the loan be prepaid?
- Maximum per year without penalty
- Method for making extra payments
- Bi-weekly payment plans

What are the other charges?
- Points
- Other closing costs
- Amount required in deposits to escrow

How long will it take for loan approval?

- Commitment to a quoted rate
- Reimbursement of deposits
- Written or verbal commitments

What are your payment policies?
- Loan payment due dates
- Late charges

Is the loan assumable?
- At the same rate or a higher rate
- Assumption fees
- Other fees or terms

Amortization Tables

A loan amortization table is used to compute the amount of monthly payment that will be required, given three factors:

1. The rate of interest
2. The time required for repayment
3. The amount of the loan

For example, a buyer will need an $80,000 mortgage. The lending institution offers a 30-year loan at a fixed rate of 10.5 percent, or a 15-year loan at 9.5%. In comparing these two loans, two offsetting points must be kept in mind:

1. The higher the rate of interest, the larger the payment required.
2. The longer the repayment term, the smaller the payment required.

A 10.5 percent loan would require a higher payment than a 9.5 percent loan, if both were compared for the same number of years. But a 15-year loan will need higher payments because the amortization period is shorter.

To use the loan amortization table, multiply the amount of the loan by the appropriate factor, following these steps for the 30-year loan:

1. Find the 10.5 percent table.
2. Locate the 30-year line.
3. Multiply the factor by the loan amount:
    $0.0091\ 473 \times \$80,000 = \$731.78$

For the second loan, follow these steps:

1. Find the 9.5 percent table.
2. Locate the 15-year line.
3. Multiply the factor by the loan amount:
    $0.0104\ 422 \times \$80,000 = \$835.38$

To further compare the two loans, the following computations should be performed:

1. The difference in monthly payment:
    $\$835.38 - \$731.78 = \$103.60$
2. Total payments for the 30-year loan:
    $\$731.78 \times 360 \text{ months} = \$263,440.80$
3. Total payments for the 15-year loan:
    $\$835.38 \times 180 \text{ months} = \$150,368.40$
4. The difference in total interest:
    $\$263,440.80 - \$150,368.40 = \$113,072.40$

Amortization Tables

A borrower can thus determine the relative cost of two different loans. If the additional $103.60 per month is affordable, a total of $113,368.40 in interest will be saved, and the loan will be fully repaid in half the time of a 30-year loan.

Estimating Mortgage Payments

The amortization tables in this volume report factors for interest rates at half-points—5.0, 5.5, 6.0, 6.5, and so forth. Actual interest rates may fall between these half-point levels.

You can estimate the monthly payment levels for rates of interest not shown by computing an average median rate. For example, an $80,000 loan is offered to a borrower at 9.25 percent for a 15-year term. To estimate the monthly payment:

1. Find the amortization tables for 9.0 percent and 9.5 percent.
2. Locate the 15-year line and add the two factors together:
    0.0101 426 + 0.0104 422 = 0.0205 848
3. Divide by 2:
    0.0205 848/2 = 0.0102 924
4. Multiply the loan amount by the estimated factor:
    $80,000 × 0.0102 924 = $823.39

The actual payment on a 9.25 percent loan for 15 years is $823.36. Interpolating the factor gives an approximation that can be used for comparisons of rates between those given on a table.

To compute the monthly payment for a loan offered at 9.125 percent, the procedure goes one step farther:

1. Find the amortization tables for 9.0 percent and 9.5 percent.
2. Estimate the factor as above, by dividing the two factors shown and dividing by 2.
3. Add your estimated factor and the factor for 9.0 percent:
    0.0102 924 + 0.0101 426 = 0.0204 435
4. Divide by 2:
    0.0204 435/2 = 0.0102 218
5. Multiply the loan amount by the estimated factor:
    $80,000 × 0.0102 218 = $817.74

AMORTIZATION TABLES

Year	5.0%	5.5%	6.0%	6.5%	Month
1	0.0856 074	0.0858 367	0.0860 664	0.0862 964	12
2	0.0438 713	0.0440 956	0.0443 206	0.0445 462	24
3	0.0299 708	0.0301 959	0.0304 219	0.0306 490	36
4	0.0230 292	0.0232 564	0.0234 850	0.0237 149	48
5	0.0188 712	0.0191 011	0.0193 328	0.0195 661	60
6	0.0161 049	0.0163 378	0.0165 728	0.0168 099	72
7	0.0141 339	0.0143 700	0.0146 085	0.0148 494	84
8	0.0126 599	0.0128 993	0.0131 414	0.0133 862	96
9	0.0115 172	0.0117 599	0.0120 057	0.0122 545	108
10	0.0106 065	0.0108 526	0.0111 020	0.0113 547	120
11	0.0098 644	0.0101 139	0.0103 670	0.0106 237	132
12	0.0092 489	0.0095 017	0.0097 585	0.0100 192	144
13	0.0087 305	0.0089 867	0.0092 472	0.0095 119	156
14	0.0082 887	0.0085 482	0.0088 123	0.0090 809	168
15	0.0079 079	0.0081 708	0.0084 385	0.0087 110	180
16	0.0075 768	0.0078 430	0.0081 143	0.0083 907	192
17	0.0072 865	0.0075 560	0.0078 310	0.0081 112	204
18	0.0070 303	0.0073 031	0.0075 816	0.0078 656	216
19	0.0068 027	0.0070 788	0.0073 608	0.0076 485	228
20	0.0065 995	0.0068 788	0.0071 643	0.0074 557	240
21	0.0064 171	0.0066 997	0.0069 885	0.0072 836	252
22	0.0062 528	0.0065 384	0.0068 307	0.0071 293	264
23	0.0061 040	0.0063 928	0.0066 884	0.0069 906	276
24	0.0059 689	0.0062 608	0.0065 597	0.0068 654	288
25	0.0058 459	0.0061 408	0.0064 430	0.0067 520	300
26	0.0057 334	0.0060 314	0.0063 367	0.0066 491	312
27	0.0056 303	0.0059 313	0.0062 398	0.0065 555	324
28	0.0055 357	0.0058 396	0.0061 512	0.0064 701	336
29	0.0054 486	0.0057 554	0.0060 700	0.0063 921	348
30	0.0053 682	0.0056 778	0.0059 955	0.0063 206	360

Amortization Tables

Year	7.0%	7.5%	8.0%	8.5%	Month
1	0.0865 267	0.0867 574	0.0869 884	0.0872 197	12
2	0.0447 725	0.0449 995	0.0452 272	0.0454 556	24
3	0.0308 770	0.0311 062	0.0313 363	0.0315 675	36
4	0.0239 462	0.0241 789	0.0244 129	0.0246 483	48
5	0.0198 011	0.0200 379	0.0202 763	0.0205 165	60
6	0.0170 490	0.0172 901	0.0175 332	0.0177 783	72
7	0.0150 926	0.0153 382	0.0155 862	0.0158 364	84
8	0.0136 337	0.0138 838	0.0141 366	0.0143 921	96
9	0.0125 062	0.0127 610	0.0130 187	0.0132 793	108
10	0.0116 108	0.0118 701	0.0121 327	0.0123 985	120
11	0.0108 841	0.0111 480	0.0114 154	0.0116 863	132
12	0.0102 838	0.0105 522	0.0108 245	0.0111 005	144
13	0.0097 807	0.0100 537	0.0103 307	0.0106 117	156
14	0.0093 540	0.0096 314	0.0099 131	0.0101 991	168
15	0.0089 882	0.0092 701	0.0095 565	0.0098 473	180
16	0.0086 720	0.0089 582	0.0092 492	0.0095 449	192
17	0.0083 966	0.0086 870	0.0089 825	0.0092 829	204
18	0.0081 550	0.0084 497	0.0087 496	0.0090 545	216
19	0.0079 419	0.0082 407	0.0085 450	0.0088 544	228
20	0.0077 529	0.0080 559	0.0083 644	0.0086 782	240
21	0.0075 847	0.0078 916	0.0082 042	0.0085 223	252
22	0.0074 342	0.0077 451	0.0080 617	0.0083 840	264
23	0.0072 991	0.0076 138	0.0079 345	0.0082 608	276
24	0.0071 775	0.0074 960	0.0078 205	0.0081 508	288
25	0.0070 677	0.0073 899	0.0077 181	0.0080 522	300
26	0.0069 683	0.0072 940	0.0076 259	0.0079 637	312
27	0.0068 781	0.0072 073	0.0075 427	0.0078 842	324
28	0.0067 960	0.0071 286	0.0074 675	0.0078 124	336
29	0.0067 213	0.0070 572	0.0073 994	0.0077 477	348
30	0.0066 530	0.0069 921	0.0073 376	0.0076 891	360

Real Estate Dictionary

Year	9.0%	9.5%	10.0%	10.5%	Month
1	0.0874 514	0.0876 835	0.0879 158	0.0881 486	12
2	0.0456 847	0.0459 144	0.0461 449	0.0463 760	24
3	0.0317 997	0.0320 329	0.0322 671	0.0325 024	36
4	0.0248 850	0.0251 231	0.0253 625	0.0256 033	48
5	0.0207 583	0.0210 018	0.0212 470	0.0214 939	60
6	0.0180 255	0.0182 746	0.0185 258	0.0187 789	72
7	0.0160 890	0.0163 439	0.0166 011	0.0168 606	84
8	0.0146 502	0.0149 108	0.0151 741	0.0154 400	96
9	0.0135 429	0.0138 093	0.0140 786	0.0143 508	108
10	0.0126 675	0.0129 397	0.0132 150	0.0134 934	120
11	0.0119 608	0.0122 386	0.0125 198	0.0128 044	132
12	0.0113 803	0.0116 637	0.0119 507	0.0122 414	144
13	0.0108 968	0.0111 857	0.0114 784	0.0117 750	156
14	0.0104 893	0.0107 836	0.0110 820	0.0113 843	168
15	0.0101 426	0.0104 422	0.0107 460	0.0110 539	180
16	0.0098 451	0.0101 498	0.0104 590	0.0107 724	192
17	0.0095 880	0.0098 978	0.0102 121	0.0105 308	204
18	0.0093 644	0.0096 791	0.0099 984	0.0103 222	216
19	0.0091 689	0.0094 883	0.0098 125	0.0101 413	228
20	0.0089 972	0.0093 213	0.0096 502	0.0099 837	240
21	0.0088 458	0.0091 743	0.0095 078	0.0098 459	252
22	0.0087 117	0.0090 446	0.0093 824	0.0097 250	264
23	0.0085 926	0.0089 297	0.0092 718	0.0096 186	276
24	0.0084 866	0.0088 277	0.0091 738	0.0095 248	288
25	0.0083 919	0.0087 369	0.0090 870	0.0094 418	300
26	0.0083 072	0.0086 559	0.0090 097	0.0093 682	312
27	0.0082 312	0.0085 836	0.0089 409	0.0093 030	324
28	0.0081 629	0.0085 188	0.0088 796	0.0092 450	336
29	0.0081 015	0.0084 607	0.0088 247	0.0091 934	348
30	0.0080 462	0.0084 085	0.0087 757	0.0091 473	360

Amortization Tables

Year	11.0%	11.5%	12.0%	12.5%	Month
1	0.0883 816	0.0886 150	0.0888 487	0.0890 828	12
2	0.0466 078	0.0468 403	0.0470 734	0.0473 073	24
3	0.0327 387	0.0329 760	0.0332 143	0.0334 536	36
4	0.0258 455	0.0260 890	0.0263 338	0.0265 799	48
5	0.0217 424	0.0219 926	0.0222 444	0.0224 979	60
6	0.0190 340	0.0192 911	0.0195 501	0.0198 111	72
7	0.0171 224	0.0173 864	0.0176 527	0.0179 212	84
8	0.0157 084	0.0159 793	0.0162 528	0.0165 288	96
9	0.0146 258	0.0149 036	0.0151 842	0.0154 675	108
10	0.0137 750	0.0140 595	0.0143 470	0.0146 376	120
11	0.0130 923	0.0133 835	0.0136 778	0.0139 754	132
12	0.0125 355	0.0128 331	0.0131 341	0.0134 385	144
13	0.0120 752	0.0123 791	0.0126 866	0.0129 976	156
14	0.0116 905	0.0120 005	0.0123 142	0.0126 316	168
15	0.0113 659	0.0116 818	0.0120 016	0.0123 252	180
16	0.0110 900	0.0114 116	0.0117 372	0.0120 666	192
17	0.0108 538	0.0111 809	0.0115 121	0.0118 472	204
18	0.0106 504	0.0109 829	0.0113 195	0.0116 600	216
19	0.0104 746	0.0108 121	0.0111 538	0.0114 995	228
20	0.0103 218	0.0106 642	0.0110 108	0.0113 614	240
21	0.0101 887	0.0105 357	0.0108 869	0.0112 421	252
22	0.0100 722	0.0104 237	0.0107 793	0.0111 389	264
23	0.0099 700	0.0103 258	0.0106 856	0.0110 493	276
24	0.0098 802	0.0102 400	0.0106 038	0.0109 714	288
25	0.0098 011	0.0101 646	0.0105 322	0.0109 035	300
26	0.0097 312	0.0100 984	0.0104 695	0.0108 442	312
27	0.0096 695	0.0100 400	0.0104 144	0.0107 924	324
28	0.0096 147	0.0099 885	0.0103 661	0.0107 471	336
29	0.0095 662	0.0099 431	0.0103 235	0.0107 074	348
30	0.0095 232	0.0099 029	0.0102 861	0.0106 725	360

Year	13.0%	13.5%	14.0%	14.5%	Month
1	0.0893 172	0.0895 520	0.0897 871	0.0900 225	12
2	0.0475 418	0.0477 770	0.0480 128	0.0482 494	24
3	0.0336 939	0.0339 352	0.0341 776	0.0344 209	36
4	0.0268 274	0.0270 763	0.0273 264	0.0275 779	48
5	0.0227 530	0.0230 098	0.0232 682	0.0235 282	60
6	0.0200 741	0.0203 389	0.0206 057	0.0208 744	72
7	0.0181 919	0.0184 648	0.0187 400	0.0190 173	84
8	0.0168 072	0.0170 881	0.0173 715	0.0176 572	96
9	0.0157 535	0.0160 423	0.0163 337	0.0166 277	108
10	0.0149 310	0.0152 274	0.0155 266	0.0158 286	120
11	0.0142 761	0.0145 798	0.0148 866	0.0151 964	132
12	0.0137 462	0.0140 571	0.0143 712	0.0146 884	144
13	0.0133 121	0.0136 299	0.0139 510	0.0142 753	156
14	0.0129 526	0.0132 770	0.0136 048	0.0139 360	168
15	0.0126 524	0.0129 831	0.0133 174	0.0136 550	180
16	0.0123 998	0.0127 366	0.0130 769	0.0134 207	192
17	0.0121 861	0.0125 286	0.0128 747	0.0132 242	204
18	0.0120 043	0.0123 523	0.0127 038	0.0130 587	216
19	0.0118 489	0.0122 021	0.0125 587	0.0129 187	228
20	0.0117 157	0.0120 737	0.0124 352	0.0127 999	240
21	0.0116 011	0.0119 636	0.0123 296	0.0126 988	252
22	0.0115 022	0.0118 691	0.0122 392	0.0126 126	264
23	0.0114 167	0.0117 876	0.0121 617	0.0125 389	276
24	0.0113 426	0.0117 172	0.0120 950	0.0124 757	288
25	0.0112 783	0.0116 564	0.0120 376	0.0124 216	300
26	0.0112 224	0.0116 037	0.0119 880	0.0123 751	312
27	0.0111 737	0.0115 581	0.0119 453	0.0123 351	324
28	0.0111 313	0.0115 184	0.0119 083	0.0123 007	336
29	0.0110 943	0.0114 840	0.0118 763	0.0122 711	348
30	0.0110 619	0.0114 541	0.0118 487	0.0122 455	360

Amortization Tables

Year	15.0%	15.5%	16.0%	16.5%	Month
1	0.0902 583	0.0904 944	0.0907 308	0.0909 676	12
2	0.0484 866	0.0487 245	0.0489 631	0.0492 023	24
3	0.0346 653	0.0349 106	0.0351 570	0.0354 043	36
4	0.0278 307	0.0280 848	0.0283 402	0.0285 970	48
5	0.0237 899	0.0240 531	0.0243 180	0.0245 845	60
6	0.0211 450	0.0214 174	0.0216 918	0.0219 680	72
7	0.0192 967	0.0195 783	0.0198 620	0.0201 478	84
8	0.0179 454	0.0182 359	0.0185 287	0.0188 239	96
9	0.0169 243	0.0172 235	0.0175 252	0.0178 294	108
10	0.0161 334	0.0164 410	0.0167 513	0.0170 642	120
11	0.0155 091	0.0158 247	0.0161 431	0.0164 643	132
12	0.0150 087	0.0153 320	0.0156 582	0.0159 873	144
13	0.0146 028	0.0149 334	0.0152 670	0.0156 035	156
14	0.0142 703	0.0146 078	0.0149 484	0.0152 919	168
15	0.0139 958	0.0143 399	0.0146 870	0.0150 370	180
16	0.0137 676	0.0141 178	0.0144 711	0.0148 272	192
17	0.0135 770	0.0139 329	0.0142 918	0.0146 537	204
18	0.0134 169	0.0137 781	0.0141 424	0.0145 096	216
19	0.0132 819	0.0136 482	0.0140 174	0.0143 894	228
20	0.0131 678	0.0135 388	0.0139 125	0.0142 890	240
21	0.0130 711	0.0134 463	0.0138 243	0.0142 048	252
22	0.0129 889	0.0133 681	0.0137 499	0.0141 341	264
23	0.0129 189	0.0133 017	0.0136 870	0.0140 747	276
24	0.0128 592	0.0132 453	0.0136 339	0.0140 246	288
25	0.0128 083	0.0131 974	0.0135 888	0.0139 824	300
26	0.0127 647	0.0131 566	0.0135 507	0.0139 468	312
27	0.0127 273	0.0131 218	0.0135 183	0.0139 166	324
28	0.0126 953	0.0130 921	0.0134 908	0.0138 912	336
29	0.0126 679	0.0130 668	0.0134 674	0.0138 697	348
30	0.0126 444	0.0130 451	0.0134 475	0.0138 514	360

Remaining Balance Tables

Remaining balance tables show the percentage of the original loan that remains outstanding at the end of each year.

The degree of remaining balance varies depending upon two factors:

1. The interest rate
2. The number of years in the loan term

The higher the interest rate, and the longer the repayment term, the slower the decline in a loan's balance. In evaluating two different loans, the comparison of time required to accumulate equity can be made with the use of these tables.

For example, a borrower needs to borrow $80,000, and has a choice between a 30-year loan at 10.5 percent, and a 15-year loan at 9.5 percent. He intends to keep the house for five years, and would like to compare equity build-up at the end of that term. Start by computing the remaining balance after five years on the 30-year loan:

1. Find the 10.5 percent remaining balance table.
2. Locate the column for 30 years.
3. Locate the "loan age" line for five years.
4. Multiply the original loan amount by the factor:
$$\$80,000 \times 96.9 = \$77,520$$

Next, compute the remaining balance after five years on the 15-year loan:

1. Find the 9.5 percent remaining balance table.
2. Locate the column for 15 years.
3. Locate the "loan age" line for five years.
4. Multiply the original loan amount by the factor:
$$\$80,000 \times 80.7 = \$64,560$$

With the 30-year loan, the principal balance has been reduced by $2,480:

	original balance	$80,000
less:	remaining balance	−77,520
equals:	equity build-up	$ 2,480

In the 15-year loan, the principal balance has been reduced by $15,440:

	original balance	$80,000
less:	remaining balance	−64,560
equals:	equity build-up	$15,440

There is $12,960 more equity build-up with the 15-year loan. To achieve this, the monthly payment must be higher than the longer term by $103.60 per month (see previous section). Over a five-year period, the increased payment equals $6,216. Under the more rapid plan, the homeowner has reduced interest costs by $6,744 in five years:

	difference in equity build-up	$12,960
less:	added payments	− 6,216
	reduced interest costs	$ 6,744

A homeowner who plans to sell a home within five to ten years after purchase date will accumulate equity at a more rapid rate by repaying a loan over a shorter term. The remaining balance tables can be used to calculate the degree of savings at different interest rates.

REMAINING BALANCE TABLES

Loan Age	5.0% Term of Loan					5.5% Term of Loan				
	10	15	20	25	30	10	15	20	25	30
1	92.1	95.4	97.0	97.9	98.5	92.3	95.6	97.2	98.1	98.7
2	83.8	90.6	93.9	95.8	97.0	84.1	90.9	94.2	96.1	97.2
3	75.0	85.5	90.6	93.5	95.3	75.5	86.0	91.0	93.9	95.7
4	65.9	80.2	87.1	91.1	93.6	66.4	80.8	87.7	91.7	94.1
5	56.2	74.6	83.5	88.6	91.8	56.8	75.3	84.2	89.3	92.5
6	46.1	68.7	79.6	85.9	89.9	46.7	69.5	80.5	86.8	90.7
7	35.4	62.5	75.6	83.2	88.0	35.9	63.3	76.5	84.1	88.8
8	24.2	56.0	71.4	80.2	85.9	24.6	56.9	72.4	81.3	86.8
9	12.4	49.1	66.9	77.2	83.7	12.6	50.0	68.0	78.3	84.8
10	0	41.9	62.2	73.9	81.3	0	42.8	63.4	75.2	82.5
11		34.3	57.3	70.5	78.9		35.1	58.5	71.8	80.2
12		26.4	52.1	67.0	76.4		27.1	53.3	68.3	77.8
13		18.0	46.7	63.2	73.7		18.5	47.9	64.6	75.1
14		9.2	41.0	59.3	70.9		9.5	42.1	60.7	72.4
15		0	35.0	55.1	67.9		0	36.0	56.6	69.5
16			28.7	50.8	64.8			29.6	52.2	66.4
17			22.0	46.2	61.5			22.8	47.6	63.2
18			15.0	41.4	58.0			15.6	42.7	59.8
19			7.7	36.3	54.4			8.0	37.6	56.1
20			0	31.0	50.6			0	32.2	52.3
21				25.4	46.6				26.4	48.3
22				19.5	42.4				20.3	44.0
23				13.3	38.0				13.9	39.5
24				6.8	33.3				7.2	34.8
25				0	28.5				0	29.7
26					23.3					24.4
27					17.9					18.8
28					12.2					12.9
29					6.3					6.6
30					0					0

Remaining Balance Tables

Loan Age	6.0% Term of Loan					6.5% Term of Loan				
	10	15	20	25	30	10	15	20	25	30
1	92.5	95.8	97.3	98.2	98.8	92.7	95.9	97.5	98.4	98.9
2	84.5	91.3	94.5	96.3	97.5	84.8	91.6	94.8	96.6	97.7
3	76.0	86.5	91.5	94.3	96.1	76.5	86.9	91.9	94.7	96.4
4	67.0	81.4	88.3	92.2	94.6	67.6	82.0	88.9	92.7	95.1
5	57.4	76.0	84.9	89.9	93.1	58.0	76.7	85.6	90.6	93.6
6	47.3	70.3	81.3	87.5	91.4	47.9	71.1	82.1	88.3	92.1
7	36.5	64.2	77.5	85.0	89.6	37.1	65.1	78.4	85.8	90.4
8	25.1	57.8	73.4	82.3	87.8	25.5	58.7	74.4	83.2	88.7
9	12.9	50.9	69.1	79.4	85.8	13.2	51.8	70.2	80.5	86.8
10	0	43.7	64.5	76.4	83.7	0	44.5	65.7	77.5	84.8
11		35.9	59.7	73.1	81.5		36.7	60.8	74.4	82.6
12		27.7	54.5	69.7	79.1		28.4	55.7	71.0	80.4
13		19.0	49.0	66.0	76.6		19.6	50.2	67.4	77.9
14		9.8	43.2	62.2	73.9		10.1	44.4	63.6	75.3
15		0	37.1	58.0	71.1		0	38.1	59.5	72.6
16			30.5	53.7	68.0			31.4	55.1	69.6
17			23.6	49.0	64.8			24.3	50.4	66.5
18			16.2	44.1	61.4			16.7	45.5	63.1
19			8.3	38.9	57.8			8.6	40.2	59.5
20			0	33.3	54.0			0	34.5	55.7
21				27.4	49.9				28.5	51.6
22				21.2	45.6				22.0	47.2
23				14.5	41.0				15.2	42.6
24				7.5	36.2				7.8	37.6
25				0	31.0				0	32.3
26					25.5					26.7
27					19.7					20.6
28					13.5					14.2
29					7.0					7.3
30					0					0

	7.0%					7.5%				
Loan	Term of Loan					Term of Loan				
Age	10	15	20	25	30	10	15	20	25	30
1	92.8	96.1	97.6	98.5	99.0	93.0	96.3	97.8	98.6	99.1
2	85.2	91.9	95.1	96.8	97.9	85.5	92.2	95.3	97.1	98.1
3	76.9	87.4	92.3	95.1	96.7	77.4	87.9	92.7	95.4	97.0
4	68.1	82.6	89.4	93.2	95.5	68.7	83.2	89.9	93.6	95.9
5	58.6	77.4	86.3	91.2	94.1	59.2	78.1	86.9	91.7	94.6
6	48.5	71.9	82.9	89.0	92.7	49.1	72.6	83.6	89.7	93.3
7	37.6	65.9	79.3	86.7	91.2	38.2	66.8	80.1	87.5	91.8
8	25.9	59.6	75.4	84.2	89.5	26.4	60.4	76.3	85.1	90.3
9	13.4	52.7	71.2	81.5	87.7	13.7	53.6	72.3	82.5	88.6
10	0	45.4	66.8	78.6	85.8	0	46.3	67.9	79.7	86.8
11		37.5	62.0	75.6	83.8		38.3	63.1	76.7	84.9
12		29.1	56.9	72.3	81.6		29.8	58.0	73.5	82.8
13		20.1	51.4	68.7	79.2		20.6	52.5	70.0	80.5
14		10.4	45.5	64.9	76.7		10.7	46.6	66.3	78.1
15		0	39.2	60.9	74.0		0	40.2	62.3	75.4
16			32.4	56.5	71.1			38.3	57.9	72.6
17			25.1	51.8	68.0			25.9	53.2	69.6
18			17.3	46.8	64.7			17.9	48.2	66.3
19			9.0	41.5	61.1			9.3	42.7	62.7
20			0	35.7	57.3			0	36.9	58.9
21				29.5	53.2				30.6	54.8
22				22.9	48.8				23.8	50.4
23				15.8	44.1				16.4	45.6
24				8.2	39.0				8.5	40.4
25				0	33.6				0	34.9
26					27.8					28.9
27					21.6					22.5
28					14.9					15.5
29					7.7					8.1
30					0					0

Remaining Balance Tables

Loan Age	8.0% Term of Loan					8.5% Term of Loan				
	10	15	20	25	30	10	15	20	25	30
1	93.2	96.4	97.9	98.7	99.2	93.4	96.6	98.0	98.8	99.2
2	85.8	92.5	95.6	97.3	98.3	86.2	92.8	95.8	97.5	98.4
3	77.8	88.3	93.1	95.7	97.3	78.3	88.7	93.5	96.0	97.5
4	69.2	83.7	90.4	94.1	96.2	69.7	84.3	90.9	94.5	96.6
5	59.8	78.8	87.5	92.3	95.1	60.4	79.4	88.1	92.8	95.5
6	49.7	73.4	84.4	90.3	93.8	50.3	74.2	85.1	90.9	94.3
7	38.7	67.6	81.0	88.2	92.5	39.3	68.4	81.8	88.9	93.1
8	26.8	61.3	77.3	85.9	91.0	27.3	62.2	78.2	86.7	91.7
9	14.0	54.5	73.3	83.5	89.4	14.2	55.4	74.3	84.4	90.2
10	0	47.1	68.9	80.8	87.7	0	48.0	70.0	81.8	88.6
11		39.2	64.3	77.9	85.9		40.0	65.4	79.0	86.8
12		30.5	59.2	74.7	83.9		31.2	60.3	75.9	84.9
13		21.1	53.7	71.3	81.7		21.7	54.8	72.5	82.8
14		11.0	47.7	67.6	79.3		11.3	48.8	68.9	80.6
15		0	41.3	63.6	76.8		0	42.3	65.0	78.1
16			34.3	59.3	74.0			35.2	60.6	75.4
17			26.7	54.6	71.0			27.5	56.0	72.5
18			18.5	49.5	67.8			19.1	50.9	69.3
19			9.6	44.0	64.3			10.0	45.3	65.8
20			0	38.1	60.5			0	39.3	62.0
21				31.6	56.4				32.7	57.9
22				24.6	51.9				25.5	53.4
23				17.1	47.1				17.7	48.6
24				8.9	41.9				9.2	43.3
25				0	36.2				0	37.5
26					30.1					31.2
27					23.4					24.4
28					16.2					16.9
29					8.4					8.8
30					0					0

	9.0%					9.5%				
Loan	Term of Loan					Term of Loan				
Age	10	15	20	25	30	10	15	20	25	30
1	93.5	96.7	98.1	98.9	99.3	93.7	96.8	98.2	99.0	99.4
2	86.5	93.1	96.1	97.7	98.6	86.8	93.4	96.3	97.8	98.7
3	78.7	89.1	93.8	96.3	97.8	79.2	89.5	94.2	96.6	98.0
4	70.3	84.8	91.4	94.9	96.9	70.8	85.3	91.8	95.2	97.1
5	61.0	80.1	88.7	93.3	95.9	61.6	80.7	89.3	93.7	96.2
6	50.9	74.9	85.8	91.5	94.8	51.5	75.6	86.4	92.1	95.3
7	39.8	69.2	82.6	89.6	93.6	40.4	70.0	83.3	90.3	94.2
8	27.7	63.0	79.1	87.5	92.4	28.2	63.9	79.9	88.3	93.0
9	14.5	56.3	75.2	85.2	91.0	14.8	57.1	76.2	86.1	91.7
10	0	48.9	71.0	82.7	89.4	0	49.7	72.0	83.7	90.2
11		40.8	66.4	80.0	87.8		41.6	67.5	81.0	88.6
12		31.9	61.4	77.0	85.9		32.6	62.5	78.1	86.9
13		22.2	55.9	73.7	83.9		22.7	57.0	74.9	85.0
14		11.6	49.9	70.2	81.7		11.9	51.1	71.4	82.8
15		0	43.3	66.3	79.3		0	44.4	67.5	80.5
16			36.2	62.0	76.7			37.1	63.3	78.0
17			28.3	57.3	73.8			29.1	58.6	75.2
18			19.7	52.2	70.7			20.3	53.5	72.1
19			10.3	46.6	67.3			10.6	47.8	68.7
20			0	40.4	63.5			0	41.6	65.0
21				33.7	59.4				34.8	60.9
22				26.4	54.9				27.3	56.4
23				18.4	50.0				19.0	51.5
24				9.6	44.6				10.0	46.0
25				0	38.8				0	40.0
26					32.3					33.5
27					25.3					26.3
28					17.6					18.3
29					9.2					9.6
30					0					0

Remaining Balance Tables

Loan Age	10.0% Term of Loan					10.5% Term of Loan				
	10	15	20	25	30	10	15	20	25	30
1	93.9	97.0	98.4	99.1	99.4	94.0	97.1	98.5	99.1	99.5
2	87.1	93.6	96.5	98.0	98.8	87.4	93.9	96.7	98.2	98.9
3	79.6	89.9	94.5	96.9	98.2	80.0	90.3	94.8	97.1	98.3
4	71.3	85.8	92.3	95.6	97.4	71.9	86.3	92.7	95.9	97.6
5	62.2	81.3	89.8	94.2	96.6	62.8	81.9	90.3	94.6	96.9
6	52.1	76.3	87.1	92.6	95.7	52.7	77.0	87.7	93.1	96.0
7	41.0	70.8	84.1	90.9	94.7	41.5	71.6	84.8	91.5	95.1
8	28.6	64.7	80.8	89.0	93.5	29.1	65.6	81.6	89.7	94.1
9	15.0	58.0	77.1	86.9	92.3	15.3	58.9	78.0	87.7	92.9
10	0	50.6	73.0	84.6	90.9	0	51.4	74.0	85.4	91.6
11		42.4	68.5	82.0	89.4		43.2	69.6	82.9	90.2
12		33.3	63.6	79.2	87.8		34.0	64.7	80.2	88.6
13		23.3	58.1	76.0	85.9		23.8	59.2	77.1	86.9
14		12.2	52.1	72.6	83.9		12.5	53.2	73.7	84.9
15		0	45.4	68.8	81.7		0	46.5	70.0	82.8
16			38.1	64.5	79.2			39.0	65.8	80.4
17			29.9	59.9	76.5			30.7	61.2	77.7
18			20.9	54.7	73.4			21.5	56.0	74.7
19			11.0	49.1	70.1			11.3	50.3	71.4
20			0	42.8	66.4			0	43.9	67.8
21				35.8	62.3				36.9	63.7
22				28.2	57.8				29.1	59.2
23				19.7	52.9				20.4	54.3
24				10.3	47.4				10.7	48.7
25				0	41.3				0	42.6
26					34.6					35.7
27					27.2					28.1
28					19.0					19.7
29					10.0					10.4
30					0					0

Real Estate Dictionary

	11.0%					11.5%				
Loan	Term of Loan					Term of Loan				
Age	10	15	20	25	30	10	15	20	25	30
1	94.2	97.2	98.5	99.2	99.6	94.3	97.3	98.6	99.3	99.6
2	87.7	94.1	96.9	98.3	99.1	88.0	94.4	97.1	98.4	99.1
3	80.5	90.7	95.1	97.3	98.5	80.9	91.0	95.4	97.5	98.6
4	72.4	86.8	93.1	96.2	97.9	72.9	87.3	93.5	96.5	98.1
5	63.4	82.5	90.8	95.0	97.2	63.9	83.1	91.3	95.3	97.4
6	53.3	77.7	88.3	93.6	96.4	53.9	78.4	88.9	94.0	96.7
7	42.1	72.4	85.5	92.0	95.5	42.6	73.1	86.2	92.6	95.9
8	29.6	66.4	82.3	90.3	94.6	30.0	67.2	83.1	90.9	95.0
9	15.6	59.7	78.8	88.4	93.5	15.9	60.6	79.7	89.1	94.0
10	0	52.3	74.9	86.2	92.3	0	53.1	75.9	87.0	92.9
11		44.0	70.6	83.8	90.9		44.8	71.6	84.7	91.6
12		34.7	65.7	81.2	89.4		35.4	66.7	82.1	90.2
13		24.4	60.3	78.2	87.7		24.9	61.3	79.2	88.6
14		12.9	54.2	74.9	85.9		13.2	55.3	76.0	86.8
15		0	47.5	71.2	83.8		0	48.5	72.3	84.8
16			39.9	67.0	81.5			40.9	68.2	82.5
17			31.5	62.4	78.9			32.3	63.6	80.0
18			22.2	57.2	76.0			22.8	58.5	77.2
19			11.7	51.5	72.7			12.0	52.7	74.0
20			0	45.1	69.1			0	46.2	70.4
21				37.9	65.1				39.0	66.5
22				29.9	60.6				30.8	62.0
23				21.0	55.6				21.7	57.0
24				11.1	50.0				11.5	51.3
25				0	43.8				0	45.0
26					36.9					38.0
27					29.1					30.0
28					20.4					21.1
29					10.8					11.2
30					0					0

Remaining Balance Tables

Loan Age	12.0% Term of Loan					12.5% Term of Loan				
	10	15	20	25	30	10	15	20	25	30
1	94.5	97.5	98.7	99.3	99.6	94.6	97.6	98.8	99.4	99.7
2	88.3	94.6	97.3	98.6	99.2	88.6	94.8	97.4	98.7	99.3
3	81.3	91.4	95.7	97.7	98.8	81.7	91.7	95.9	97.9	98.9
4	73.4	87.8	93.8	96.7	98.3	73.9	88.2	94.2	97.0	98.4
5	64.5	83.7	91.7	95.7	97.7	65.1	84.2	92.2	96.0	97.9
6	54.5	79.0	89.4	94.4	97.0	55.1	79.7	89.9	94.8	97.3
7	43.2	73.8	86.8	93.1	96.3	43.8	74.6	87.4	93.5	96.6
8	30.5	68.0	83.8	91.5	95.4	30.9	68.8	84.5	92.0	95.8
9	16.2	61.4	80.5	89.7	94.5	16.4	62.2	81.3	90.4	94.9
10	0	54.0	76.8	87.8	93.4	0	54.8	77.6	88.5	93.9
11		45.6	72.5	85.5	92.2		46.4	73.5	86.3	92.8
12		36.1	67.8	83.0	90.9		36.8	68.7	83.9	91.5
13		25.5	62.4	80.2	89.4		26.1	63.4	81.1	90.1
14		13.5	56.3	77.0	87.6		13.8	57.4	78.0	88.5
15		0	49.5	73.4	85.7		0	50.5	74.5	86.6
16			41.8	69.4	83.5			42.7	70.5	84.5
17			33.2	64.8	81.1			34.0	66.0	82.1
18			23.4	59.7	78.3			24.0	60.8	79.4
19			12.4	53.9	75.2			12.8	55.0	76.4
20			0	47.4	71.7			0	48.5	72.9
21				40.0	67.7				41.0	69.0
22				31.7	63.3				32.6	64.6
23				22.4	58.3				23.1	59.6
24				11.9	52.6				12.2	53.9
25				0	46.2				0	47.4
26					39.1					40.2
27					31.0					31.9
28					21.9					22.6
29					11.6					12.0
30					0					0

Loan Age	13.0% Term of Loan					13.5% Term of Loan				
	10	15	20	25	30	10	15	20	25	30
1	94.8	97.7	98.9	99.4	99.7	94.9	97.8	99.0	99.5	99.7
2	88.8	95.0	97.6	98.8	99.4	89.1	95.3	97.7	98.9	99.4
3	82.1	92.0	96.1	98.1	99.0	82.5	92.4	96.4	98.2	99.1
4	74.4	88.6	94.5	97.2	98.6	74.9	89.1	94.8	97.4	98.7
5	65.6	84.7	92.6	96.3	98.1	66.2	85.3	93.0	96.5	98.3
6	55.7	80.3	90.5	95.2	97.5	56.2	80.9	90.9	95.5	97.8
7	44.3	75.3	88.0	94.0	96.9	44.9	76.0	88.6	94.4	97.2
8	31.4	69.6	85.2	92.6	96.2	31.9	70.3	85.9	93.0	96.5
9	16.7	63.0	82.1	91.0	95.4	17.0	63.8	82.8	91.5	95.7
10	0	55.6	78.5	89.1	94.4	0	56.4	79.3	89.8	94.9
11		47.2	74.4	87.1	93.4		48.0	75.3	87.8	93.9
12		37.6	69.7	84.7	92.2		38.3	70.7	85.5	92.7
13		26.6	64.4	82.1	90.8		27.2	65.4	82.9	91.4
14		14.2	58.4	79.0	89.2		14.5	59.4	80.0	89.9
15		0	51.5	75.5	87.4		0	52.5	76.6	88.2
16			43.7	71.6	85.4			44.6	72.7	86.3
17			34.8	67.1	83.1			35.6	68.2	84.0
18			24.6	62.0	80.5			25.3	63.1	81.5
19			13.1	56.2	77.5			13.5	57.3	78.6
20			0	49.6	74.1			0	50.7	75.2
21				42.0	70.2				43.1	71.4
22				33.5	65.8				34.4	67.0
23				23.7	60.8				24.4	62.0
24				12.6	55.1				13.0	56.3
25				0	48.6				0	49.8
26					41.2					42.3
27					32.8					33.8
28					23.3					24.0
29					12.4					12.8
30					0					0

Remaining Balance Tables

Loan Age	14.0% Term of Loan					14.5% Term of Loan				
	10	15	20	25	30	10	15	20	25	30
1	95.1	97.9	99.0	99.5	99.8	95.2	98.0	99.1	99.6	99.8
2	89.4	95.5	97.9	99.0	99.5	89.6	95.7	98.0	99.1	99.6
3	82.9	92.7	96.6	98.4	99.2	83.2	93.0	96.8	98.5	99.3
4	75.4	89.5	95.1	97.6	98.8	75.8	89.9	95.4	97.8	99.0
5	66.7	85.8	93.4	96.8	98.4	67.3	86.3	93.7	97.0	98.6
6	56.8	81.5	91.4	95.9	98.0	57.4	82.1	91.9	96.2	98.2
7	45.4	76.7	89.1	94.8	97.4	46.0	77.3	89.7	95.1	97.7
8	32.3	71.1	86.5	93.5	96.8	32.8	71.8	87.1	93.9	97.1
9	17.3	64.6	83.5	92.1	96.1	17.6	65.4	84.2	92.6	96.4
10	0	57.2	80.1	90.4	95.3	0	58.0	80.9	91.0	95.7
11		48.7	76.1	88.5	94.4		49.5	77.0	89.1	94.8
12		39.0	71.6	86.3	93.3		39.7	72.5	87.0	93.8
13		27.7	66.4	83.8	92.0		28.3	67.3	84.6	92.6
14		14.8	60.4	80.9	90.6		15.2	61.3	81.7	91.2
15		0	53.4	77.5	89.0		0	54.4	78.5	89.7
16			45.5	73.7	87.1			46.4	74.5	87.9
17			36.4	69.3	84.9			37.2	70.4	85.8
18			25.9	64.2	82.5			26.5	65.3	83.4
19			13.9	58.4	79.6			14.2	59.5	80.6
20			0	51.7	76.3			0	52.8	77.4
21				44.1	72.5				45.0	73.7
22				35.2	68.2				36.1	69.4
23				25.1	63.2				25.7	64.4
24				13.4	57.5				13.8	58.7
25				0	50.9				0	52.1
26					43.4					44.4
27					34.7					35.6
28					24.7					25.4
29					13.2					13.6
30					0					0

Loan Age	15.0% Term of Loan					15.5% Term of Loan				
	10	15	20	25	30	10	15	20	25	30
1	95.3	98.1	99.1	99.6	99.8	95.5	98.2	99.2	99.6	99.8
2	89.9	95.8	98.1	99.1	99.6	90.2	96.0	98.3	99.2	99.6
3	83.6	93.3	97.0	98.6	99.4	84.0	93.5	97.2	98.7	99.4
4	76.3	90.2	95.6	98.0	99.1	76.8	90.6	95.9	98.2	99.2
5	67.8	86.8	94.1	97.3	98.7	68.4	87.2	94.4	97.5	98.9
6	58.0	82.7	92.3	96.4	98.3	58.5	83.3	92.7	96.7	98.5
7	46.5	78.0	90.2	95.5	97.9	47.1	78.6	90.7	95.8	98.1
8	33.3	72.5	87.7	94.3	97.4	33.7	73.2	88.3	94.7	97.6
9	17.9	66.2	84.9	93.0	96.7	18.2	67.0	85.6	93.5	97.0
10	0	58.8	81.6	91.5	96.0	0	59.6	82.4	92.0	96.4
11		50.3	77.8	89.8	95.2		51.1	78.6	90.3	95.6
12		40.4	73.4	87.7	94.2		41.1	74.2	88.4	94.7
13		28.9	68.2	85.3	93.1		29.4	69.2	86.1	93.6
14		15.5	62.3	82.6	91.8		15.9	63.2	83.4	92.4
15		0	55.4	79.4	90.3		0	56.3	80.3	91.0
16			47.3	75.7	88.6			48.2	76.6	89.3
17			38.0	71.4	86.6			38.8	72.4	87.4
18			27.2	66.4	84.3			27.8	67.4	85.1
19			14.6	60.6	81.5			15.0	61.6	82.4
20			0	53.8	78.4			0	54.9	79.4
21				46.0	74.7				47.0	75.7
22				37.0	70.5				37.8	71.5
23				26.4	65.5				27.1	66.6
24				14.2	59.8				14.6	60.9
25				0	53.2				0	54.2
26					45.4					46.5
27					36.5					37.4
28					26.1					26.8
29					14.0					14.4
30					0					0

Remaining Balance Tables

Loan Age	16.0% Term of Loan					16.5% Term of Loan				
	10	15	20	25	30	10	15	20	25	30
1	95.6	98.3	99.3	99.7	99.9	95.7	98.3	99.3	99.7	99.9
2	90.4	96.2	98.4	99.3	99.7	90.7	96.4	98.5	99.3	99.7
3	84.3	93.8	97.4	98.8	99.5	84.7	94.1	97.5	98.9	99.5
4	77.2	91.0	96.1	98.3	99.2	77.7	91.3	96.4	98.4	99.3
5	68.9	87.7	94.7	97.7	99.0	69.4	88.1	95.0	97.9	99.1
6	59.1	83.8	93.1	96.9	98.7	59.7	84.3	93.4	97.2	98.8
7	47.7	79.3	91.1	96.1	98.3	48.2	79.9	91.6	96.4	98.4
8	34.2	74.0	88.9	95.1	97.8	34.7	74.6	89.4	95.4	98.0
9	18.5	67.7	86.2	93.9	97.3	18.8	68.5	86.8	94.3	97.5
10	0	60.4	83.1	92.5	96.7	0	61.2	83.7	93.0	96.9
11		51.8	79.4	90.9	95.9		52.6	80.1	91.4	96.3
12		41.8	75.1	89.0	95.1		42.5	75.9	89.6	95.5
13		30.0	70.1	86.8	94.1		30.6	70.9	87.5	94.5
14		16.2	64.1	84.2	92.9		16.5	65.0	84.9	93.4
15		0	57.2	81.1	91.6		0	58.1	81.9	92.1
16			49.1	77.5	90.0			50.0	78.4	90.6
17			39.6	73.3	88.1			40.4	74.3	88.8
18			28.4	68.4	85.9			29.0	69.4	86.6
19			15.3	62.7	83.3			15.7	63.7	84.1
20			0	55.9	80.3			0	56.9	81.2
21				48.0	76.7				48.9	77.7
22				38.7	72.6				39.5	73.6
23				27.8	67.7				28.4	68.8
24				15.0	62.0				15.4	63.1
25				0	55.3				0	56.3
26					47.5					48.4
27					38.3					39.1
28					27.5					28.2
29					14.8					15.2
30					0					0

Abbreviations

ACRS	Accelerated Cost Recovery System
ACV	Actual Cash Value
AIREA	American Institute of Real Estate Appraisers
ALT	Alternative Minimum Tax
ALTA	American Land Title Association
APR	Annual Percentage Rate
ARM	Adjustable Rate Mortgage
ASA	American Society of Appraisers
ASHI	American Society of Home Inspectors
ASREC	American Society of Real Estate Counselors
CCIM	Certified Commercial Investment Member
CMB	Certified Mortgage Banker
CMO	Collaterized Mortgage Obligation
Co-Op	Bank for Cooperatives
CPM	Certified Property Manager
CRB	Certified Residential Broker
CRE	Counselor of Real Estate
CRS	Certified Residential Specialist
DCR	Debt Coverage Ratio
ECOA	Equal Credit Opportunity Act
ERTA	Economic Recovery Tax Act of 1981
FAR	Floor-Area Ratio
FCA	Farm Credit Administration
FCRA	Fair Credit Reporting Act
FFCB	Federal Farm Credit Banks
FFHA	Federal Fair Housing Act
FFMC	Federal Farm Mortgage Corporation
FHA	Federal Housing Administration
FHLB	Federal Home Loan Bank
FHLMC	Federal Home Loan Mortgage Corporation
FICB	Federal Intermediate Credit Bank
FISBO	For Sale By Owner
FLB	Federal Land Bank
FmHA	Farmer's Home Administration
FMV	Fair Market Value
FNMA	Federal National Mortgage Association
FRM	Fixed Rate Mortgage
FRM	Flexible Rate Mortgage
FSBO	see **FISBO**
GEM	Growing Equity Mortgage

Abbreviations

GMC	Guaranteed Mortgage Certificate
GNMA	Government National Mortgage Association
GPM	Graduated Payment Mortgage
GRI	Graduate Realtors Institute
GRM	Gross Rent Multiplier
HLC	Homeowner's Land Corporation
HOW	Homeowner's Warranty Program
HUD	Department of Housing and Urban Development
IAAO	International Association of Assessing Officers
ILSA	Interstate Land Sales Full Disclosure Act
IREM	Institute of Real Estate Management
IRR	Internal Rate of Return
JTWROS	Joint Tenants With Rights Of Survivorship
LRM	Low-Rate Mortgage
LTV	Loan-To-Value Ratio
MAI	Member Appraisal Institute
MBA	Mortgage Banker's Association
MGIC	Mortgage Guarantee Insurance Company
MLP	Master Limited Partnership
MLS	Multiple Listing Service
NAHB	National Association of Home Builders
NAR	National Association of Realtors
NAREB	National Association of Real Estate Brokers
NAREIT	National Association of Real Estate Investment Trusts
NOI	Net Operating Income
NPV	Net Present Value
OEO	Office of Equal Opportunity
OILSR	Office of Interstate Land Sales Registration
PAM	Pledged Account Mortgage
PC	Participation Certificate
PITI	Principal, Interest, Taxes and Insurance
PMI	Private Mortgage Insurance
PMM	Purchase Money Mortgage
PUD	Planned Unit Development
RAM	Reverse Annuity Mortgage
REIT	Real Estate Investment Trust
RELP	Real Estate Limited Partnership
REMIC	Real Estate Mortgage Investment Company
RESPA	Real Estate Settlement Procedures Act
RESSI	Real Estate Securities and Syndication Institution
RM	Residential Member
RM	Rollover Mortgage
RNMI	Realtors National Marketing Institute
RPM	Rapid Payoff Mortgage
RRM	Renegotiated Rate Mortgage
SAM	Shared Appreciation Mortgage
SEM	Shared Equity Mortgage
SRA	Senior Residential Appraiser
SREA	Senior Real Estate Appraiser
SREA	Society of Real Estate Appraisers

Real Estate Dictionary

TEFRA	Tax Equity and Fiscal Responsibility Act of 1982
TEIP	Tax-Exempt Investor Program
UBI	Unrelated Business Income
ULPA	Uniform Limited Partnership Act
UPA	Uniform Partnership Act
VA	Veteran's Administration
VRM	Variable Rate Mortgage
WCR	Women's Council of Realtors
YAL	Yield to Average Life
YTM	Yield To Maturity
ZRM	Zero Rate Mortgage